THE UNTAMED

KILLING FLOOR

I would kill the world
and die in Hell
For her to live
in Heaven

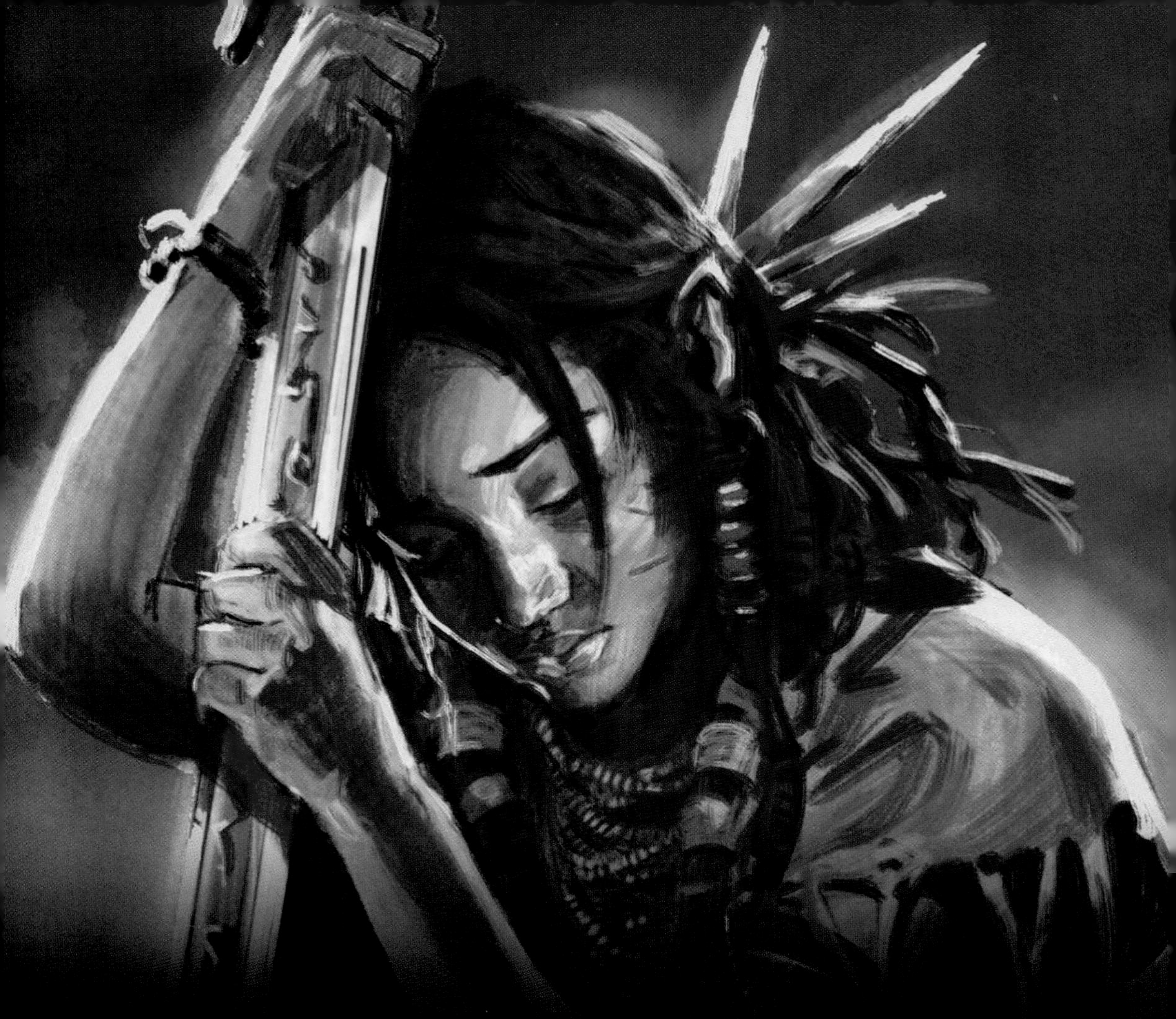

THE UNTAMED
KILLING FLOOR

STRANGER COMICS

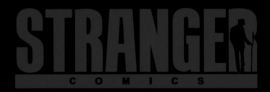

WRITER
SEBASTIAN A. JONES

ARTIST
PETER BERGTING

LAYOUT ARTIST
DARRELL MAY

LETTERERS AND DESIGNERS
A LARGER WORLD STUDIOS

EDITOR
JOSHUA COZINE

ASSOCIATES
KEN LOCSMANDI
MARK HAMMOND
TERRANCE BOULDIN-JOHNSON

CHIEF CREATIVE OFFICER
DARRELL MAY

EDITOR-IN-CHIEF
JOSHUA COZINE

PUBLISHER
SEBASTIAN A. JONES

BASED IN THE WORLD OF ASUNDA CREATED BY SEBASTIAN A. JONES

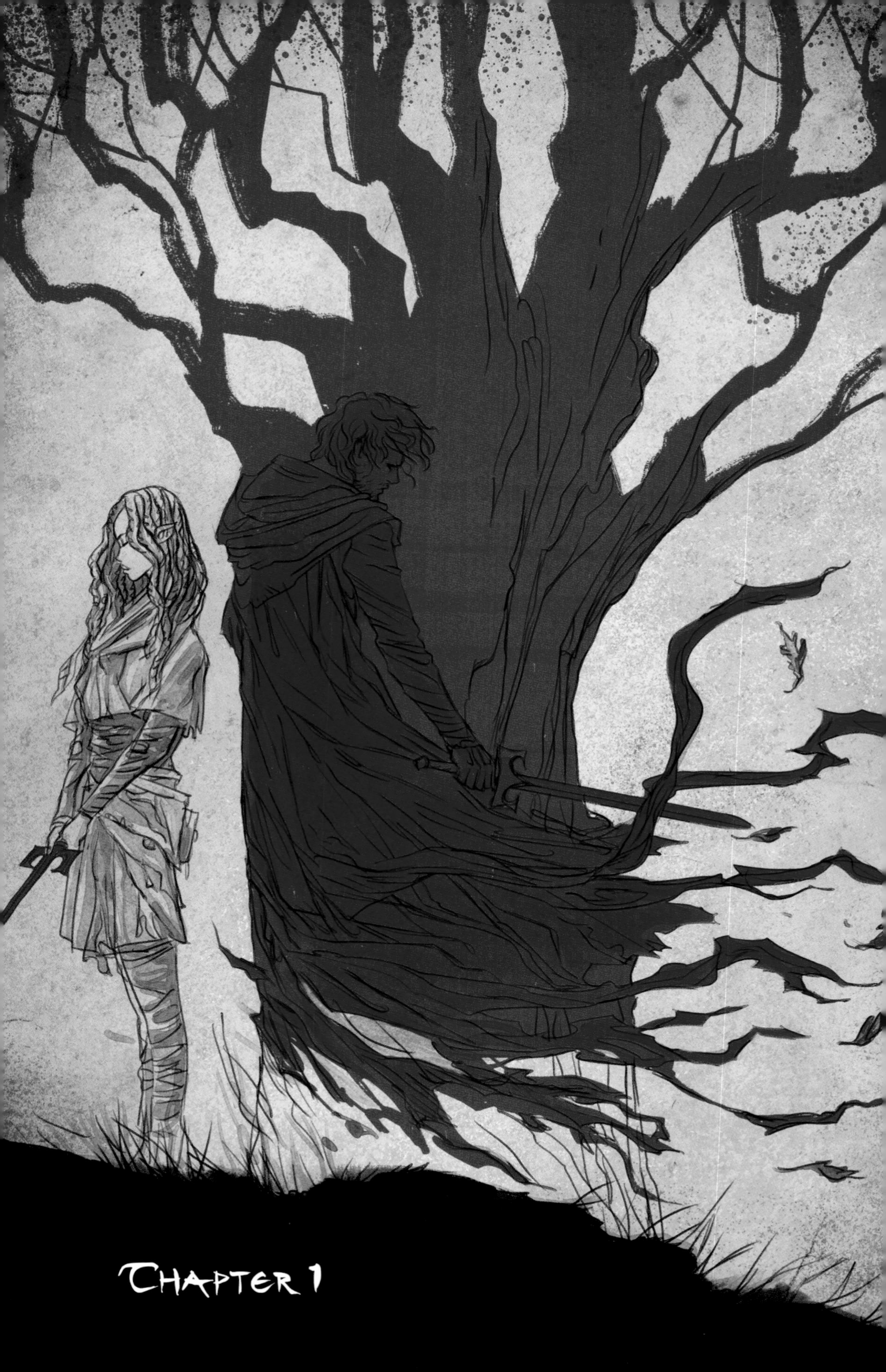
Chapter 1

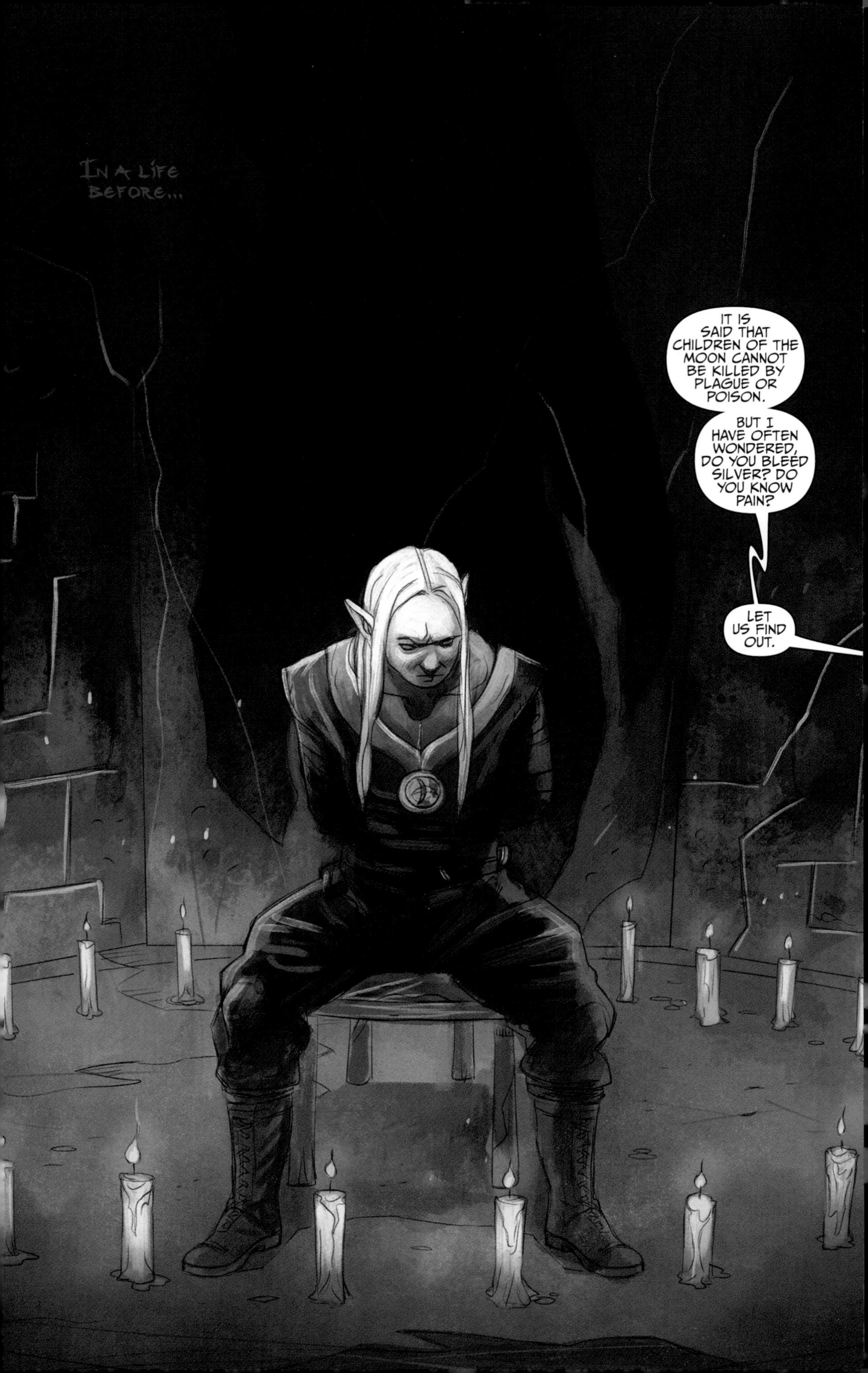
IN A LIFE BEFORE...
IT IS SAID THAT CHILDREN OF THE MOON CANNOT BE KILLED BY PLAGUE OR POISON.
BUT I HAVE OFTEN WONDERED, DO YOU BLEED SILVER? DO YOU KNOW PAIN?
LET US FIND OUT.

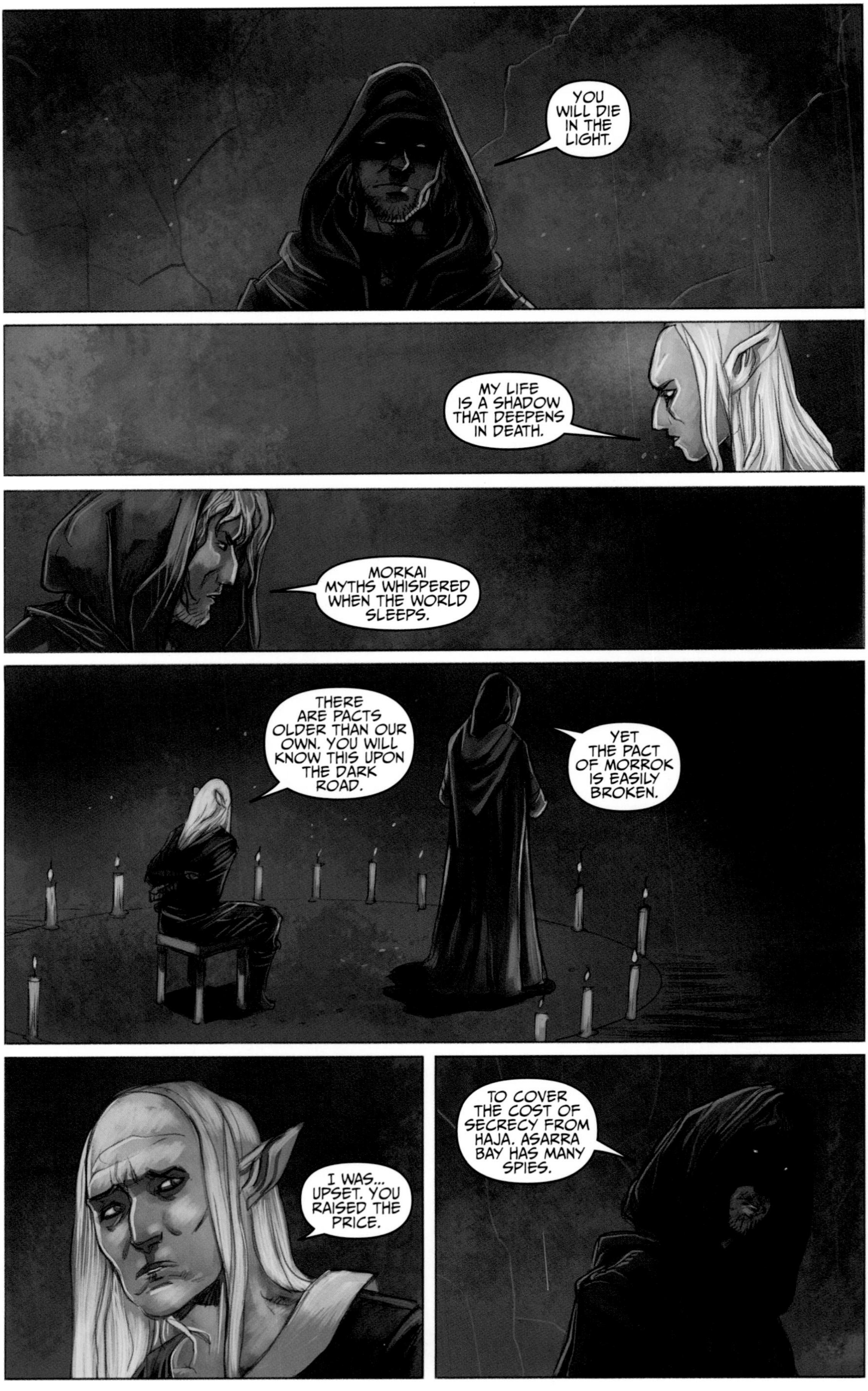
YOU WILL DIE IN THE LIGHT.
MY LIFE IS A SHADOW THAT DEEPENS IN DEATH.
MORKAI MYTHS WHISPERED WHEN THE WORLD SLEEPS.
THERE ARE PACTS OLDER THAN OUR OWN. YOU WILL KNOW THIS UPON THE DARK ROAD.
YET THE PACT OF MORROK IS EASILY BROKEN.
I WAS... UPSET. YOU RAISED THE PRICE.
TO COVER THE COST OF SECRECY FROM HAJA. ASARRA BAY HAS MANY SPIES.

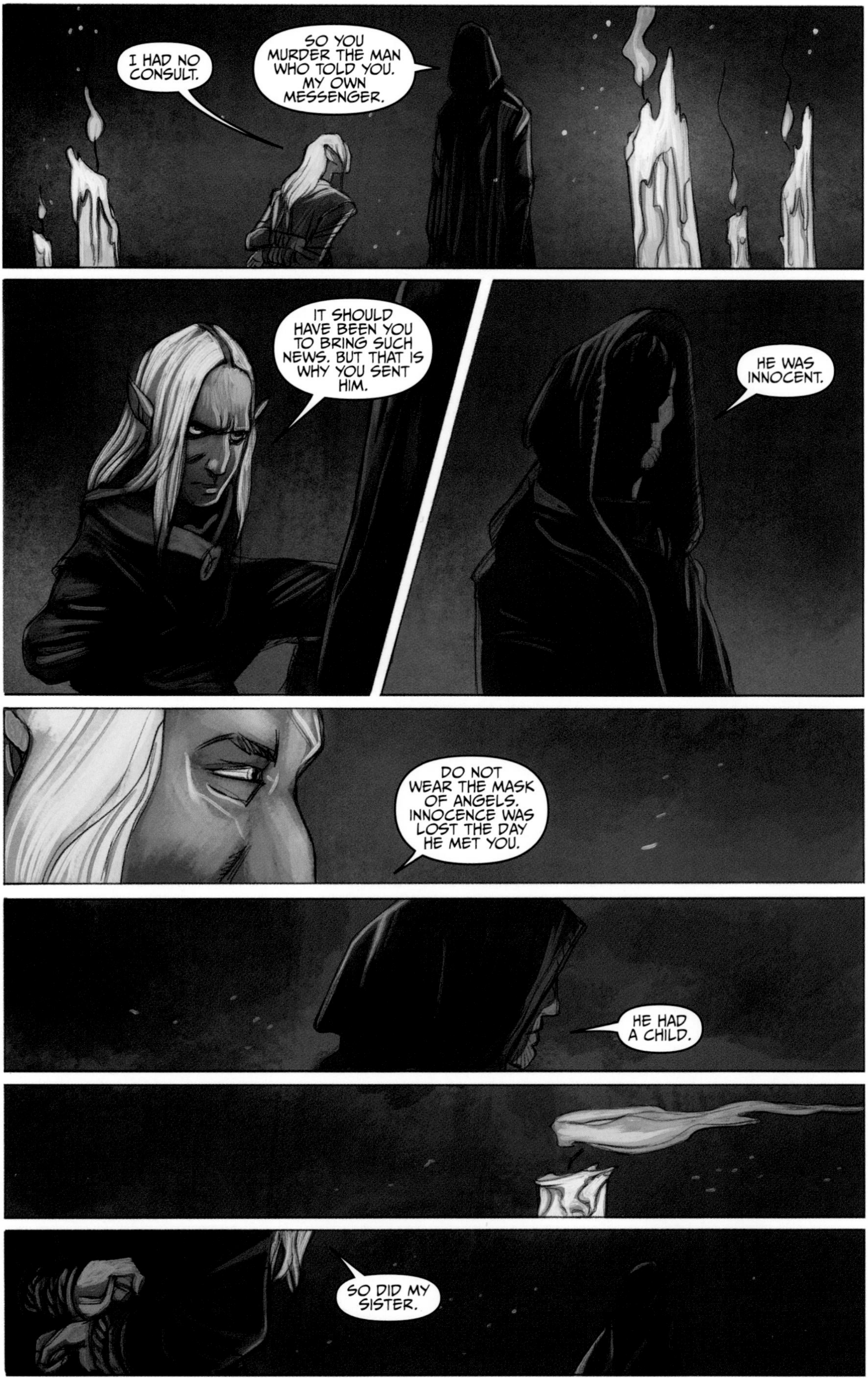
I HAD NO CONSULT.
SO YOU MURDER THE MAN WHO TOLD YOU. MY OWN MESSENGER.
IT SHOULD HAVE BEEN YOU TO BRING SUCH NEWS. BUT THAT IS WHY YOU SENT HIM.
HE WAS INNOCENT.
DO NOT WEAR THE MASK OF ANGELS. INNOCENCE WAS LOST THE DAY HE MET YOU.
HE HAD A CHILD.
SO DID MY SISTER.

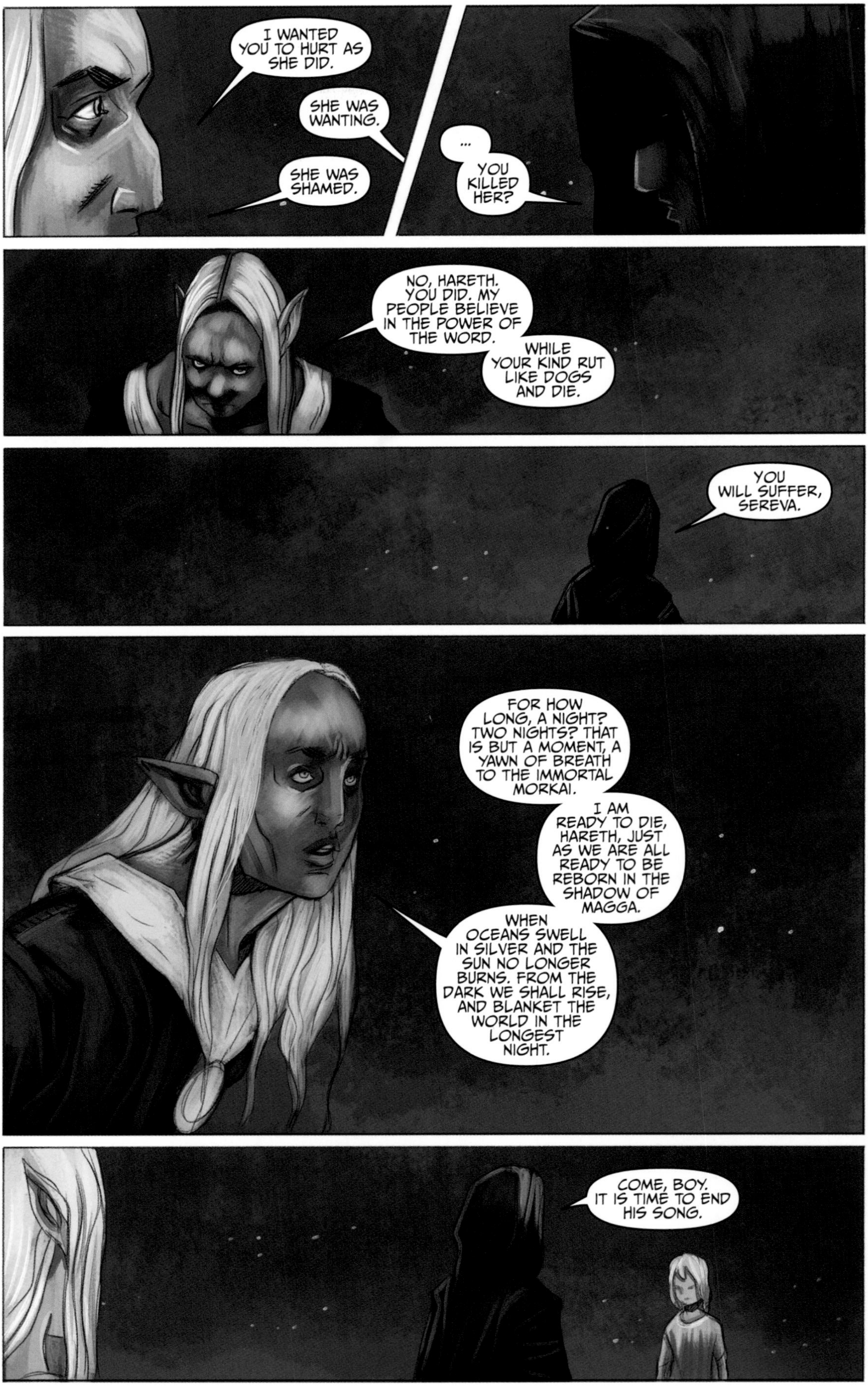
I WANTED YOU TO HURT AS SHE DID.
SHE WAS WANTING.
SHE WAS SHAMED.
...
YOU KILLED HER?
NO, HARETH. YOU DID. MY PEOPLE BELIEVE IN THE POWER OF THE WORD.
WHILE YOUR KIND RUT LIKE DOGS AND DIE.
YOU WILL SUFFER, SEREVA.
FOR HOW LONG, A NIGHT? TWO NIGHTS? THAT IS BUT A MOMENT, A YAWN OF BREATH TO THE IMMORTAL MORKAI.
I AM READY TO DIE, HARETH, JUST AS WE ARE ALL READY TO BE REBORN IN THE SHADOW OF MAGGA.
WHEN OCEANS SWELL IN SILVER AND THE SUN NO LONGER BURNS. FROM THE DARK WE SHALL RISE, AND BLANKET THE WORLD IN THE LONGEST NIGHT.
COME, BOY. IT IS TIME TO END HIS SONG.

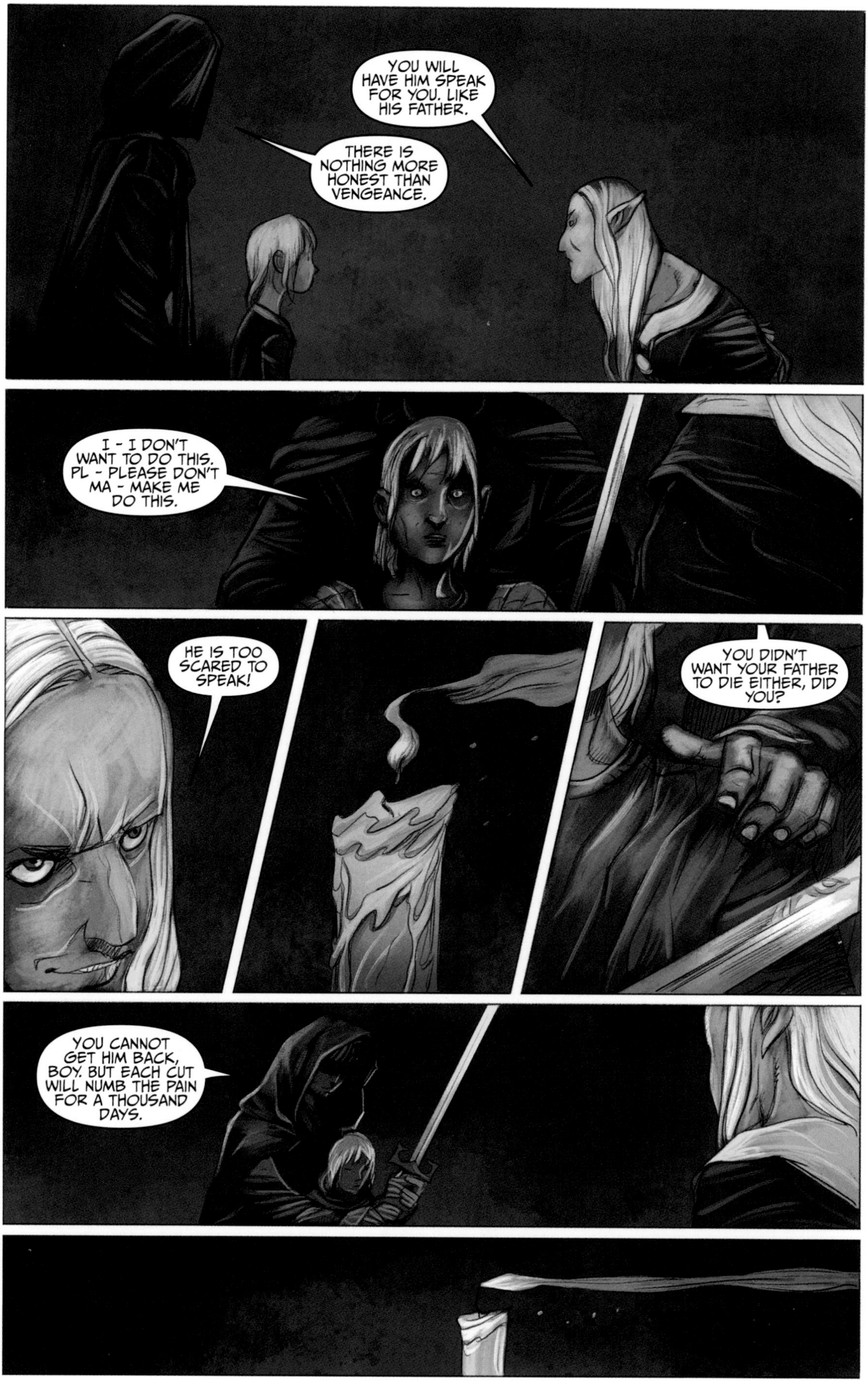
YOU WILL HAVE HIM SPEAK FOR YOU. LIKE HIS FATHER.
THERE IS NOTHING MORE HONEST THAN VENGEANCE.
I - I DON'T WANT TO DO THIS. PL - PLEASE DON'T MA - MAKE ME DO THIS.
HE IS TOO SCARED TO SPEAK!
YOU DIDN'T WANT YOUR FATHER TO DIE EITHER, DID YOU?
YOU CANNOT GET HIM BACK, BOY. BUT EACH CUT WILL NUMB THE PAIN FOR A THOUSAND DAYS.

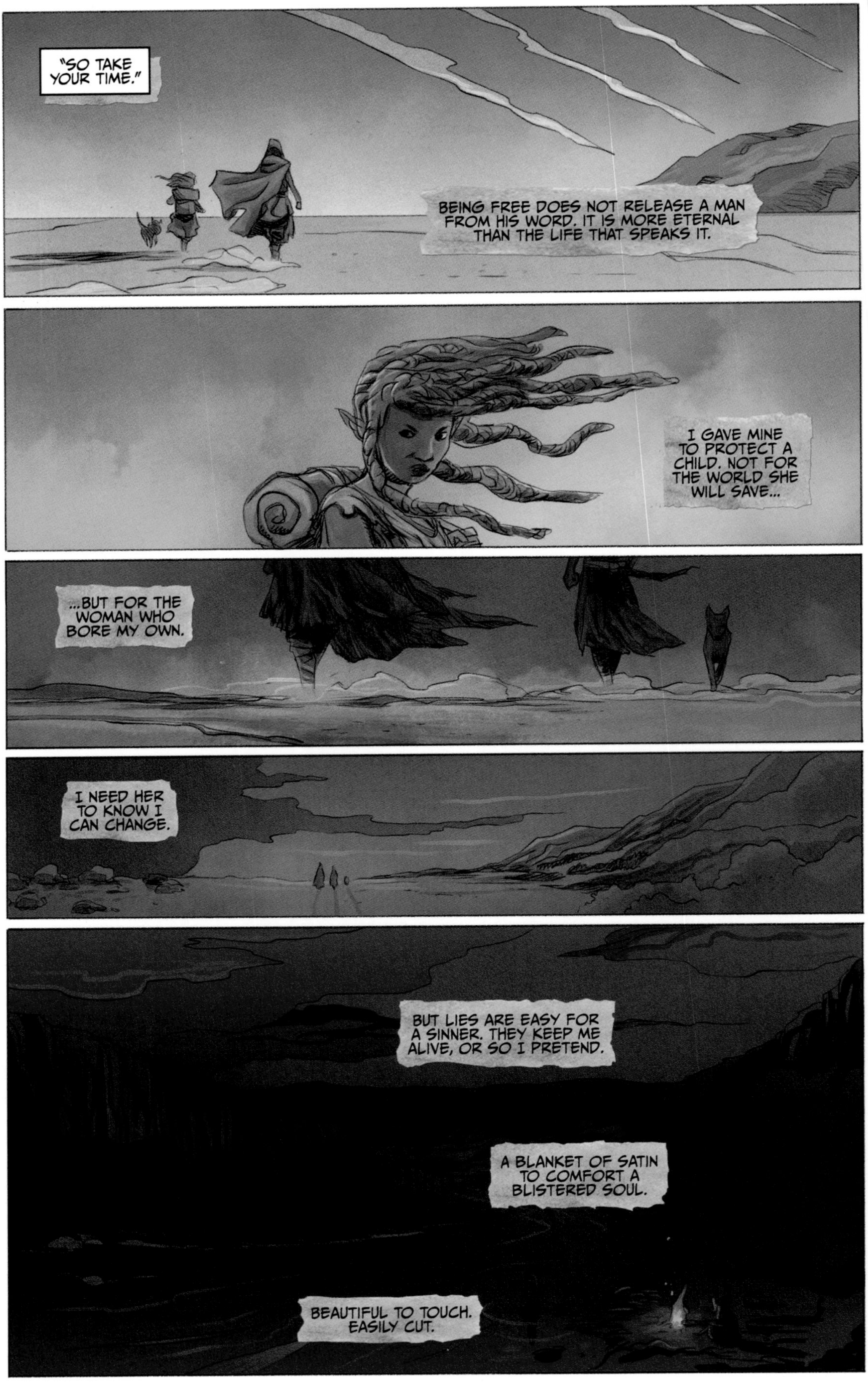
"SO TAKE YOUR TIME."
BEING FREE DOES NOT RELEASE A MAN FROM HIS WORD. IT IS MORE ETERNAL THAN THE LIFE THAT SPEAKS IT.
I GAVE MINE TO PROTECT A CHILD. NOT FOR THE WORLD SHE WILL SAVE...
...BUT FOR THE WOMAN WHO BORE MY OWN.
I NEED HER TO KNOW I CAN CHANGE.
BUT LIES ARE EASY FOR A SINNER. THEY KEEP ME ALIVE, OR SO I PRETEND.
A BLANKET OF SATIN TO COMFORT A BLISTERED SOUL.
BEAUTIFUL TO TOUCH. EASILY CUT.

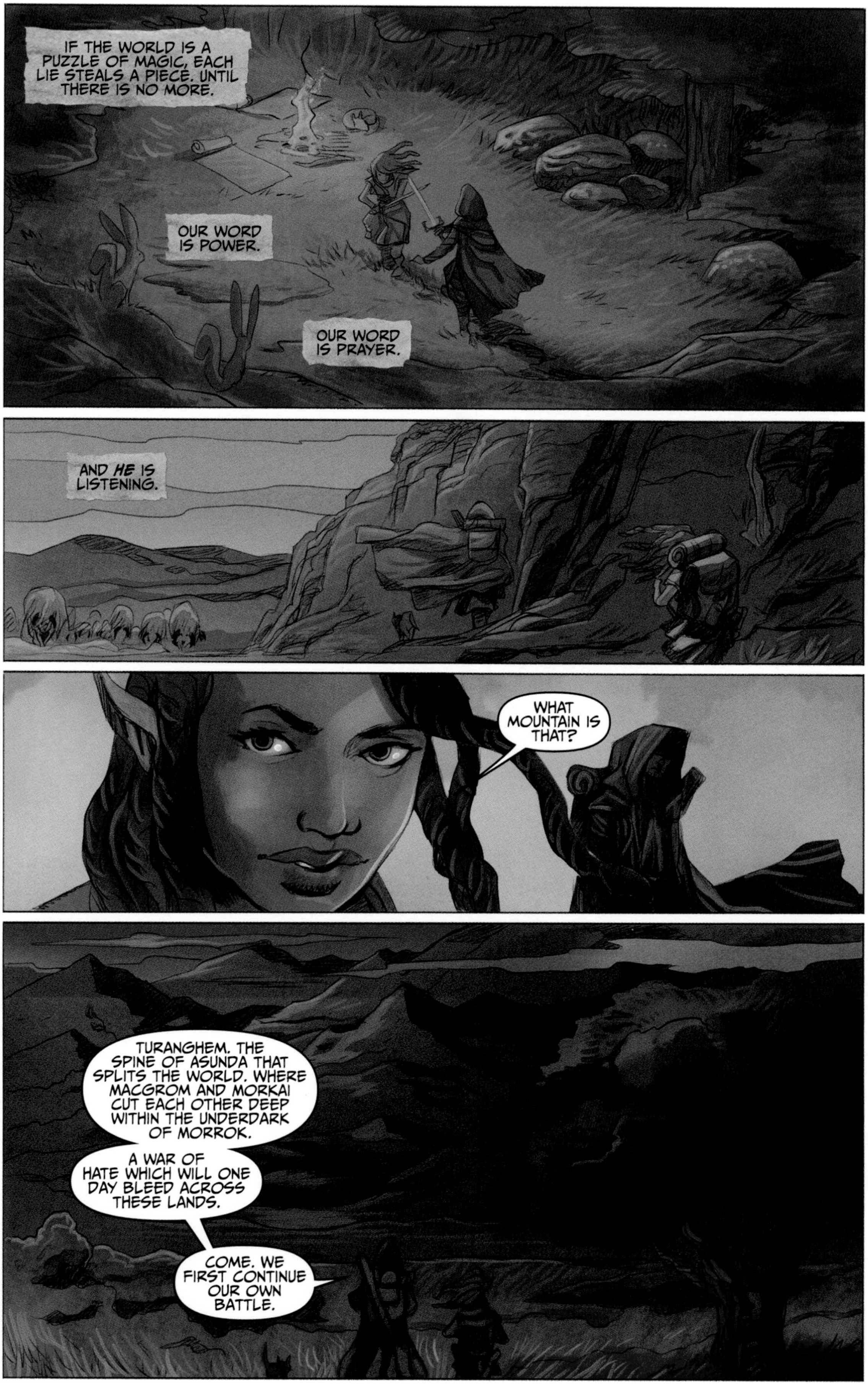
IF THE WORLD IS A PUZZLE OF MAGIC, EACH LIE STEALS A PIECE. UNTIL THERE IS NO MORE.
OUR WORD IS POWER.
OUR WORD IS PRAYER.
AND *HE* IS LISTENING.
WHAT MOUNTAIN IS THAT?
TURANGHEM. THE SPINE OF ASUNDA THAT SPLITS THE WORLD. WHERE MACGROM AND MORKAI CUT EACH OTHER DEEP WITHIN THE UNDERDARK OF MORROK.
A WAR OF HATE WHICH WILL ONE DAY BLEED ACROSS THESE LANDS.
COME. WE FIRST CONTINUE OUR OWN BATTLE.

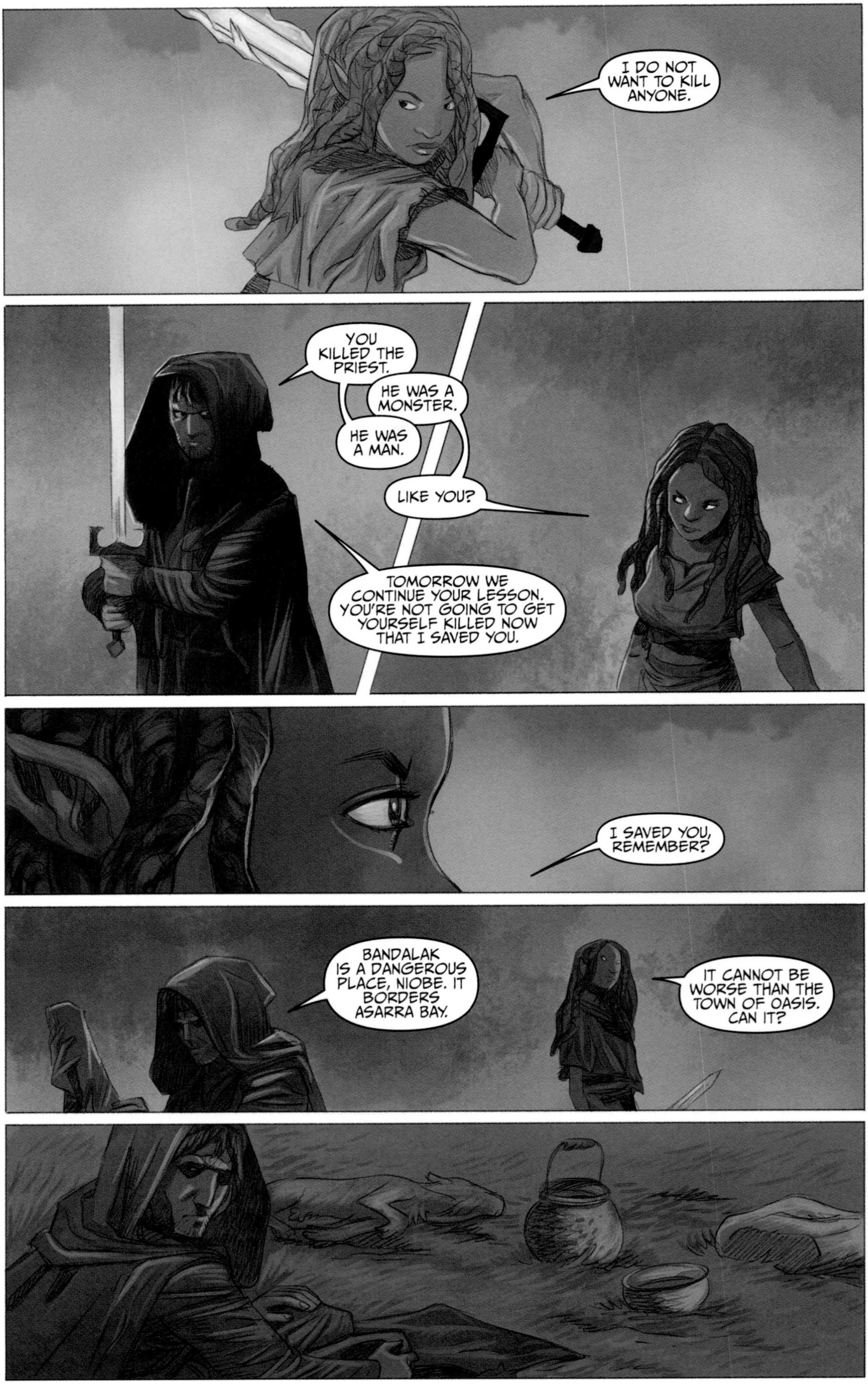
I DO NOT WANT TO KILL ANYONE.
YOU KILLED THE PRIEST.
HE WAS A MONSTER.
HE WAS A MAN.
LIKE YOU?
TOMORROW WE CONTINUE YOUR LESSON. YOU'RE NOT GOING TO GET YOURSELF KILLED NOW THAT I SAVED YOU.
I SAVED YOU, REMEMBER?
BANDALAK IS A DANGEROUS PLACE, NIOBE. IT BORDERS ASARRA BAY.
IT CANNOT BE WORSE THAN THE TOWN OF OASIS. CAN IT?

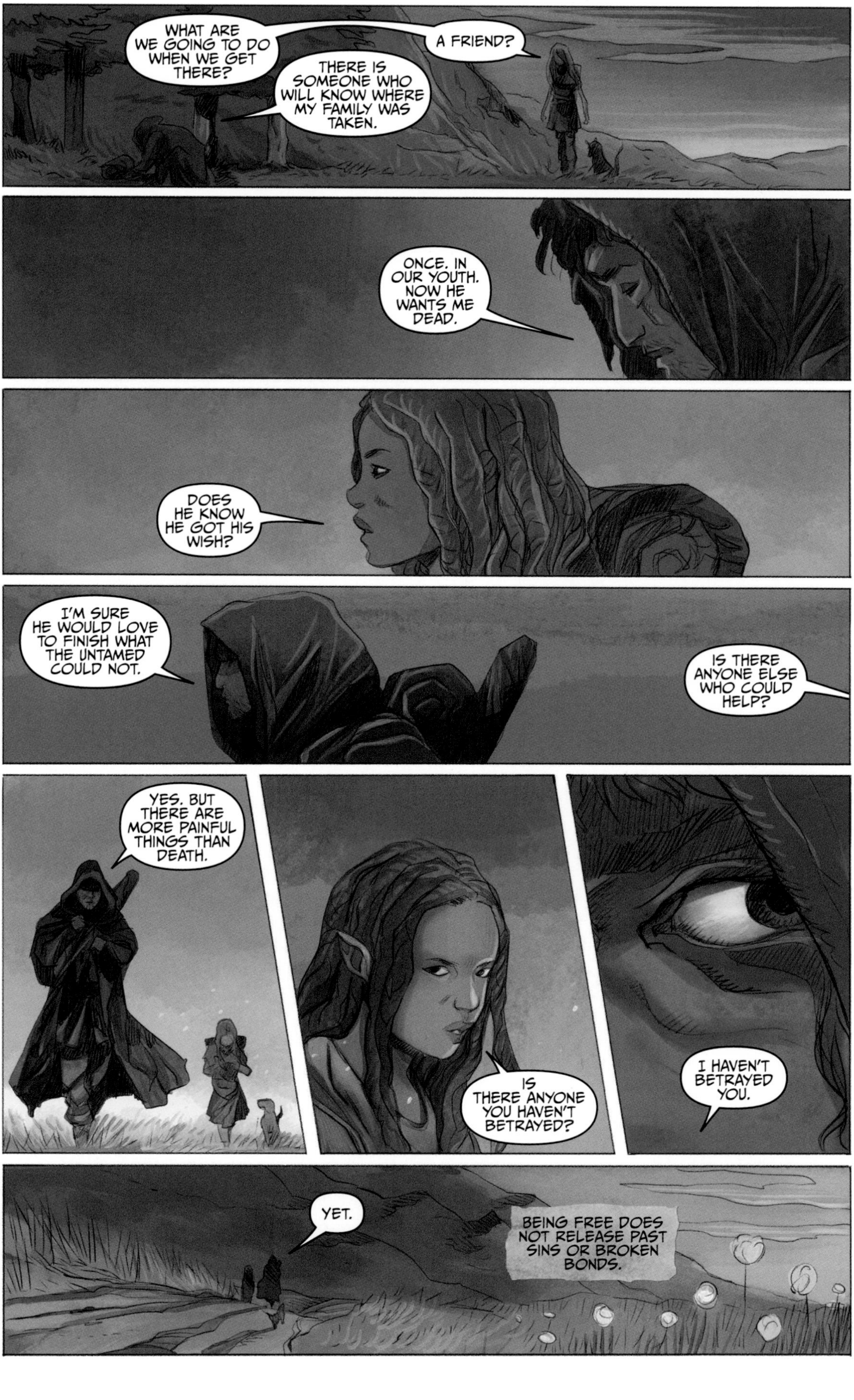
WHAT ARE WE GOING TO DO WHEN WE GET THERE?
THERE IS SOMEONE WHO WILL KNOW WHERE MY FAMILY WAS TAKEN.
A FRIEND?
ONCE. IN OUR YOUTH. NOW HE WANTS ME DEAD.
DOES HE KNOW HE GOT HIS WISH?
I'M SURE HE WOULD LOVE TO FINISH WHAT THE UNTAMED COULD NOT.
IS THERE ANYONE ELSE WHO COULD HELP?
YES. BUT THERE ARE MORE PAINFUL THINGS THAN DEATH.
IS THERE ANYONE YOU HAVEN'T BETRAYED?
I HAVEN'T BETRAYED YOU.
YET.
BEING FREE DOES NOT RELEASE PAST SINS OR BROKEN BONDS.

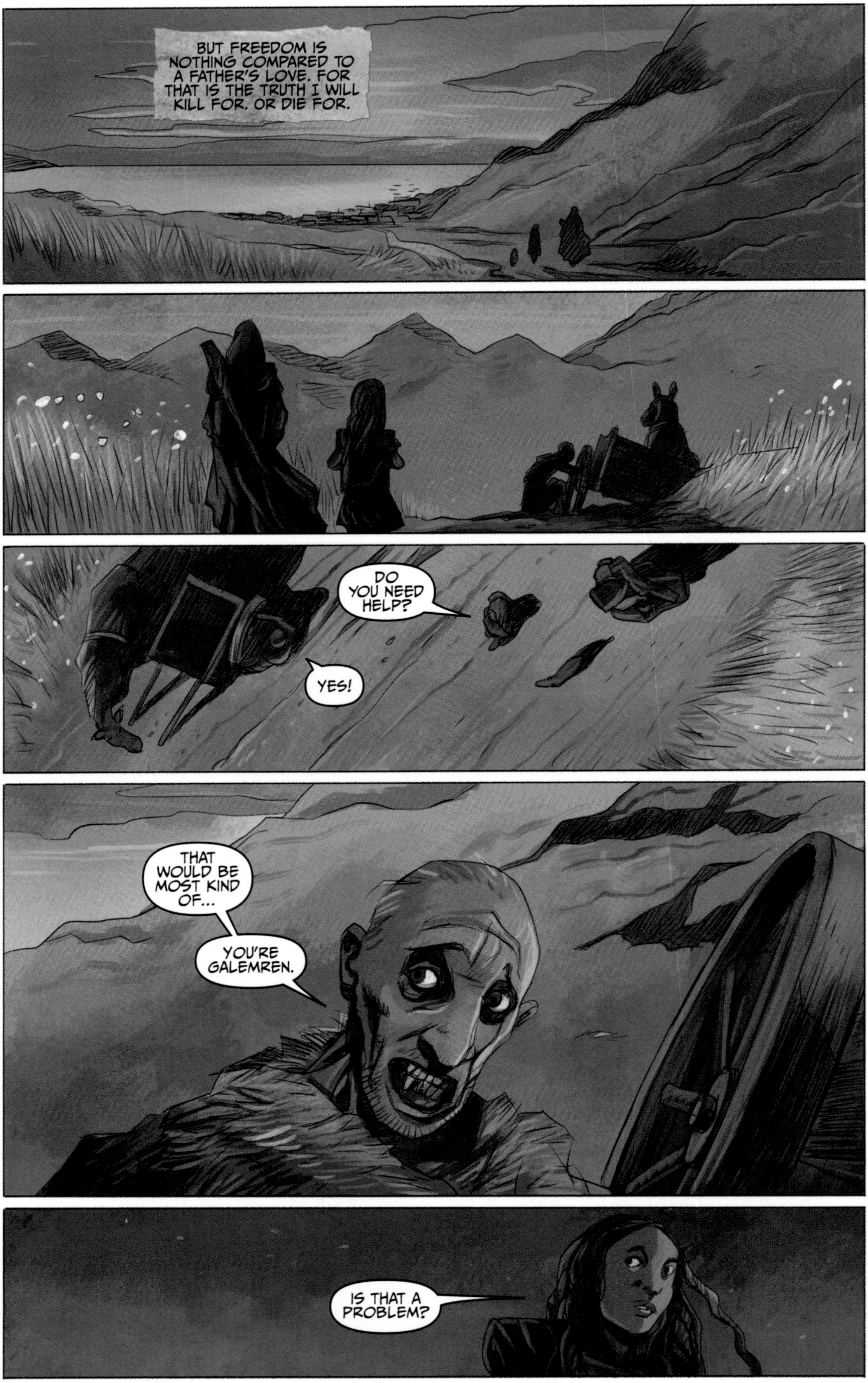
BUT FREEDOM IS NOTHING COMPARED TO A FATHER'S LOVE. FOR THAT IS THE TRUTH I WILL KILL FOR. OR DIE FOR.
DO YOU NEED HELP?
YES!
THAT WOULD BE MOST KIND OF...
YOU'RE GALEMREN.
IS THAT A PROBLEM?

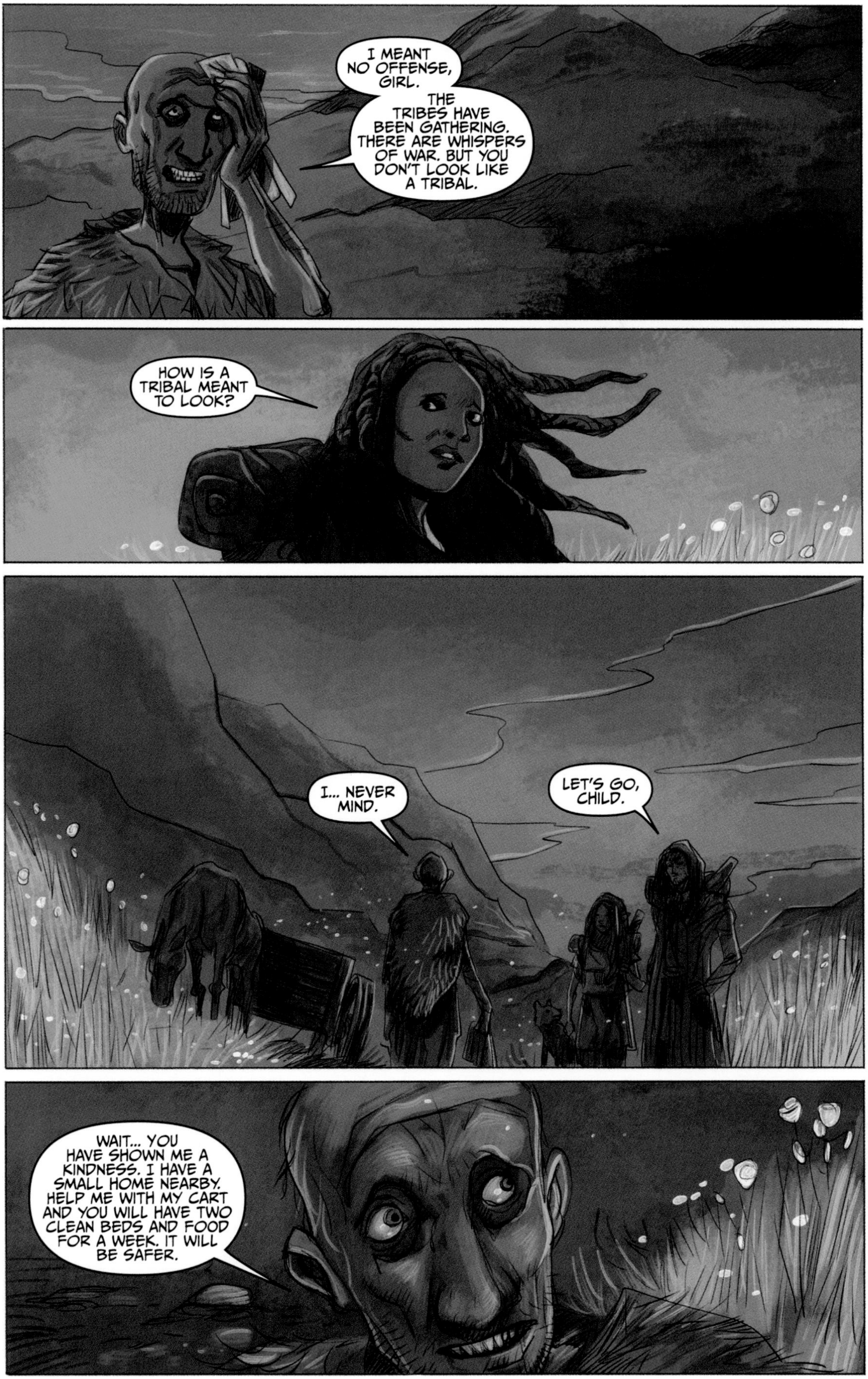
I MEANT NO OFFENSE, GIRL.
THE TRIBES HAVE BEEN GATHERING. THERE ARE WHISPERS OF WAR. BUT YOU DON'T LOOK LIKE A TRIBAL.
HOW IS A TRIBAL MEANT TO LOOK?
I... NEVER MIND.
LET'S GO, CHILD.
WAIT... YOU HAVE SHOWN ME A KINDNESS. I HAVE A SMALL HOME NEARBY. HELP ME WITH MY CART AND YOU WILL HAVE TWO CLEAN BEDS AND FOOD FOR A WEEK. IT WILL BE SAFER.

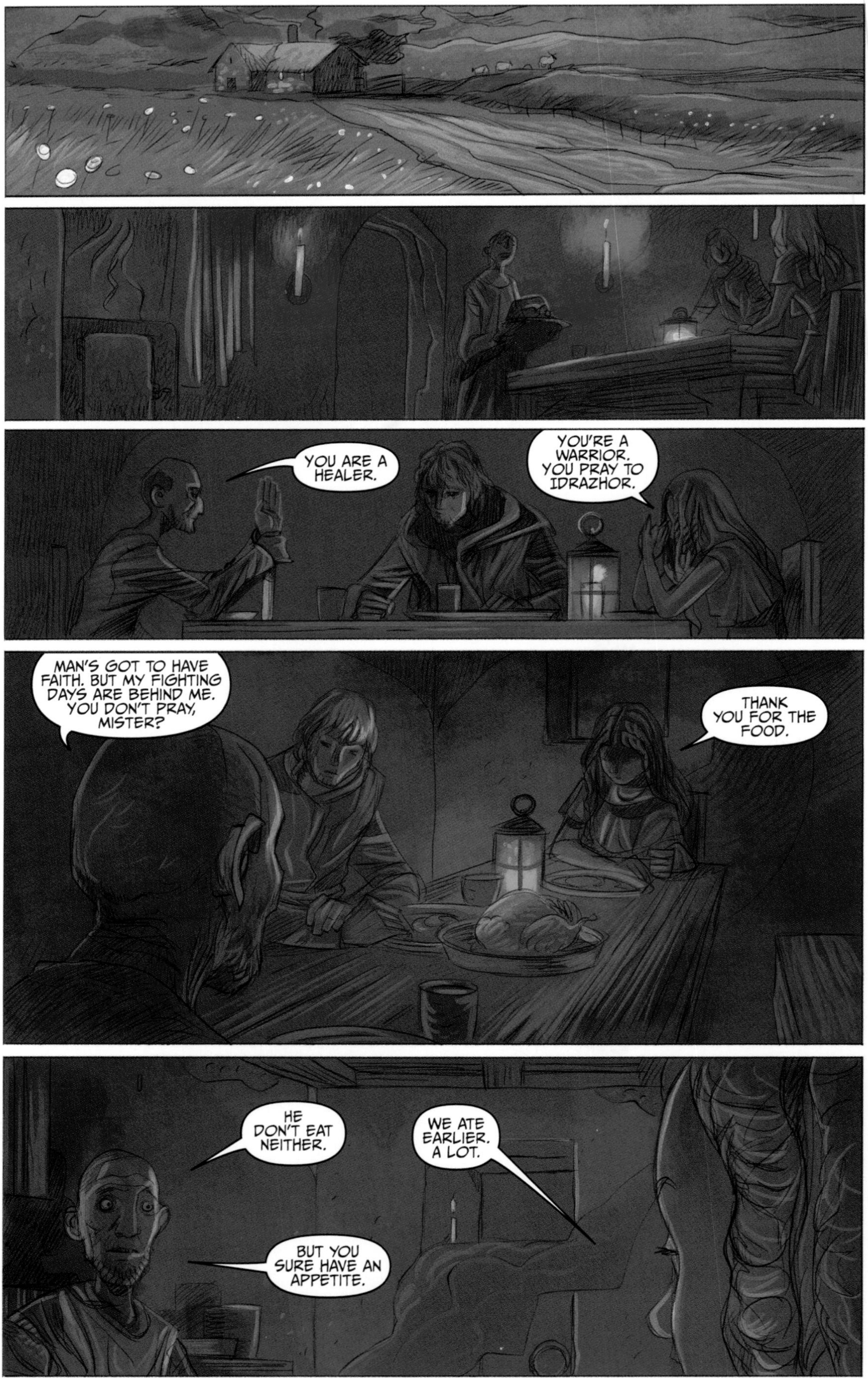
YOU ARE A HEALER.
YOU'RE A WARRIOR. YOU PRAY TO IDRAZHOR.
MAN'S GOT TO HAVE FAITH. BUT MY FIGHTING DAYS ARE BEHIND ME. YOU DON'T PRAY, MISTER?
THANK YOU FOR THE FOOD.
HE DON'T EAT NEITHER.
WE ATE EARLIER. A LOT.
BUT YOU SURE HAVE AN APPETITE.

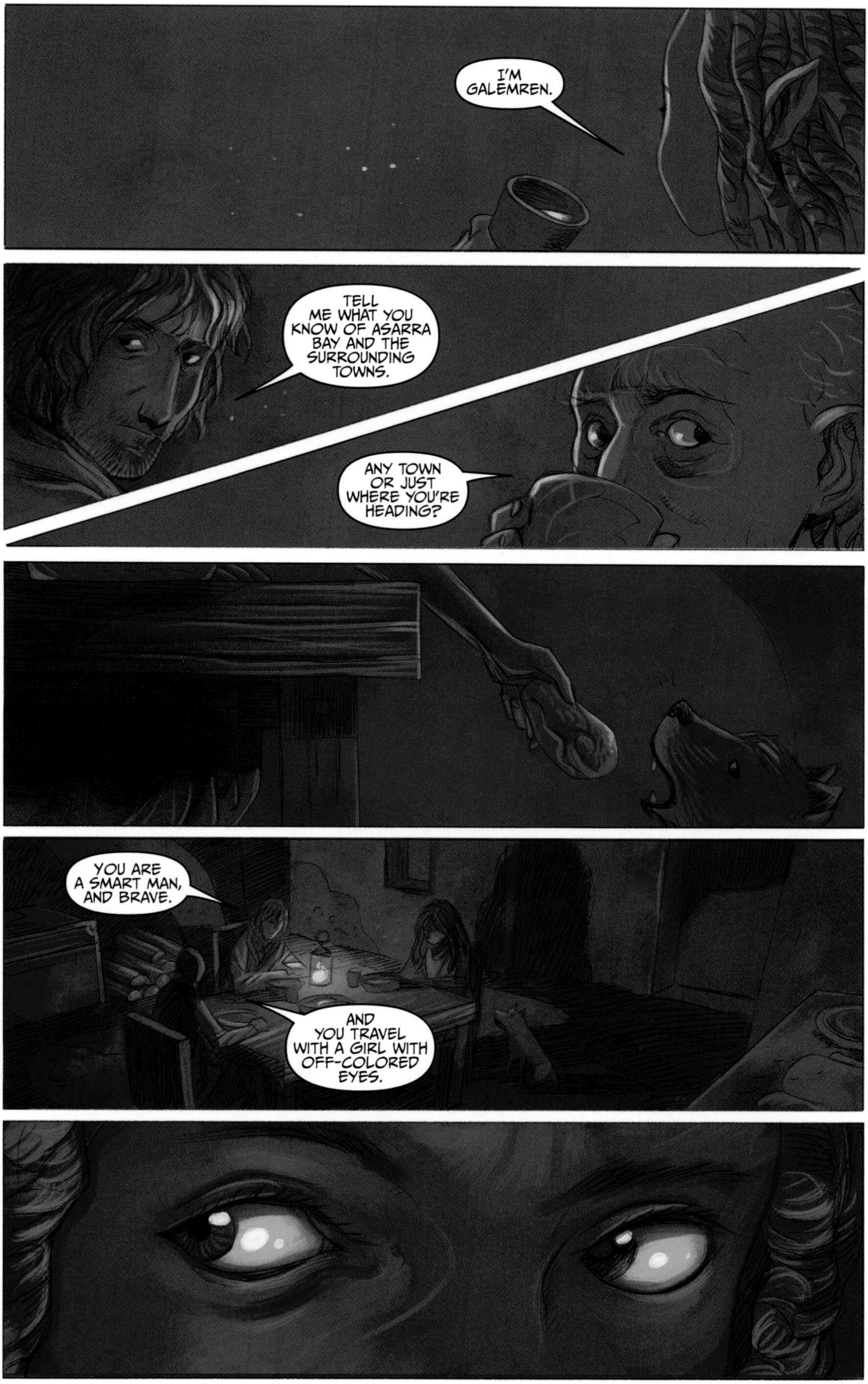
I'M GALEMREN.
TELL ME WHAT YOU KNOW OF ASARRA BAY AND THE SURROUNDING TOWNS.
ANY TOWN OR JUST WHERE YOU'RE HEADING?
YOU ARE A SMART MAN, AND BRAVE.
AND YOU TRAVEL WITH A GIRL WITH OFF-COLORED EYES.

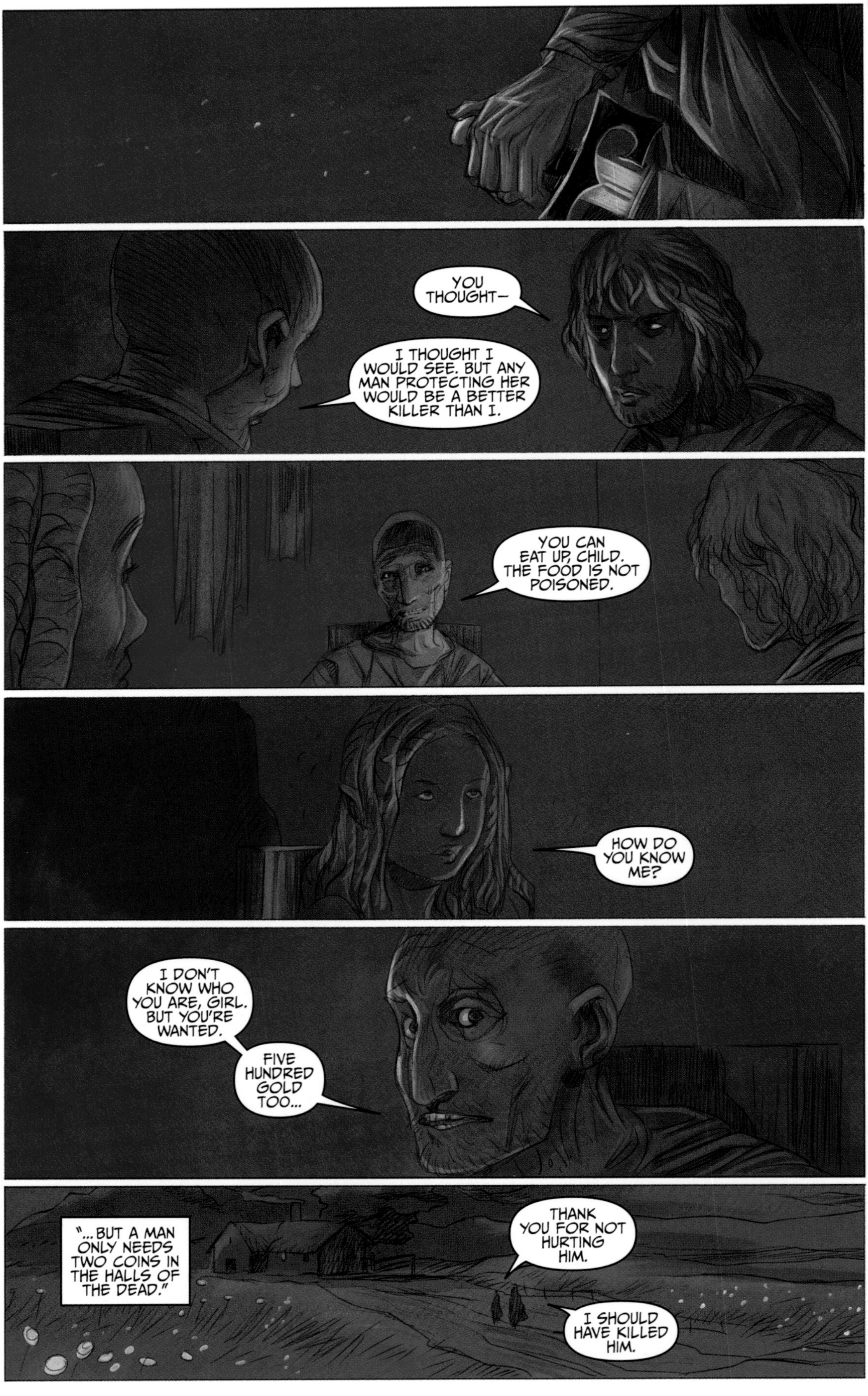
YOU THOUGHT--
I THOUGHT I WOULD SEE. BUT ANY MAN PROTECTING HER WOULD BE A BETTER KILLER THAN I.
YOU CAN EAT UP, CHILD. THE FOOD IS NOT POISONED.
HOW DO YOU KNOW ME?
I DON'T KNOW WHO YOU ARE, GIRL. BUT YOU'RE WANTED.
FIVE HUNDRED GOLD TOO...
"...BUT A MAN ONLY NEEDS TWO COINS IN THE HALLS OF THE DEAD."
THANK YOU FOR NOT HURTING HIM.
I SHOULD HAVE KILLED HIM.

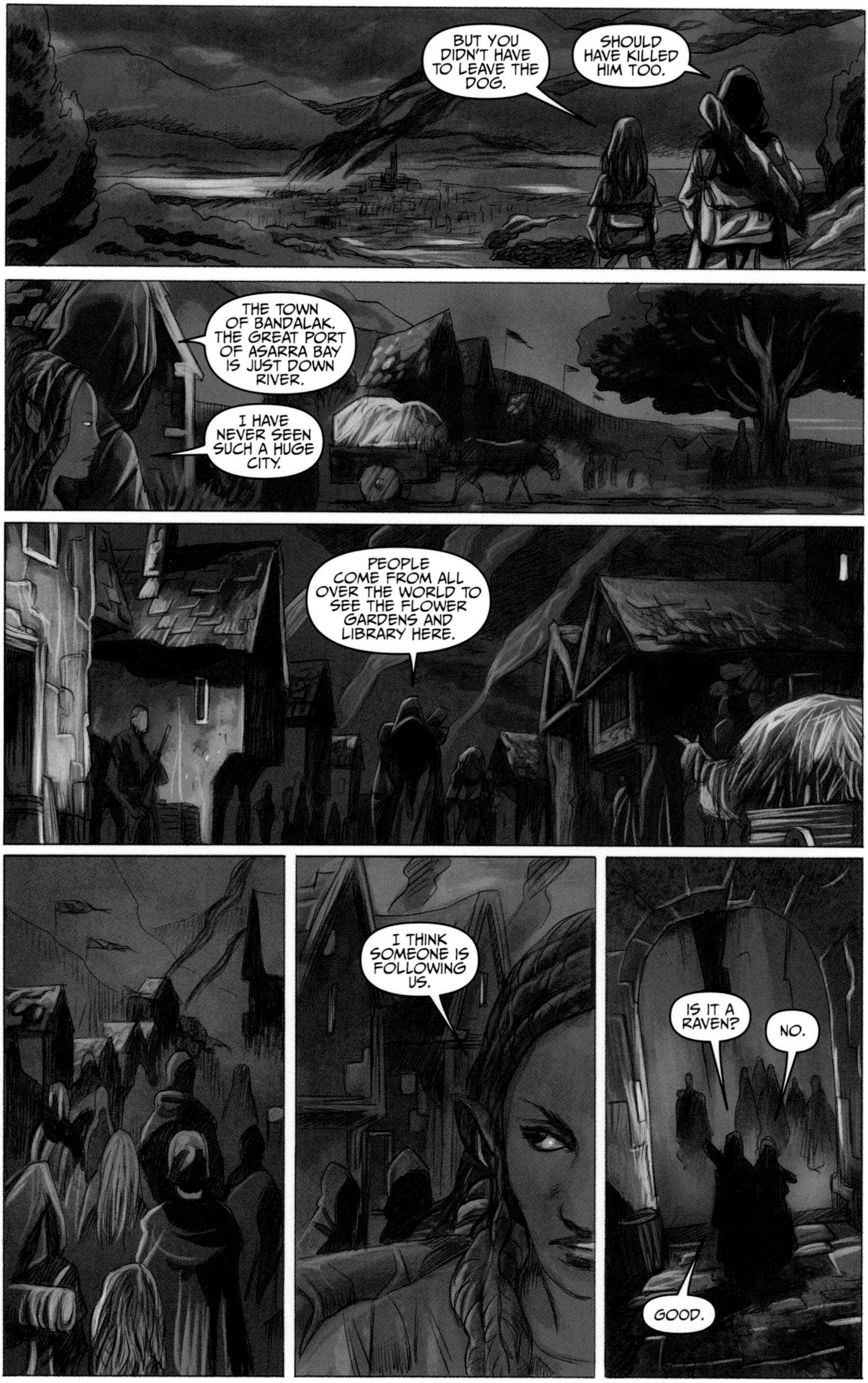
BUT YOU DIDN'T HAVE TO LEAVE THE DOG.
SHOULD HAVE KILLED HIM TOO.
THE TOWN OF BANDALAK. THE GREAT PORT OF ASARRA BAY IS JUST DOWN RIVER.
I HAVE NEVER SEEN SUCH A HUGE CITY.
PEOPLE COME FROM ALL OVER THE WORLD TO SEE THE FLOWER GARDENS AND LIBRARY HERE.
I THINK SOMEONE IS FOLLOWING US.
IS IT A RAVEN?
NO.
GOOD.

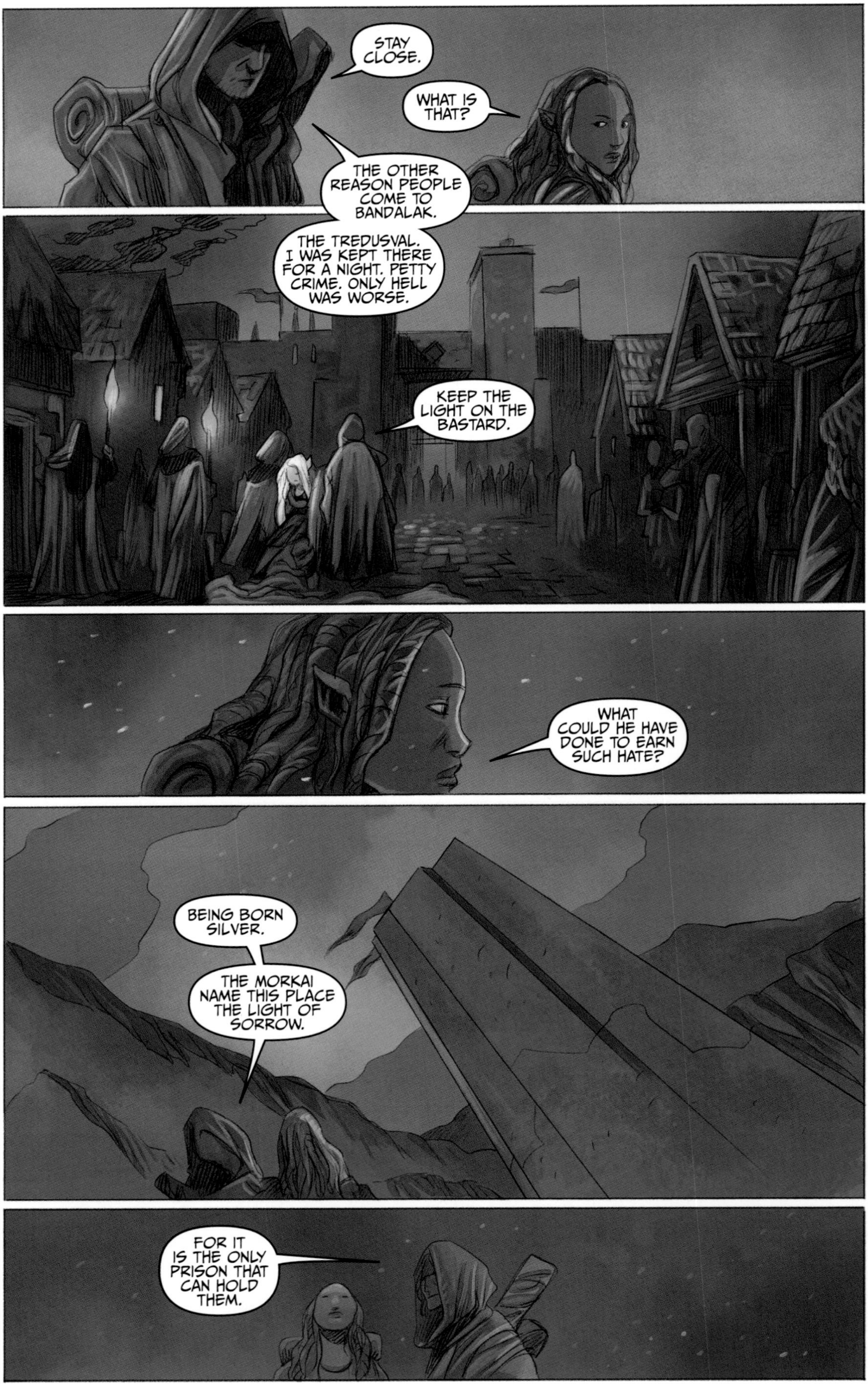
STAY CLOSE.
WHAT IS THAT?
THE OTHER REASON PEOPLE COME TO BANDALAK.
THE TREDUSVAL. I WAS KEPT THERE FOR A NIGHT. PETTY CRIME. ONLY HELL WAS WORSE.
KEEP THE LIGHT ON THE BASTARD.
WHAT COULD HE HAVE DONE TO EARN SUCH HATE?
BEING BORN SILVER.
THE MORKAI NAME THIS PLACE THE LIGHT OF SORROW.
FOR IT IS THE ONLY PRISON THAT CAN HOLD THEM.

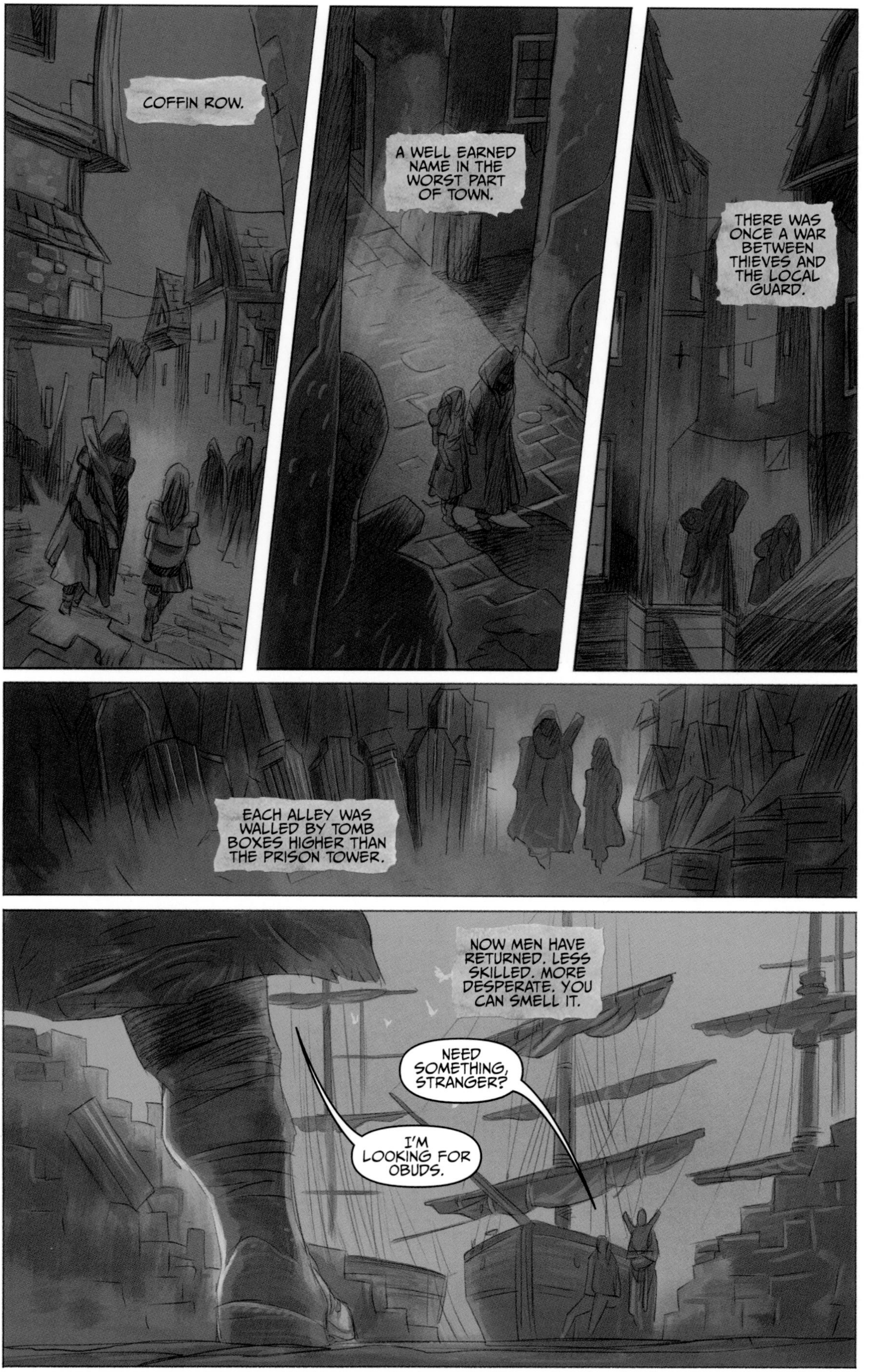
COFFIN ROW.
A WELL EARNED NAME IN THE WORST PART OF TOWN.
THERE WAS ONCE A WAR BETWEEN THIEVES AND THE LOCAL GUARD.
EACH ALLEY WAS WALLED BY TOMB BOXES HIGHER THAN THE PRISON TOWER.
NOW MEN HAVE RETURNED. LESS SKILLED. MORE DESPERATE. YOU CAN SMELL IT.
NEED SOMETHING, STRANGER?
I'M LOOKING FOR OBUDS.

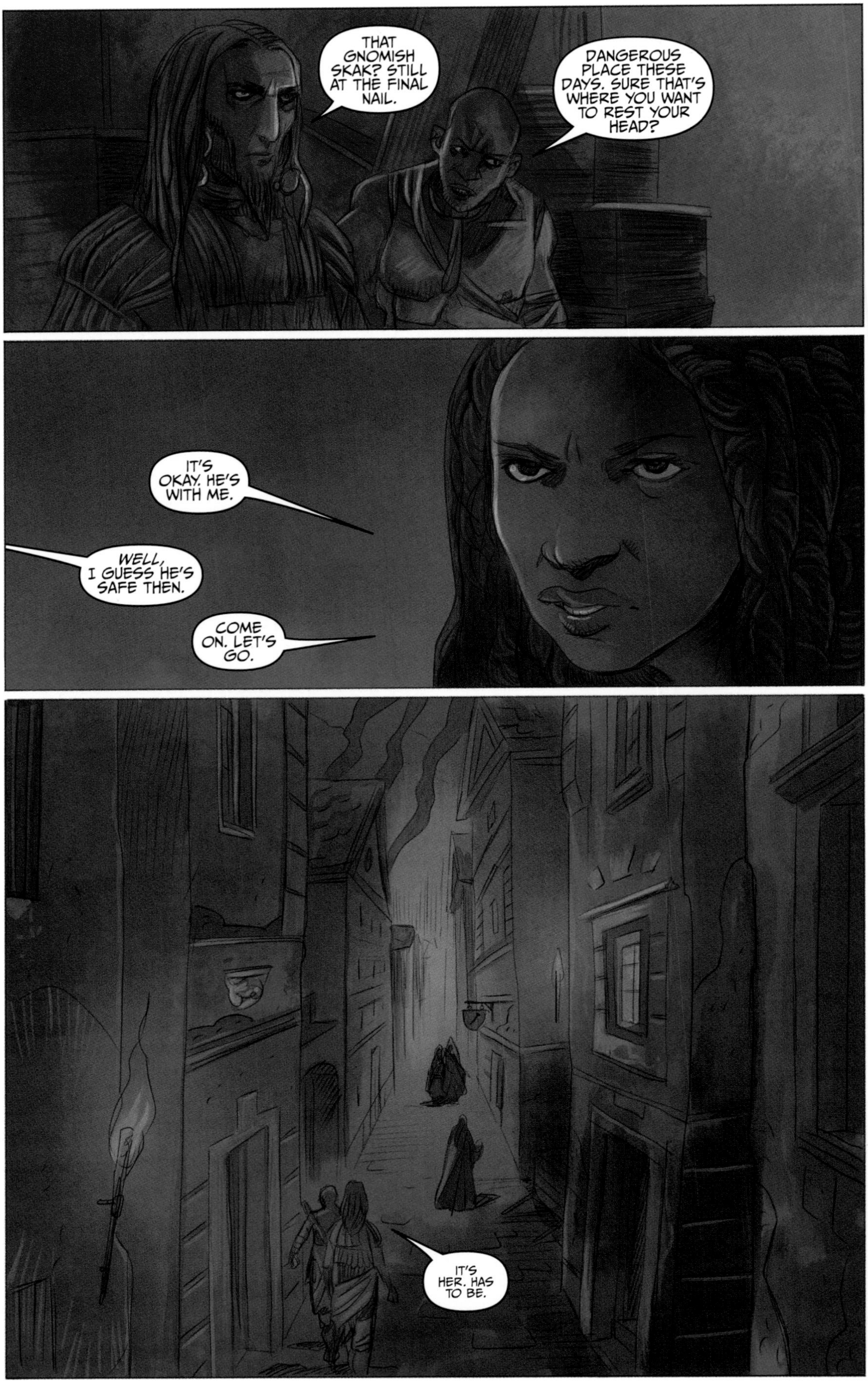
THAT GNOMISH SKAK? STILL AT THE FINAL NAIL.
DANGEROUS PLACE THESE DAYS. SURE THAT'S WHERE YOU WANT TO REST YOUR HEAD?
IT'S OKAY. HE'S WITH ME.
WELL, I GUESS HE'S SAFE THEN.
COME ON. LET'S GO.
IT'S HER. HAS TO BE.

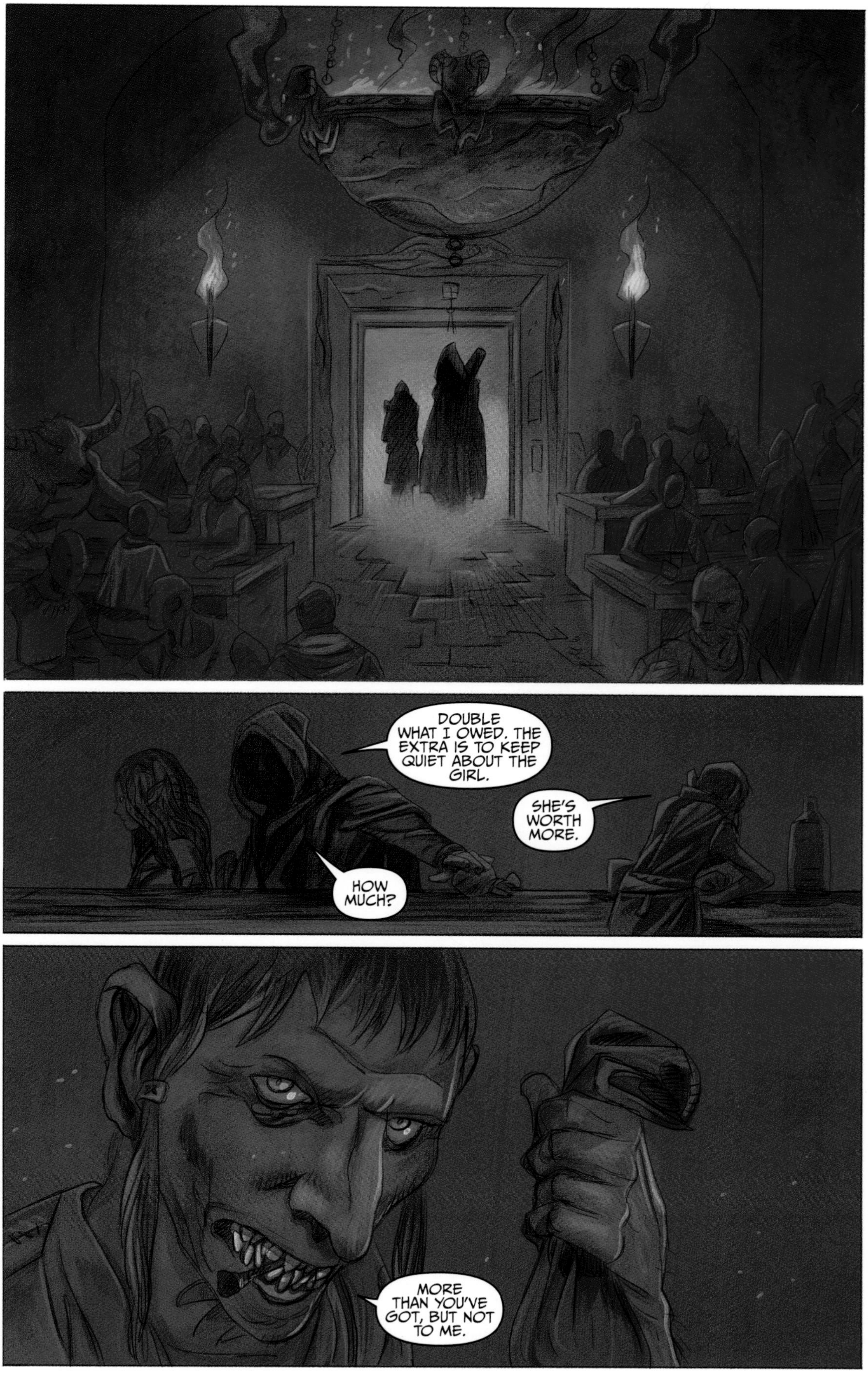
DOUBLE WHAT I OWED. THE EXTRA IS TO KEEP QUIET ABOUT THE GIRL.
SHE'S WORTH MORE.
HOW MUCH?
MORE THAN YOU'VE GOT, BUT NOT TO ME.

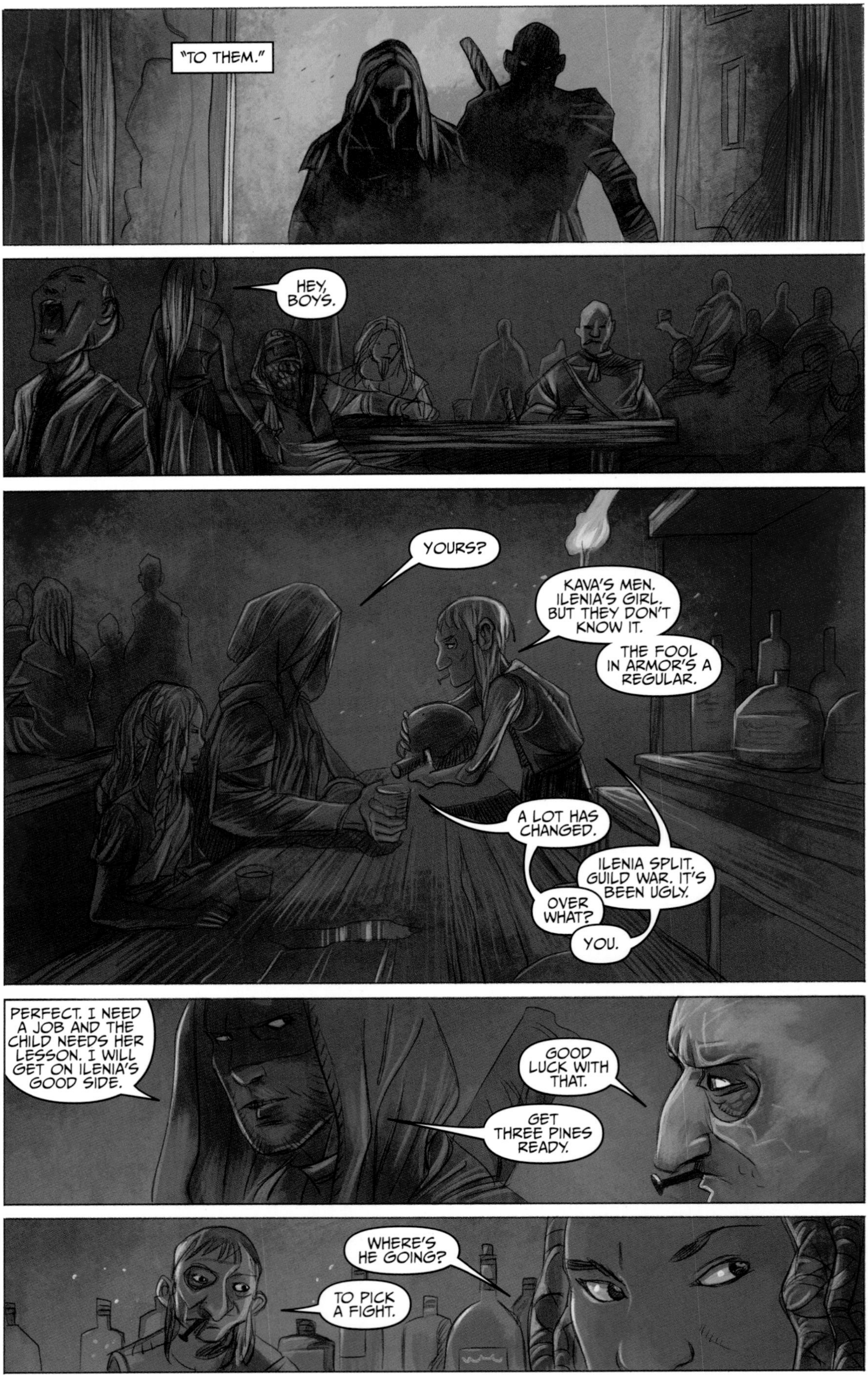
"TO THEM."
HEY, BOYS.
YOURS?
KAVA'S MEN. ILENIA'S GIRL. BUT THEY DON'T KNOW IT.
THE FOOL IN ARMOR'S A REGULAR.
A LOT HAS CHANGED.
ILENIA SPLIT. GUILD WAR. IT'S BEEN UGLY.
OVER WHAT?
YOU.
PERFECT. I NEED A JOB AND THE CHILD NEEDS HER LESSON. I WILL GET ON ILENIA'S GOOD SIDE.
GOOD LUCK WITH THAT.
GET THREE PINES READY.
WHERE'S HE GOING?
TO PICK A FIGHT.

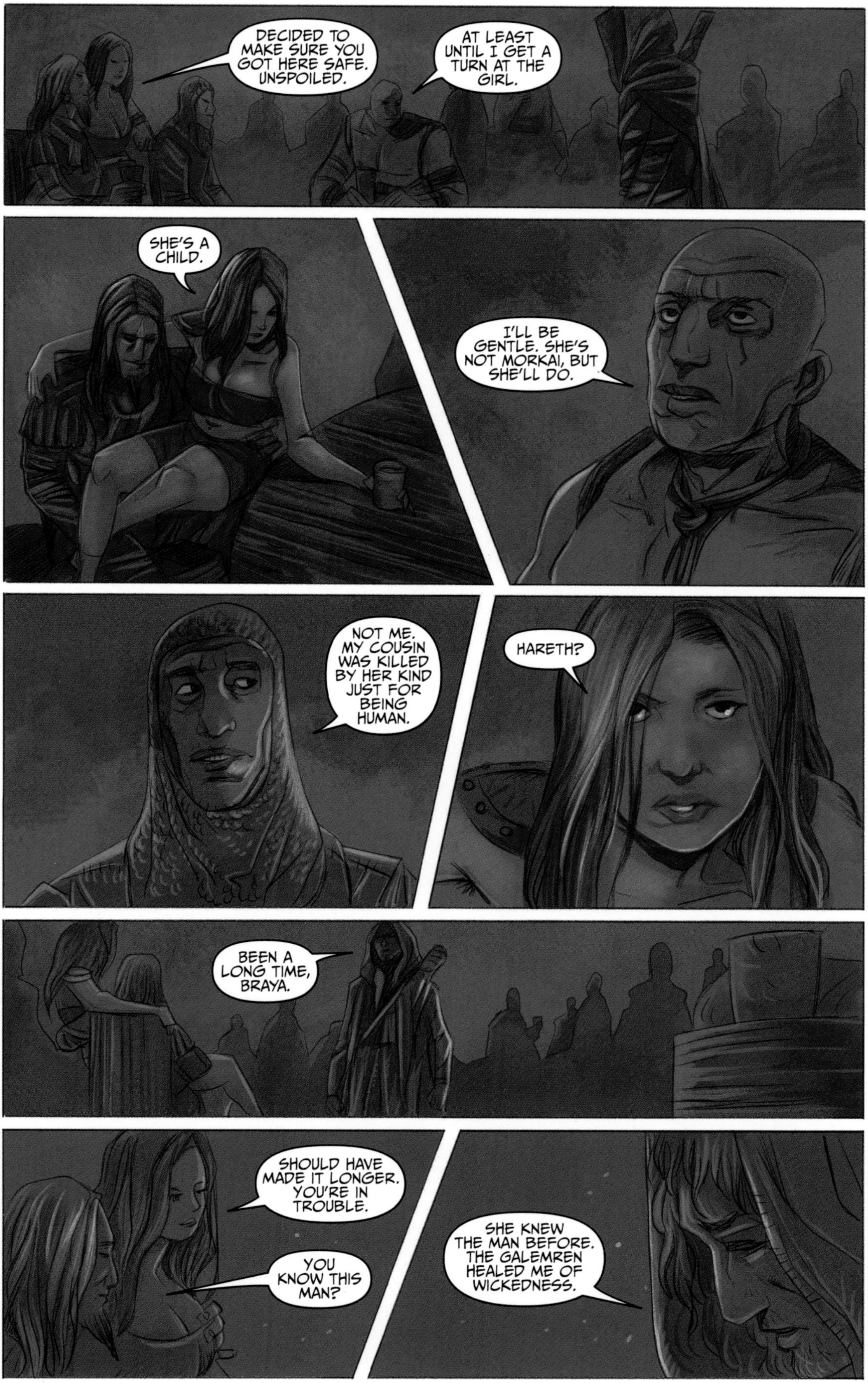
DECIDED TO MAKE SURE YOU GOT HERE SAFE. UNSPOILED.
AT LEAST UNTIL I GET A TURN AT THE GIRL.
SHE'S A CHILD.
I'LL BE GENTLE. SHE'S NOT MORKAI, BUT SHE'LL DO.
NOT ME. MY COUSIN WAS KILLED BY HER KIND JUST FOR BEING HUMAN.
HARETH?
BEEN A LONG TIME, BRAYA.
SHOULD HAVE MADE IT LONGER. YOU'RE IN TROUBLE.
YOU KNOW THIS MAN?
SHE KNEW THE MAN BEFORE. THE GALEMREN HEALED ME OF WICKEDNESS.

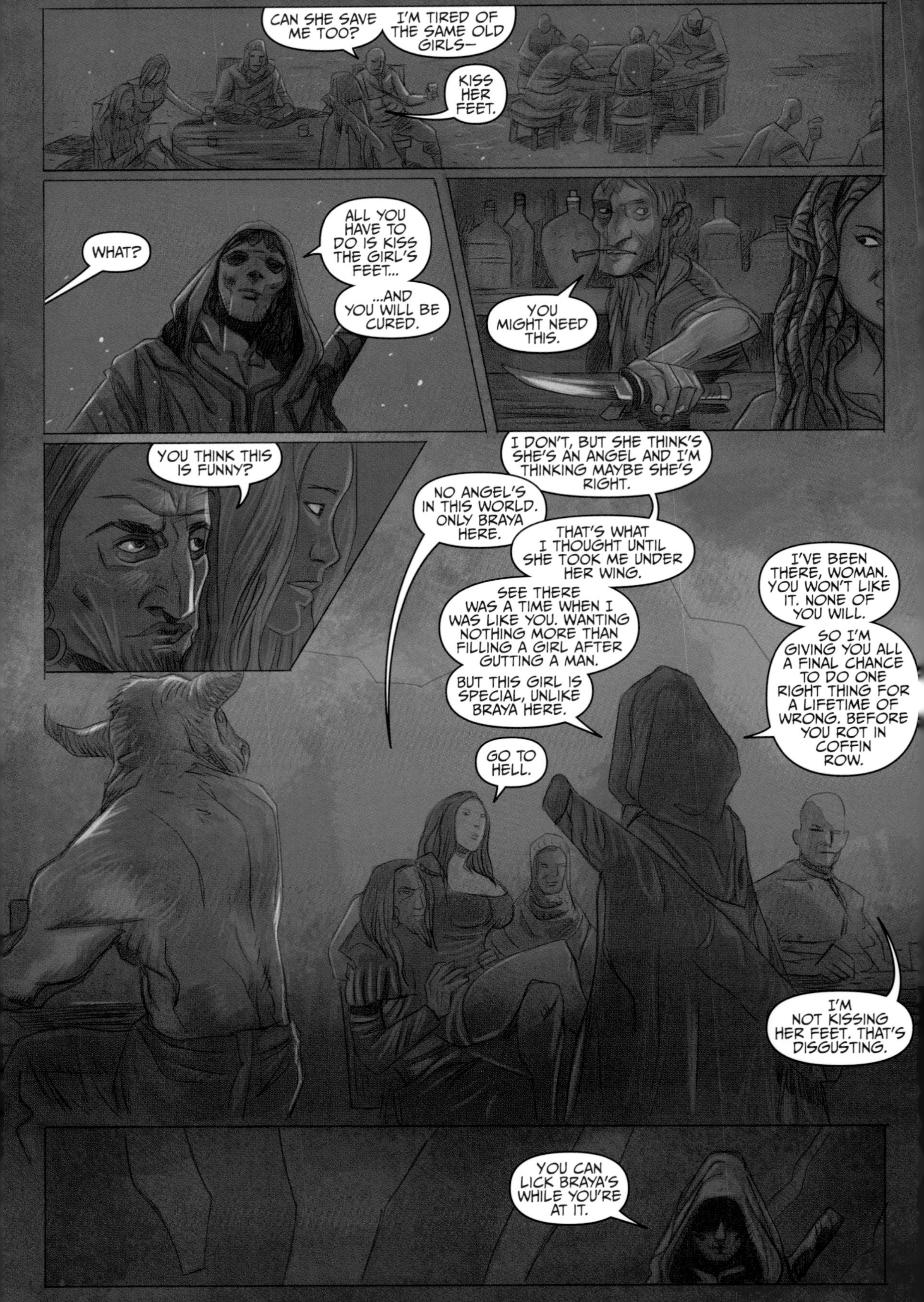
CAN SHE SAVE ME TOO?
I'M TIRED OF THE SAME OLD GIRLS—
KISS HER FEET.
WHAT?
ALL YOU HAVE TO DO IS KISS THE GIRL'S FEET...
...AND YOU WILL BE CURED.
YOU MIGHT NEED THIS.
YOU THINK THIS IS FUNNY?
I DON'T, BUT SHE THINK'S SHE'S AN ANGEL AND I'M THINKING MAYBE SHE'S RIGHT.
NO ANGEL'S IN THIS WORLD. ONLY BRAYA HERE.
THAT'S WHAT I THOUGHT UNTIL SHE TOOK ME UNDER HER WING.
SEE THERE WAS A TIME WHEN I WAS LIKE YOU. WANTING NOTHING MORE THAN FILLING A GIRL AFTER GUTTING A MAN.
BUT THIS GIRL IS SPECIAL, UNLIKE BRAYA HERE.
I'VE BEEN THERE, WOMAN. YOU WON'T LIKE IT. NONE OF YOU WILL.
SO I'M GIVING YOU ALL A FINAL CHANCE TO DO ONE RIGHT THING FOR A LIFETIME OF WRONG. BEFORE YOU ROT IN COFFIN ROW.
GO TO HELL.
I'M NOT KISSING HER FEET. THAT'S DISGUSTING.
YOU CAN LICK BRAYA'S WHILE YOU'RE AT IT.

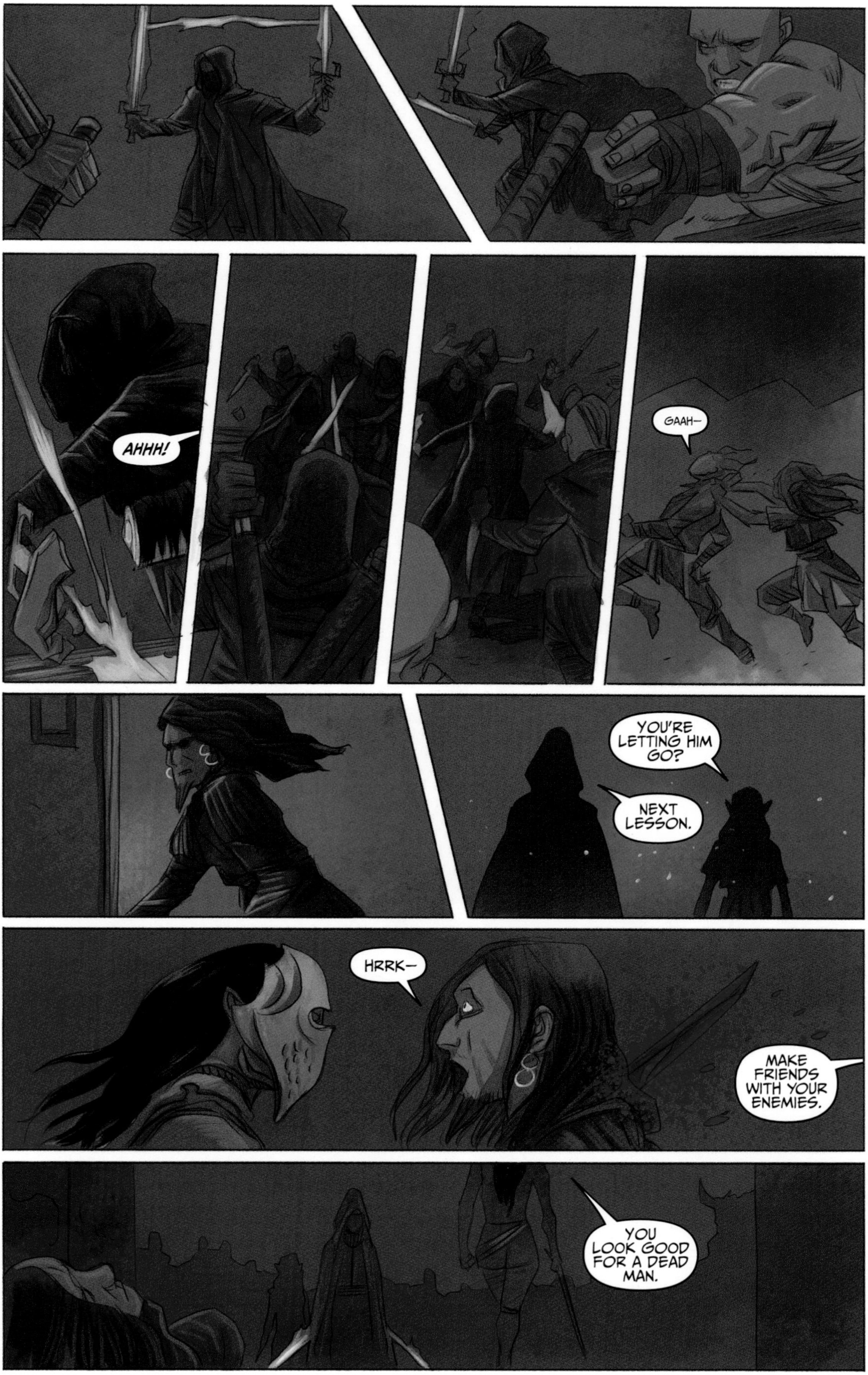
AHHH!
GAAH—
YOU'RE LETTING HIM GO?
NEXT LESSON.
HRRK—
MAKE FRIENDS WITH YOUR ENEMIES.
YOU LOOK GOOD FOR A DEAD MAN.

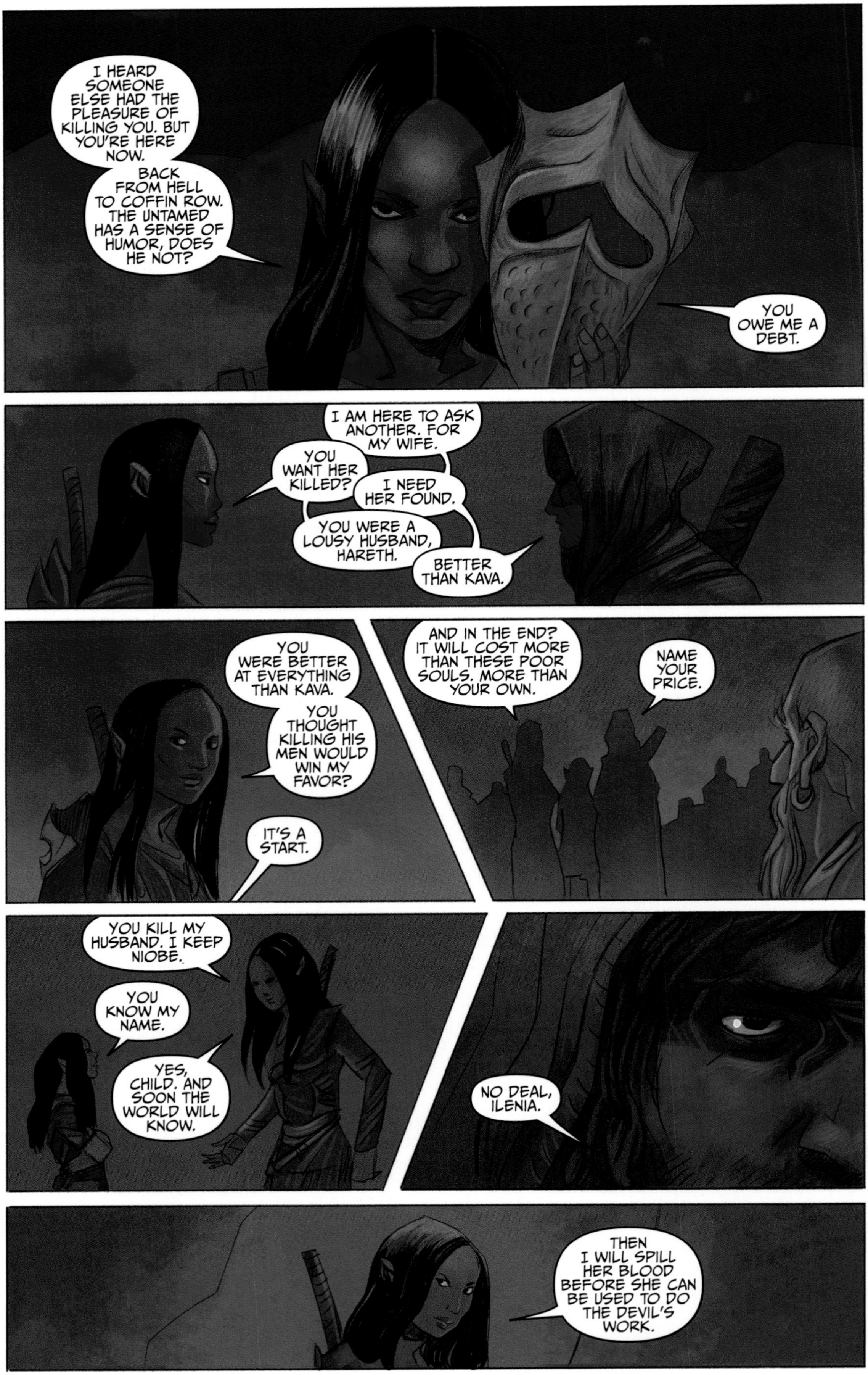
I HEARD SOMEONE ELSE HAD THE PLEASURE OF KILLING YOU. BUT YOU'RE HERE NOW.
BACK FROM HELL TO COFFIN ROW. THE UNTAMED HAS A SENSE OF HUMOR, DOES HE NOT?
YOU OWE ME A DEBT.
I AM HERE TO ASK ANOTHER. FOR MY WIFE.
YOU WANT HER KILLED?
I NEED HER FOUND.
YOU WERE A LOUSY HUSBAND, HARETH.
BETTER THAN KAVA.
YOU WERE BETTER AT EVERYTHING THAN KAVA.
YOU THOUGHT KILLING HIS MEN WOULD WIN MY FAVOR?
IT'S A START.
AND IN THE END? IT WILL COST MORE THAN THESE POOR SOULS. MORE THAN YOUR OWN.
NAME YOUR PRICE.
YOU KILL MY HUSBAND. I KEEP NIOBE.
YOU KNOW MY NAME.
YES, CHILD. AND SOON THE WORLD WILL KNOW.
NO DEAL, ILENIA.
THEN I WILL SPILL HER BLOOD BEFORE SHE CAN BE USED TO DO THE DEVIL'S WORK.

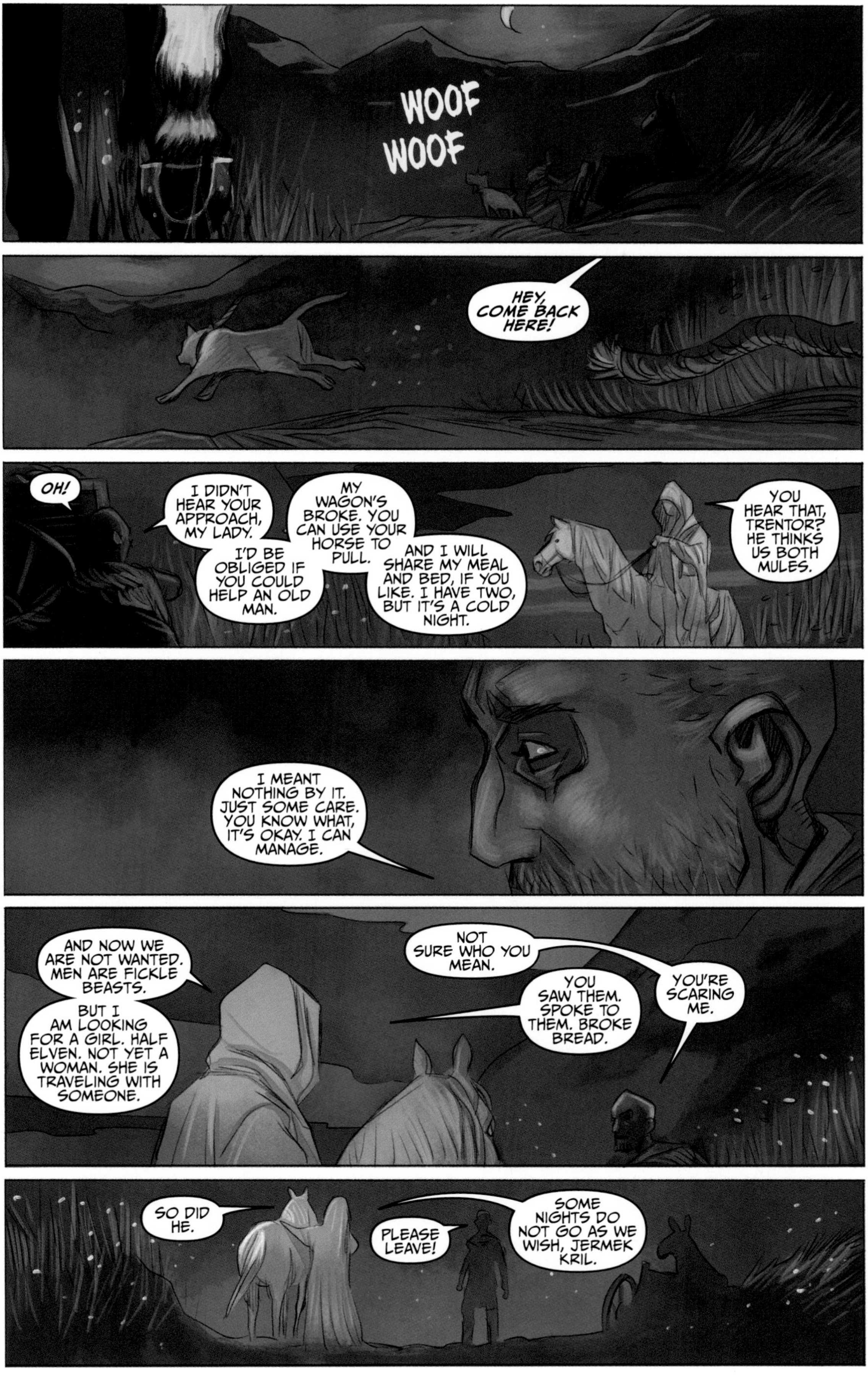
WOOF
WOOF
HEY, COME BACK HERE!
OH!
I DIDN'T HEAR YOUR APPROACH, MY LADY.
I'D BE OBLIGED IF YOU COULD HELP AN OLD MAN.
MY WAGON'S BROKE. YOU CAN USE YOUR HORSE TO PULL.
AND I WILL SHARE MY MEAL AND BED, IF YOU LIKE. I HAVE TWO, BUT IT'S A COLD NIGHT.
YOU HEAR THAT, TRENTOR? HE THINKS US BOTH MULES.
I MEANT NOTHING BY IT. JUST SOME CARE. YOU KNOW WHAT, IT'S OKAY. I CAN MANAGE.
AND NOW WE ARE NOT WANTED. MEN ARE FICKLE BEASTS.
BUT I AM LOOKING FOR A GIRL. HALF ELVEN. NOT YET A WOMAN. SHE IS TRAVELING WITH SOMEONE.
NOT SURE WHO YOU MEAN.
YOU SAW THEM. SPOKE TO THEM. BROKE BREAD.
YOU'RE SCARING ME.
SO DID HE.
PLEASE LEAVE!
SOME NIGHTS DO NOT GO AS WE WISH, JERMEK KRIL.

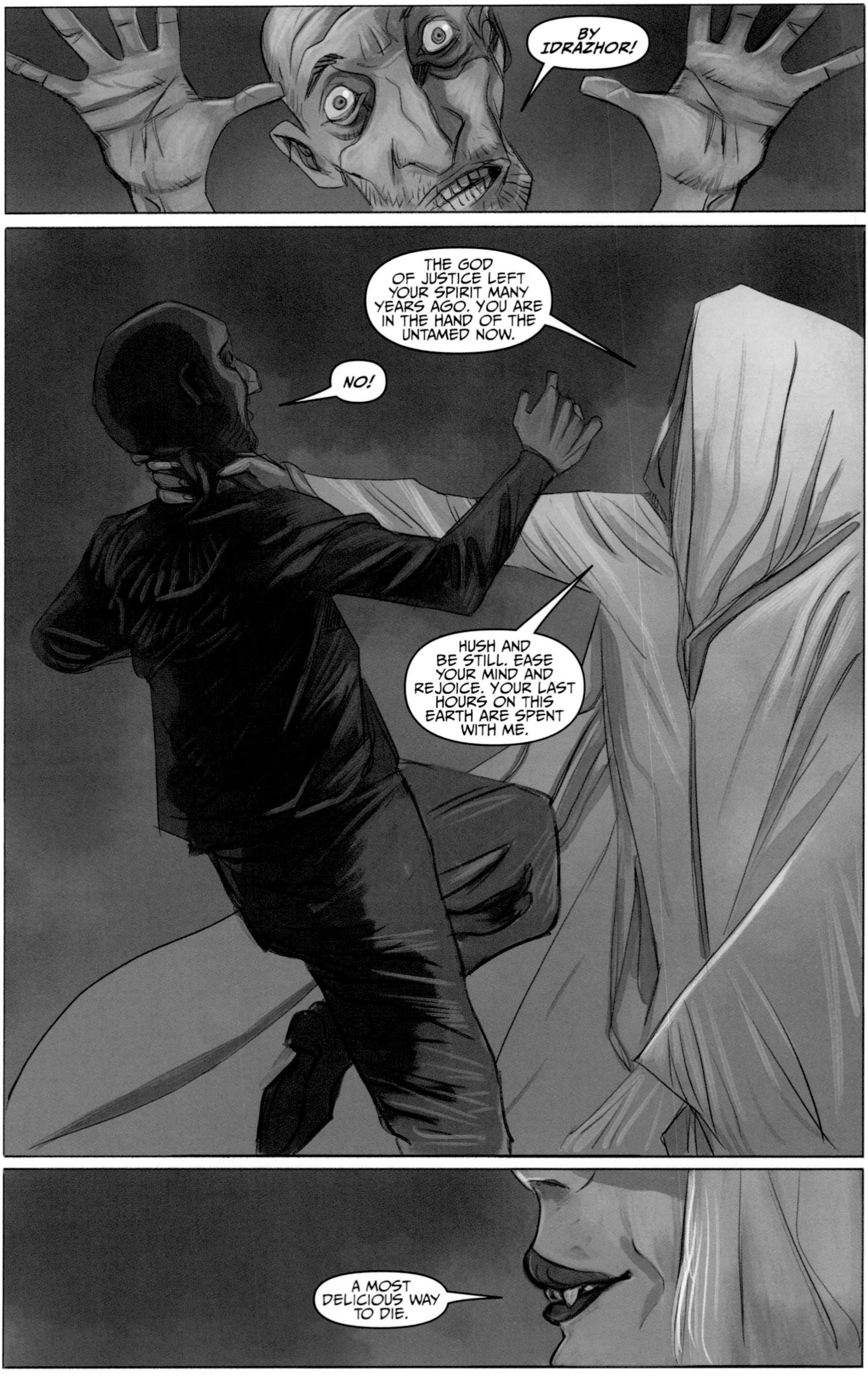
BY IDRAZHOR!
THE GOD OF JUSTICE LEFT YOUR SPIRIT MANY YEARS AGO. YOU ARE IN THE HAND OF THE UNTAMED NOW.
NO!
HUSH AND BE STILL. EASE YOUR MIND AND REJOICE. YOUR LAST HOURS ON THIS EARTH ARE SPENT WITH ME.
A MOST DELICIOUS WAY TO DIE.

Hello Stranger,

What would you do with a second chance?

The Stranger had been given one. Or rather, he'd taken it by force, defying the devil to perform one good deed in a lifetime of wickedness. One selfless decision with the world in the balance.

It would not, however, absolve him of his past, nor did he wish it to. He could never forgive himself for the evil he had done when living. He had never been a good man, although his wife saw the possibility in him. She thought that love and patience could bring it out, but she had been taken from him before she could succeed. The small light of goodness she had nurtured in him quickly became a blazing inferno of vengeance instead, a wildfire that was eventually snuffed out by the executioner's axe.

But for ten years, the embers burned, and when he returned from Hell, they stoked another fire. This one cold and devastating. But as the Town of Oasis fell around them, a young girl turned his flame into one of purification.

Niobe was an angel, or so he liked to think. She was not his daughter, he knew, but on some plane, their spirits were kin. He had not stopped to think how or why until they were far from the hellhole where they had met, where he had saved her life, and she had saved his soul. He had killed the wicked men who wanted them dead, but she had renewed the task that his wife had started.

It was a long road still to walk, but in death he would be better. For her.

For his wife.

Until the moment when he could hold his family in truth, the angel would be that flickering light guiding him from the shadows of his mind, across the vast and volatile world of...

Chapter 1

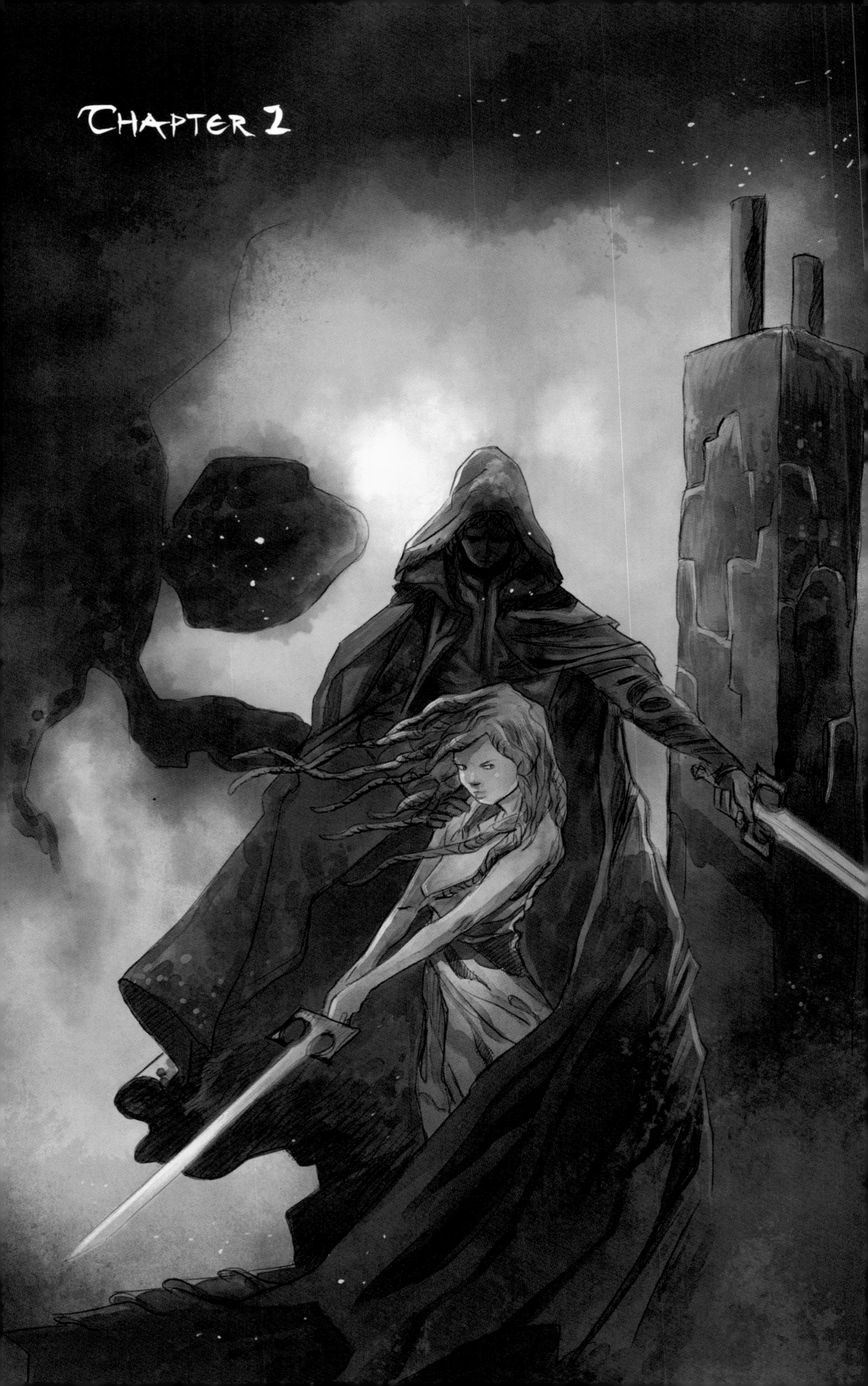

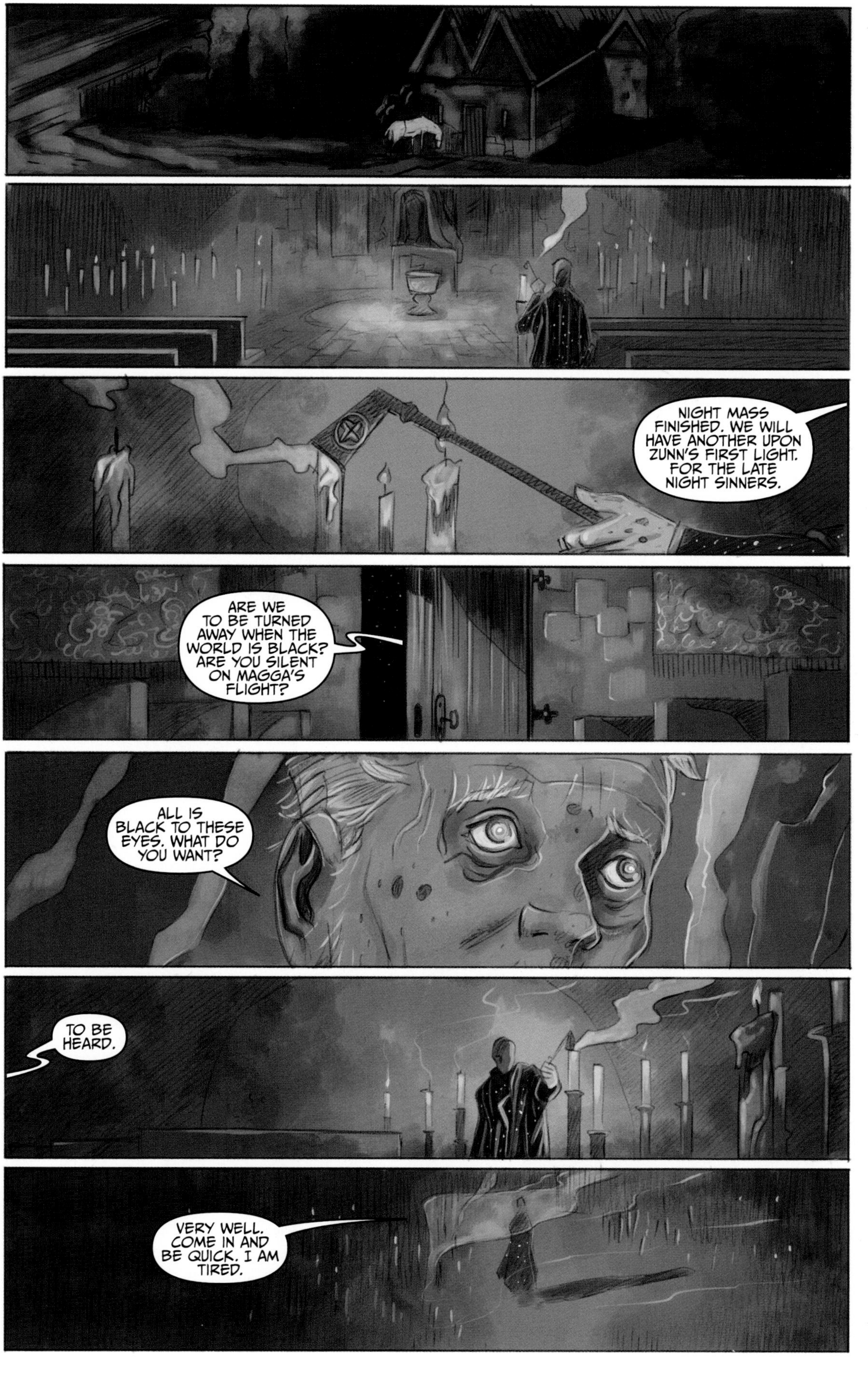
NIGHT MASS FINISHED. WE WILL HAVE ANOTHER UPON ZUNN'S FIRST LIGHT. FOR THE LATE NIGHT SINNERS.
ARE WE TO BE TURNED AWAY WHEN THE WORLD IS BLACK? ARE YOU SILENT ON MAGGA'S FLIGHT?
ALL IS BLACK TO THESE EYES. WHAT DO YOU WANT?
TO BE HEARD.
VERY WELL. COME IN AND BE QUICK. I AM TIRED.

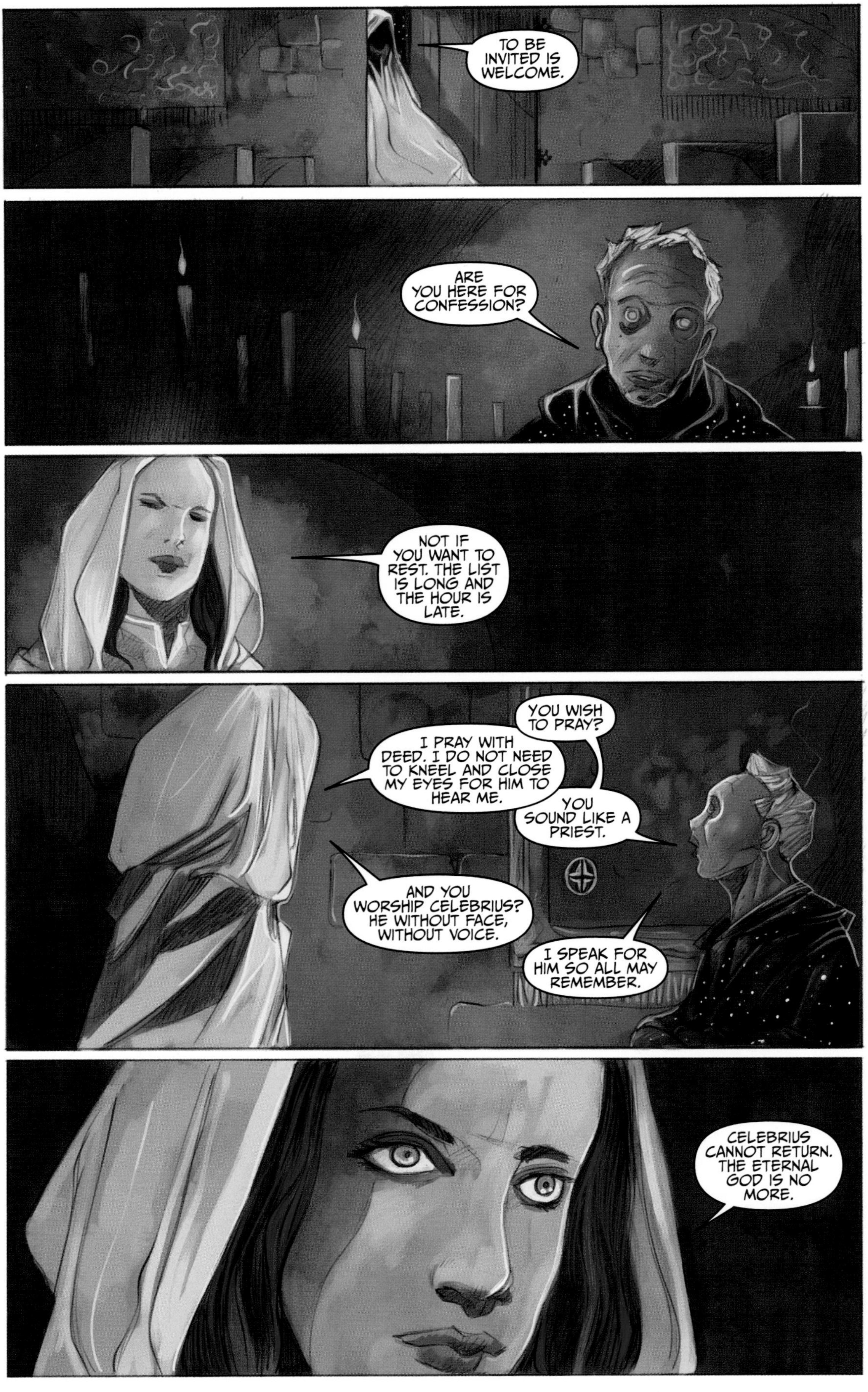
TO BE INVITED IS WELCOME.
ARE YOU HERE FOR CONFESSION?
NOT IF YOU WANT TO REST. THE LIST IS LONG AND THE HOUR IS LATE.
YOU WISH TO PRAY?
I PRAY WITH DEED. I DO NOT NEED TO KNEEL AND CLOSE MY EYES FOR HIM TO HEAR ME.
YOU SOUND LIKE A PRIEST.
AND YOU WORSHIP CELEBRIUS? HE WITHOUT FACE, WITHOUT VOICE.
I SPEAK FOR HIM SO ALL MAY REMEMBER.
CELEBRIUS CANNOT RETURN. THE ETERNAL GOD IS NO MORE.

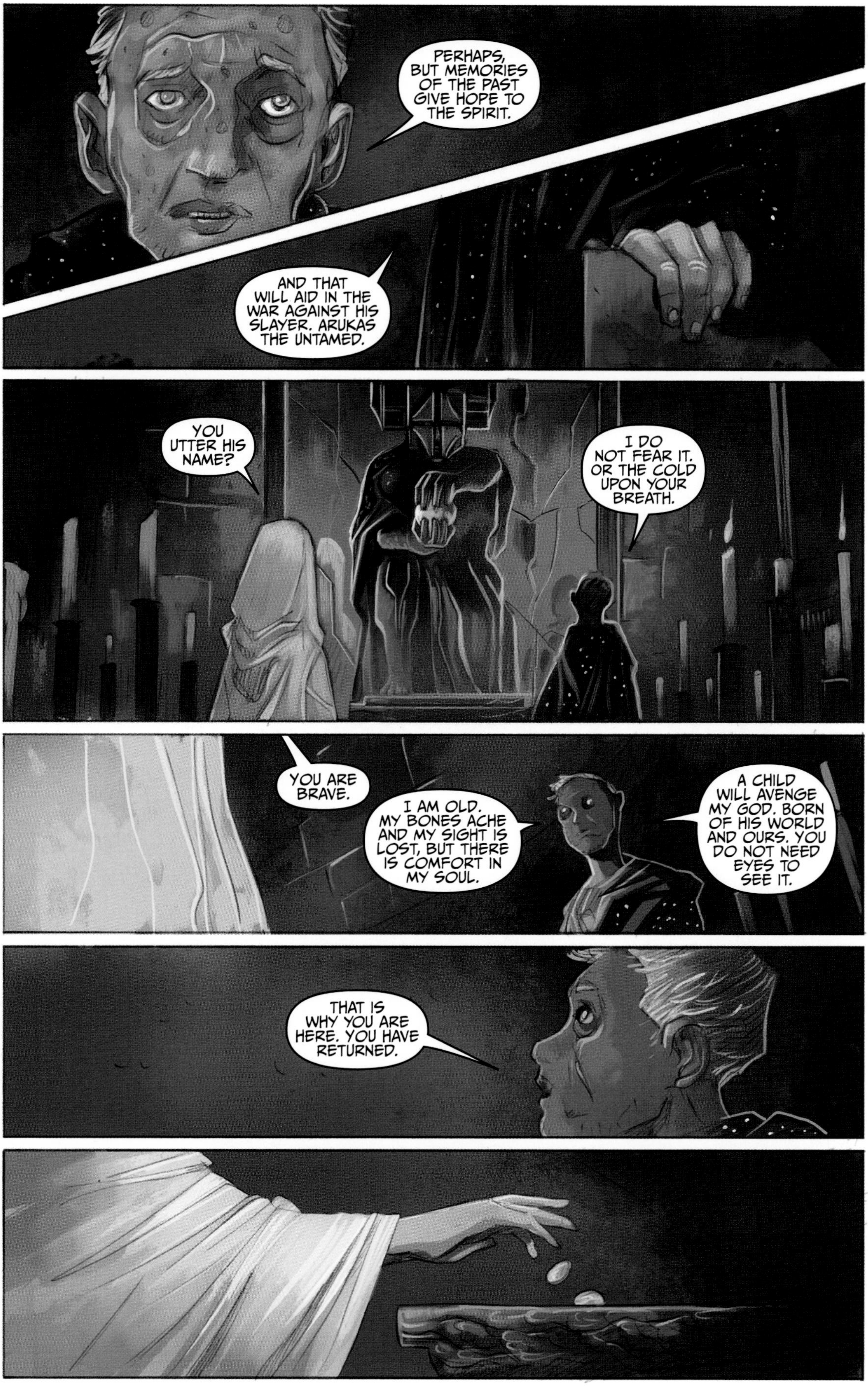
PERHAPS, BUT MEMORIES OF THE PAST GIVE HOPE TO THE SPIRIT.
AND THAT WILL AID IN THE WAR AGAINST HIS SLAYER. ARUKAS THE UNTAMED.
YOU UTTER HIS NAME?
I DO NOT FEAR IT. OR THE COLD UPON YOUR BREATH.
YOU ARE BRAVE.
I AM OLD. MY BONES ACHE AND MY SIGHT IS LOST, BUT THERE IS COMFORT IN MY SOUL.
A CHILD WILL AVENGE MY GOD. BORN OF HIS WORLD AND OURS. YOU DO NOT NEED EYES TO SEE IT.
THAT IS WHY YOU ARE HERE. YOU HAVE RETURNED.

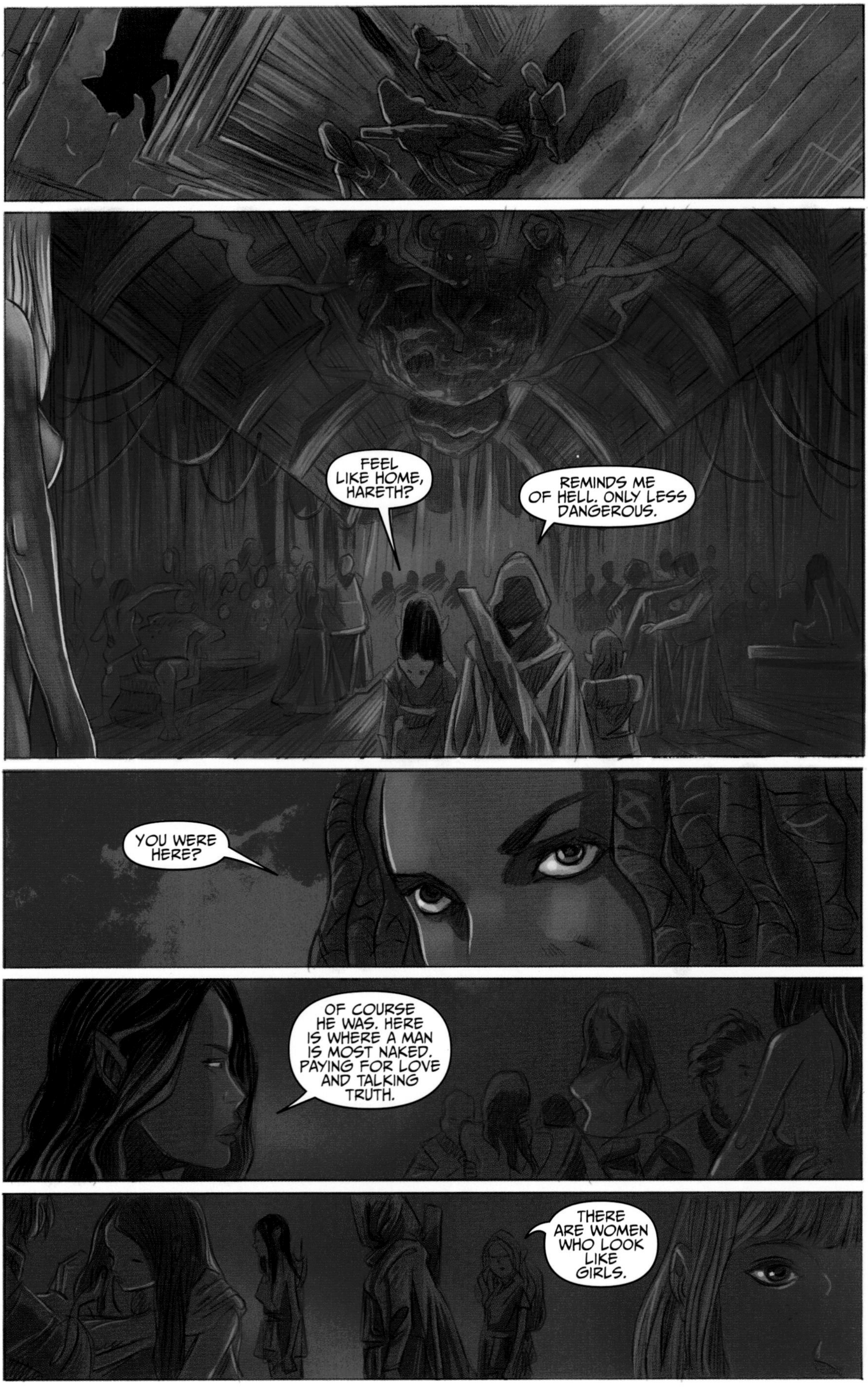
FEEL LIKE HOME, HARETH?
REMINDS ME OF HELL. ONLY LESS DANGEROUS.
YOU WERE HERE?
OF COURSE HE WAS. HERE IS WHERE A MAN IS MOST NAKED. PAYING FOR LOVE AND TALKING TRUTH.
THERE ARE WOMEN WHO LOOK LIKE GIRLS.

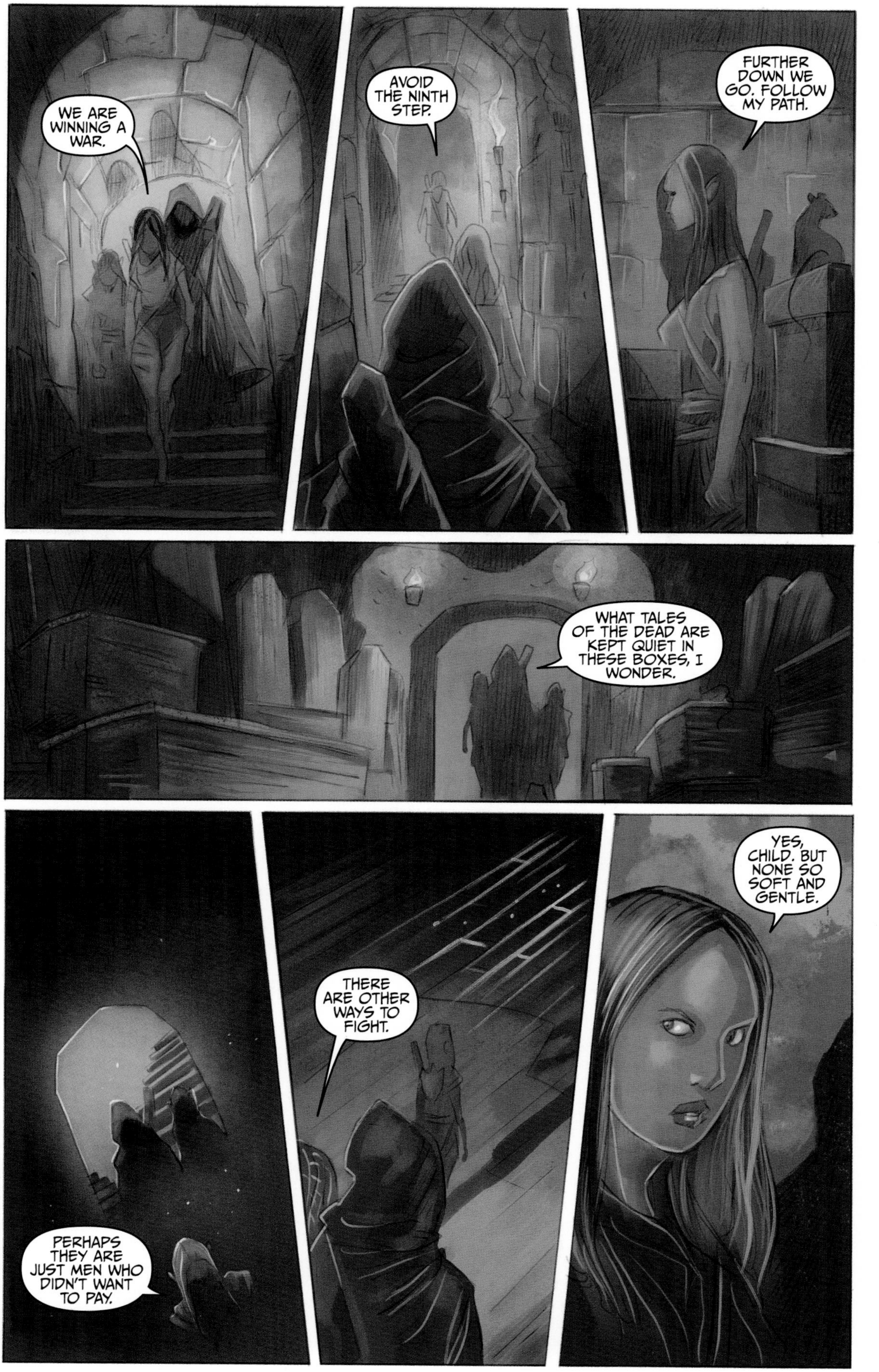
WE ARE WINNING A WAR.
AVOID THE NINTH STEP.
FURTHER DOWN WE GO. FOLLOW MY PATH.
WHAT TALES OF THE DEAD ARE KEPT QUIET IN THESE BOXES, I WONDER.
PERHAPS THEY ARE JUST MEN WHO DIDN'T WANT TO PAY.
THERE ARE OTHER WAYS TO FIGHT.
YES, CHILD. BUT NONE SO SOFT AND GENTLE.

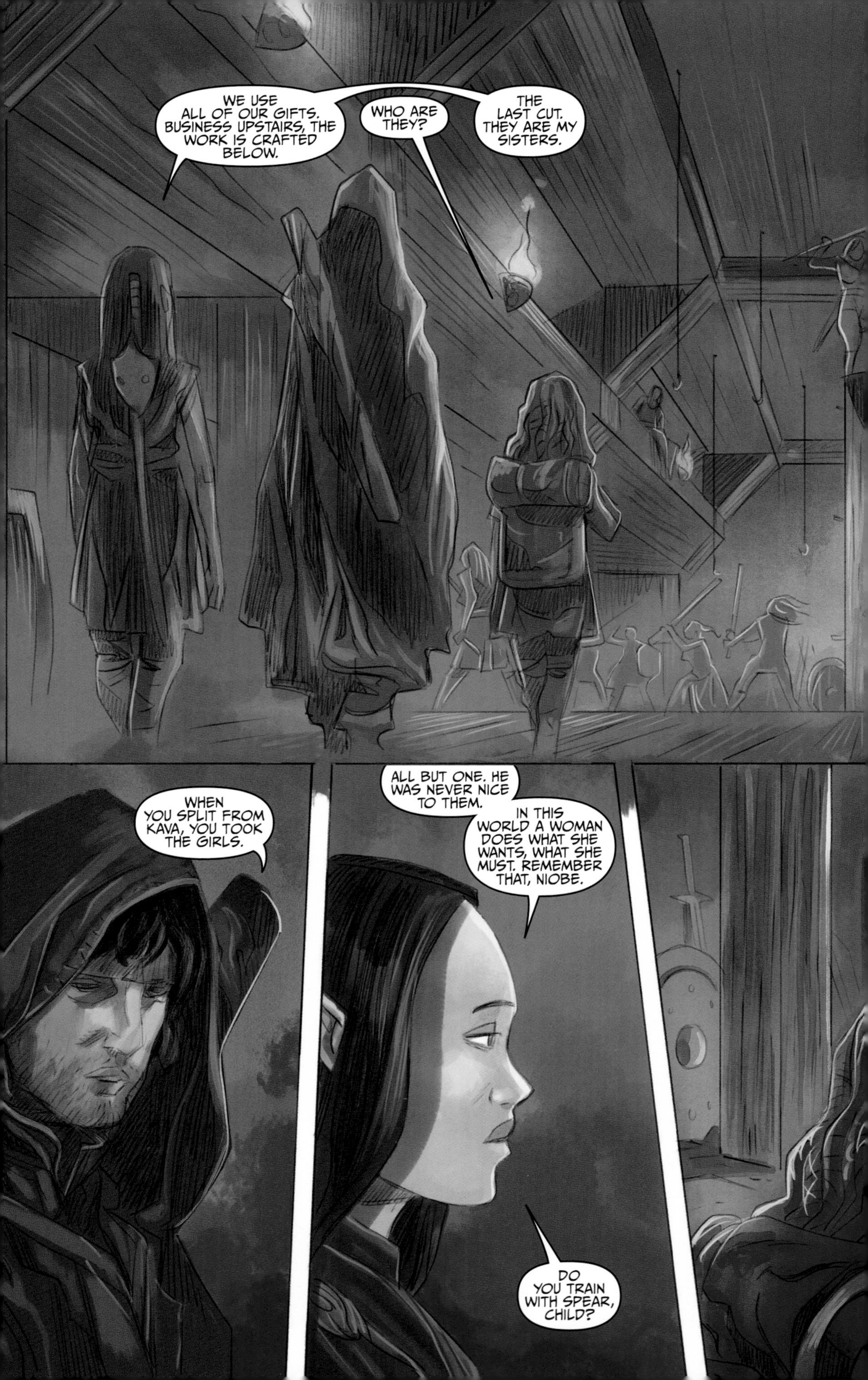
WE USE ALL OF OUR GIFTS. BUSINESS UPSTAIRS, THE WORK IS CRAFTED BELOW.
WHO ARE THEY?
THE LAST CUT. THEY ARE MY SISTERS.
WHEN YOU SPLIT FROM KAVA, YOU TOOK THE GIRLS.
ALL BUT ONE. HE WAS NEVER NICE TO THEM.
IN THIS WORLD A WOMAN DOES WHAT SHE WANTS, WHAT SHE MUST. REMEMBER THAT, NIOBE.
DO YOU TRAIN WITH SPEAR, CHILD?

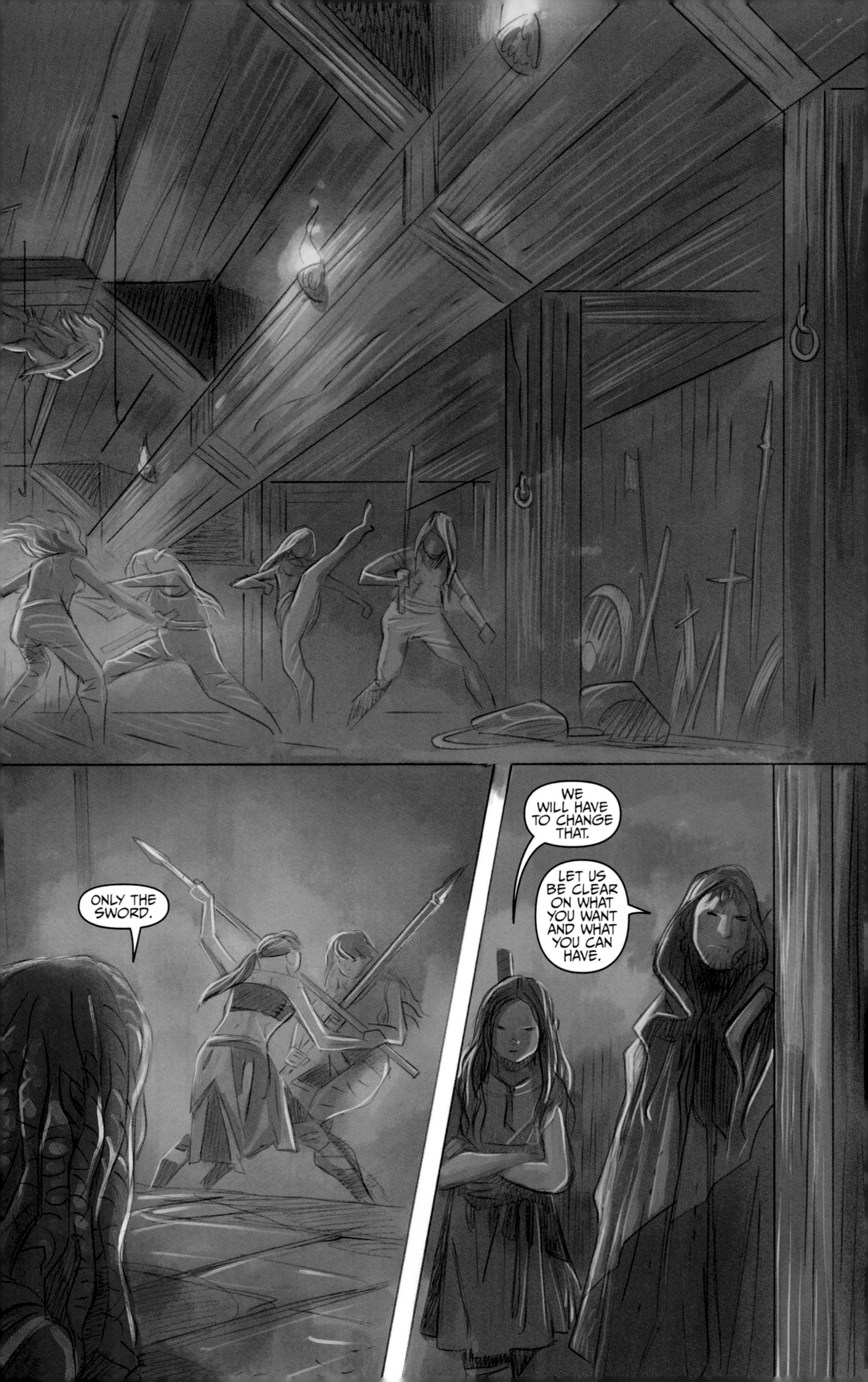
ONLY THE SWORD.
WE WILL HAVE TO CHANGE THAT.
LET US BE CLEAR ON WHAT YOU WANT AND WHAT YOU CAN HAVE.

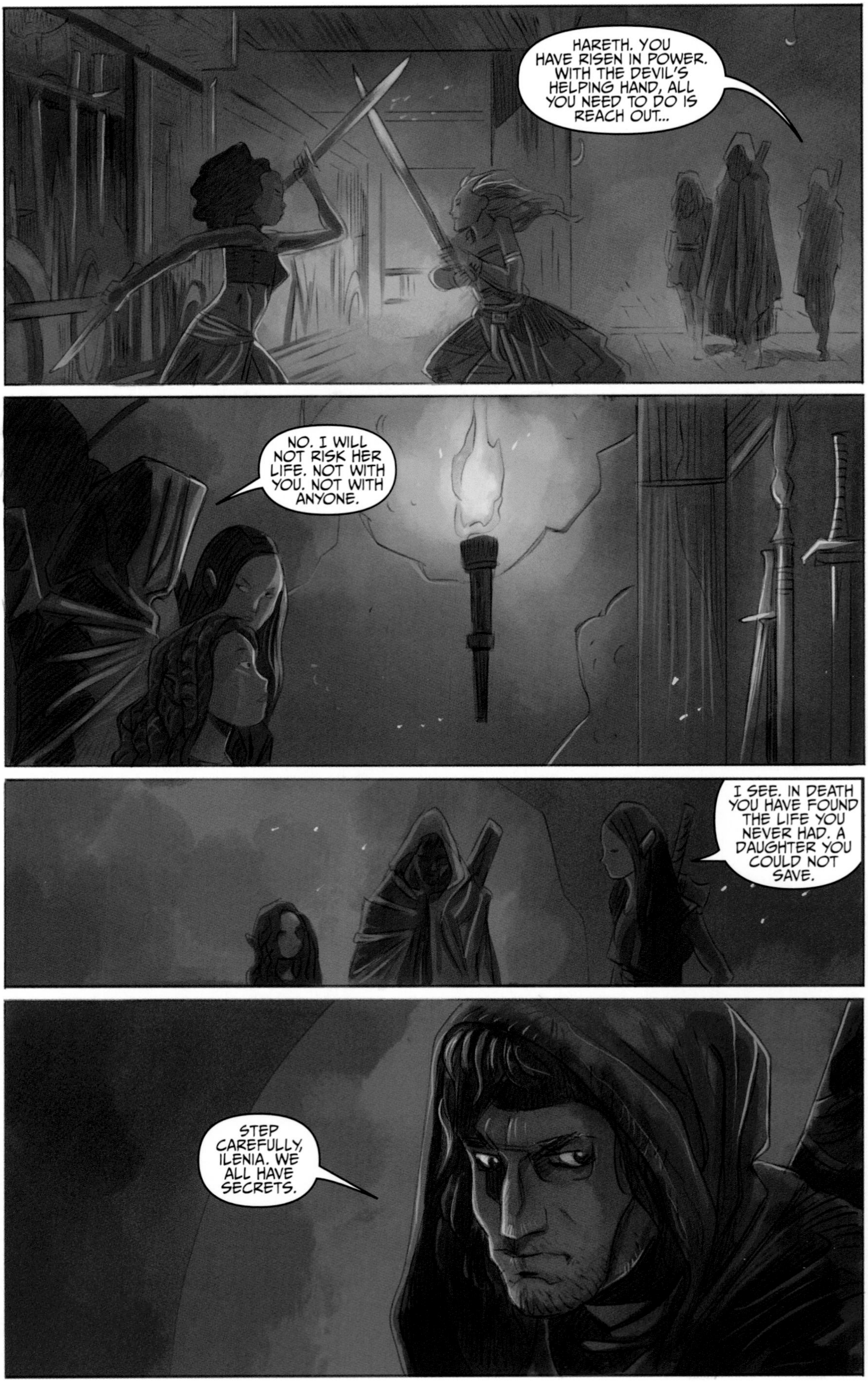
HARETH. YOU HAVE RISEN IN POWER. WITH THE DEVIL'S HELPING HAND, ALL YOU NEED TO DO IS REACH OUT...
NO. I WILL NOT RISK HER LIFE. NOT WITH YOU. NOT WITH ANYONE.
I SEE. IN DEATH YOU HAVE FOUND THE LIFE YOU NEVER HAD. A DAUGHTER YOU COULD NOT SAVE.
STEP CAREFULLY, ILENIA. WE ALL HAVE SECRETS.

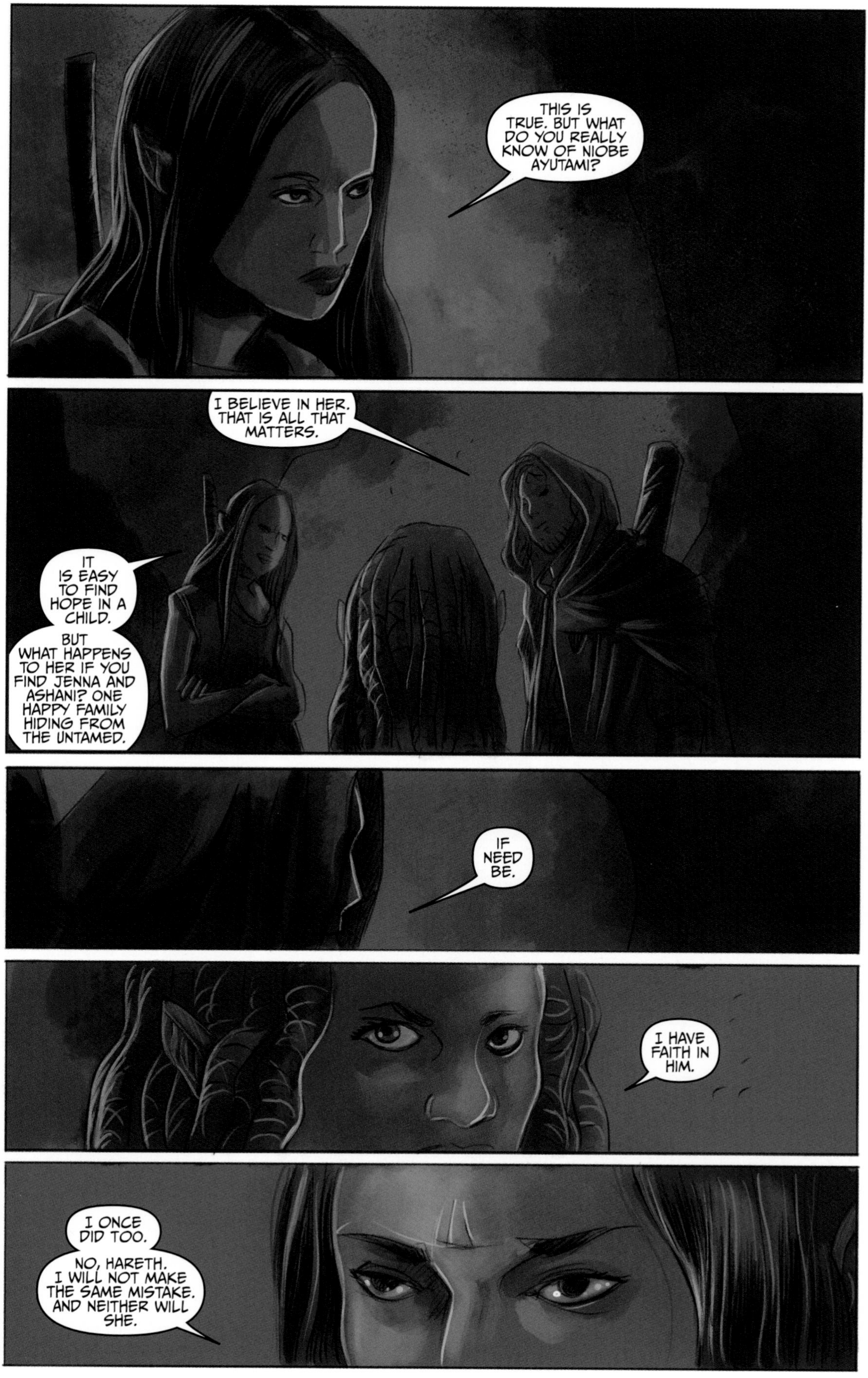
THIS IS TRUE. BUT WHAT DO YOU REALLY KNOW OF NIOBE AYUTAMI?
I BELIEVE IN HER. THAT IS ALL THAT MATTERS.
IT IS EASY TO FIND HOPE IN A CHILD.
BUT WHAT HAPPENS TO HER IF YOU FIND JENNA AND ASHANI? ONE HAPPY FAMILY HIDING FROM THE UNTAMED.
IF NEED BE.
I HAVE FAITH IN HIM.
I ONCE DID TOO.
NO, HARETH. I WILL NOT MAKE THE SAME MISTAKE. AND NEITHER WILL SHE.

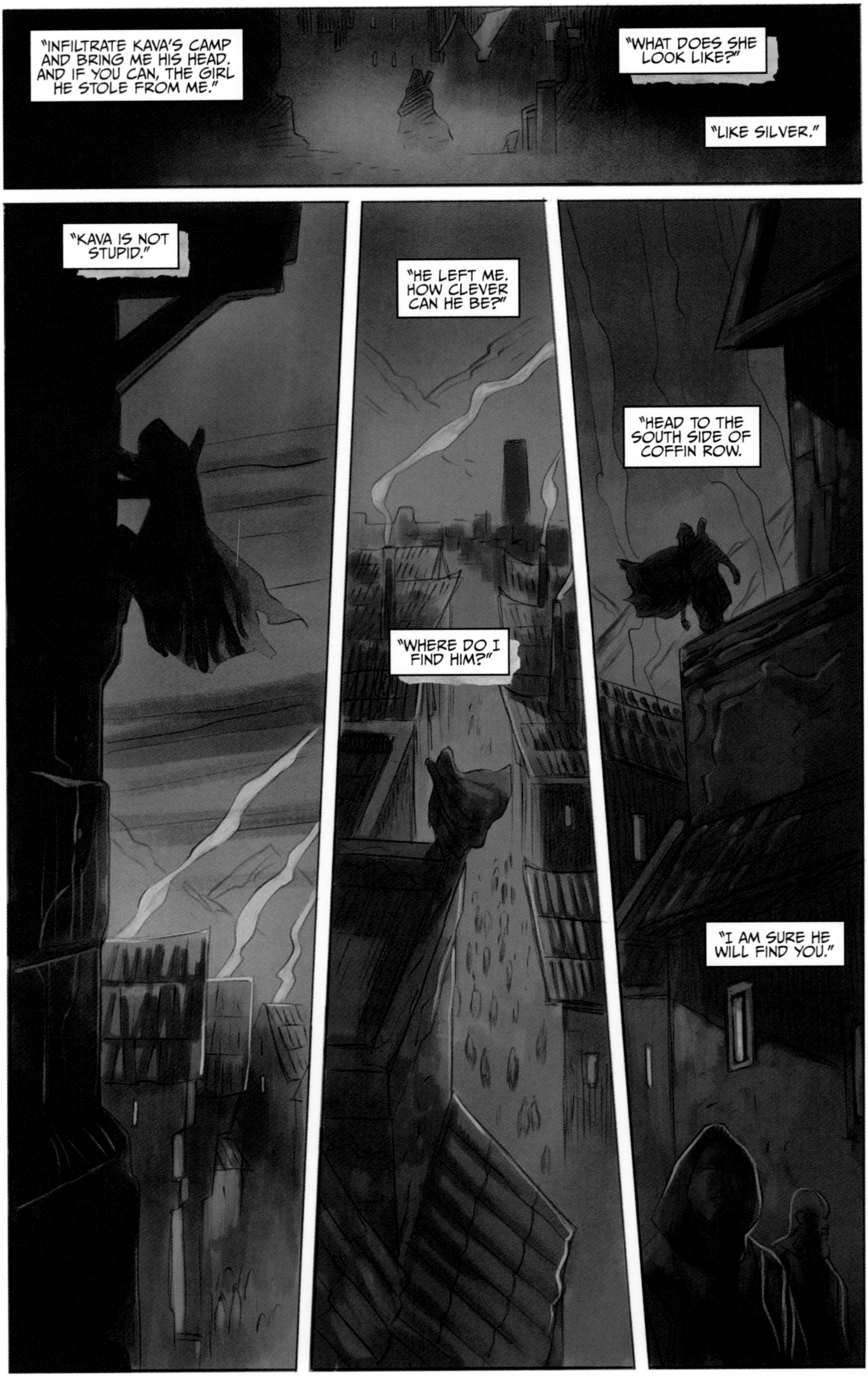
"INFILTRATE KAVA'S CAMP AND BRING ME HIS HEAD. AND IF YOU CAN, THE GIRL HE STOLE FROM ME."
"WHAT DOES SHE LOOK LIKE?"
"LIKE SILVER."
"KAVA IS NOT STUPID."
"HE LEFT ME. HOW CLEVER CAN HE BE?"
"WHERE DO I FIND HIM?"
"HEAD TO THE SOUTH SIDE OF COFFIN ROW.
"I AM SURE HE WILL FIND YOU."

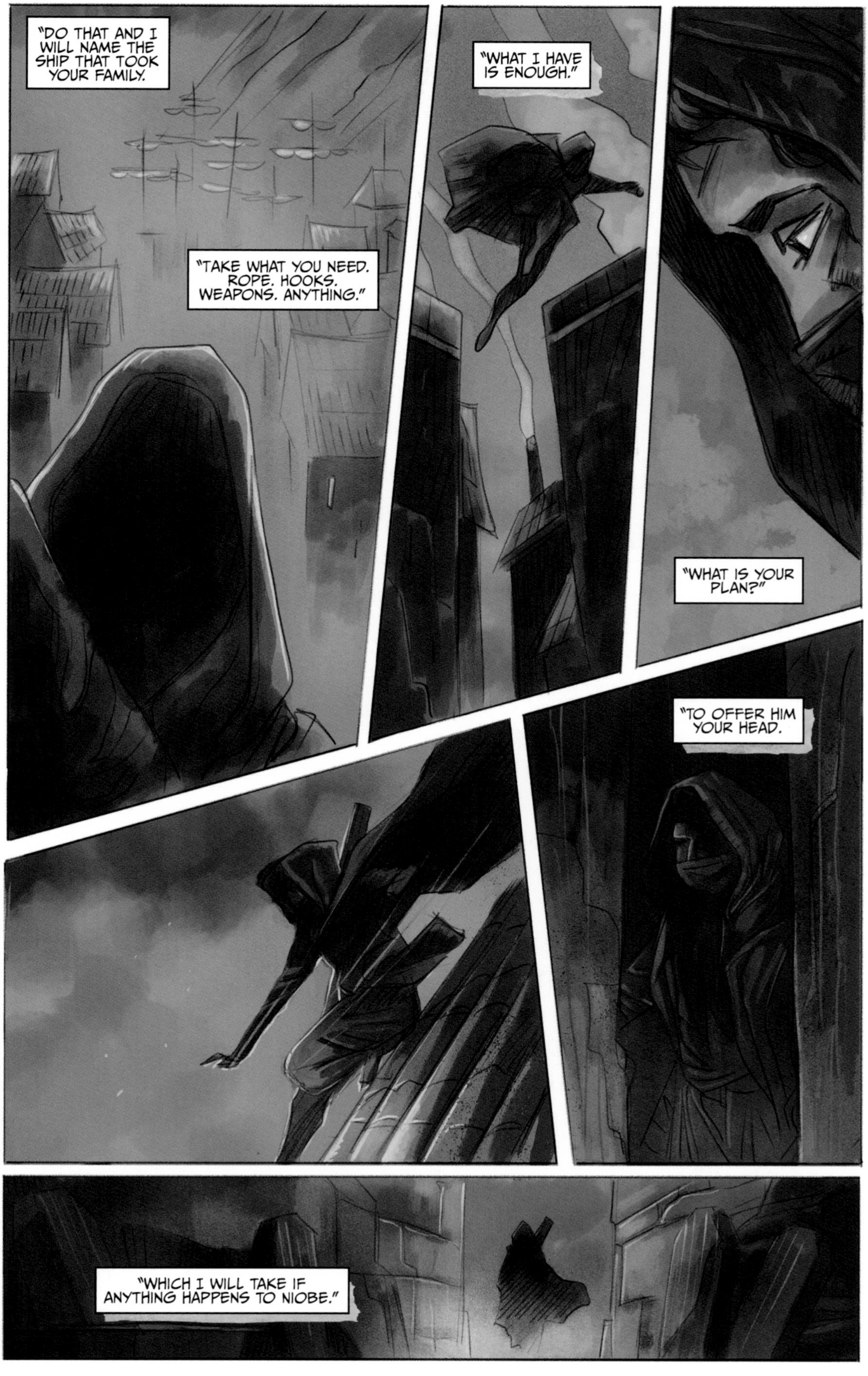
"DO THAT AND I WILL NAME THE SHIP THAT TOOK YOUR FAMILY.
"TAKE WHAT YOU NEED. ROPE. HOOKS. WEAPONS. ANYTHING."
"WHAT I HAVE IS ENOUGH."
"WHAT IS YOUR PLAN?"
"TO OFFER HIM YOUR HEAD.
"WHICH I WILL TAKE IF ANYTHING HAPPENS TO NIOBE."

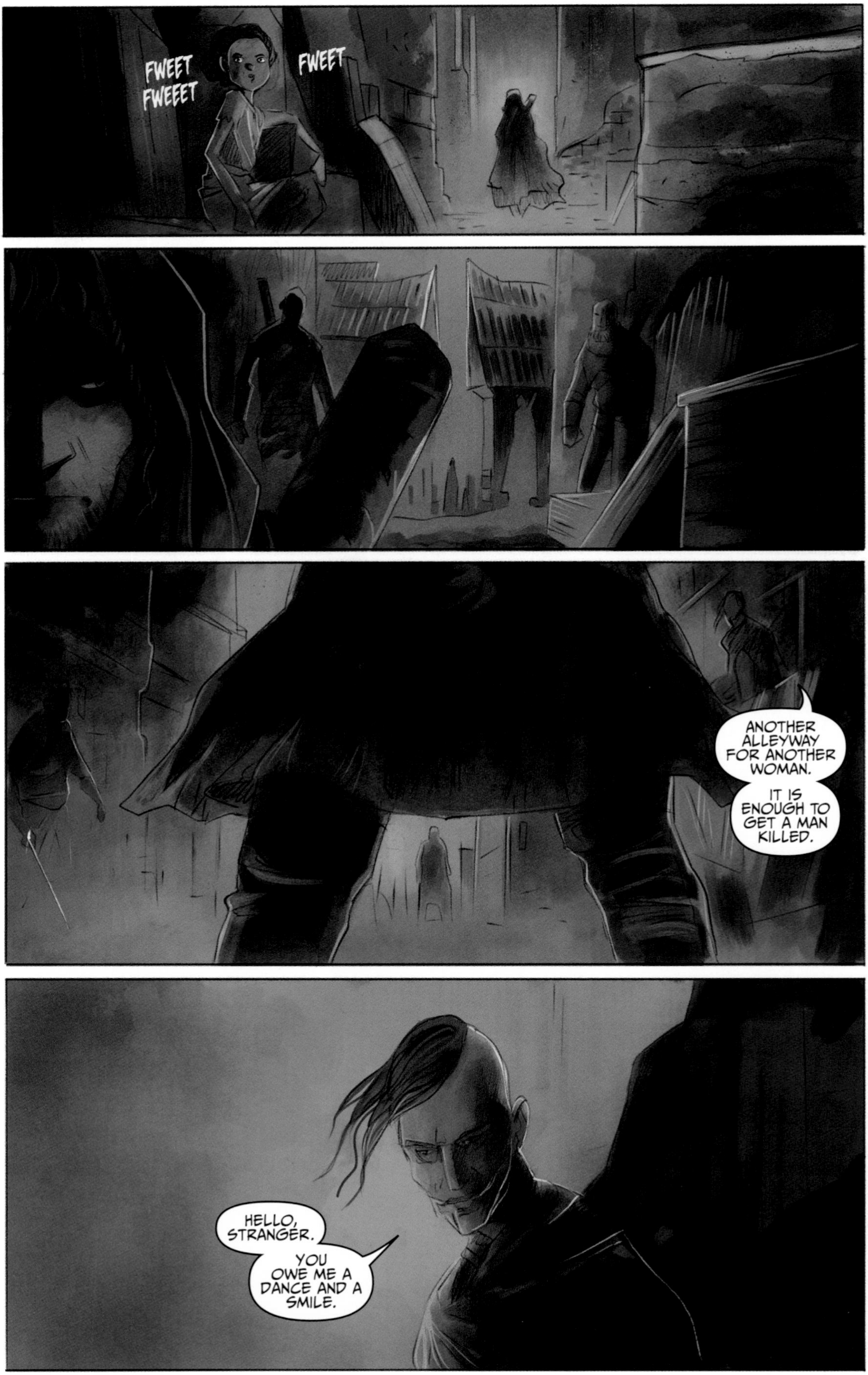
FWEET FWEEET
FWEET
ANOTHER ALLEYWAY FOR ANOTHER WOMAN.
IT IS ENOUGH TO GET A MAN KILLED.
HELLO, STRANGER.
YOU OWE ME A DANCE AND A SMILE.

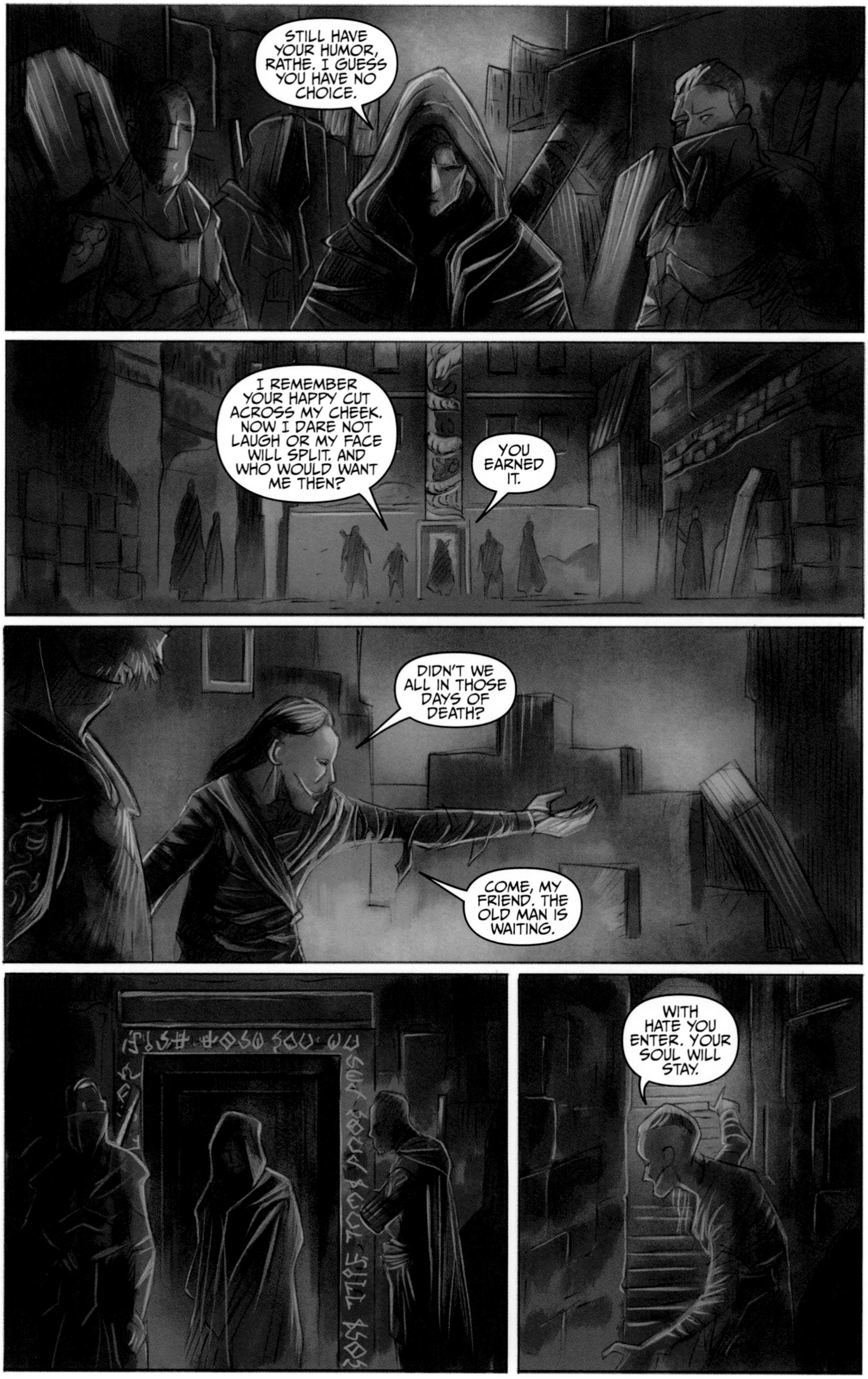
STILL HAVE YOUR HUMOR, RATHE. I GUESS YOU HAVE NO CHOICE.
I REMEMBER YOUR HAPPY CUT ACROSS MY CHEEK. NOW I DARE NOT LAUGH OR MY FACE WILL SPLIT. AND WHO WOULD WANT ME THEN?
YOU EARNED IT.
DIDN'T WE ALL IN THOSE DAYS OF DEATH?
COME, MY FRIEND. THE OLD MAN IS WAITING.
WITH HATE YOU ENTER. YOUR SOUL WILL STAY.

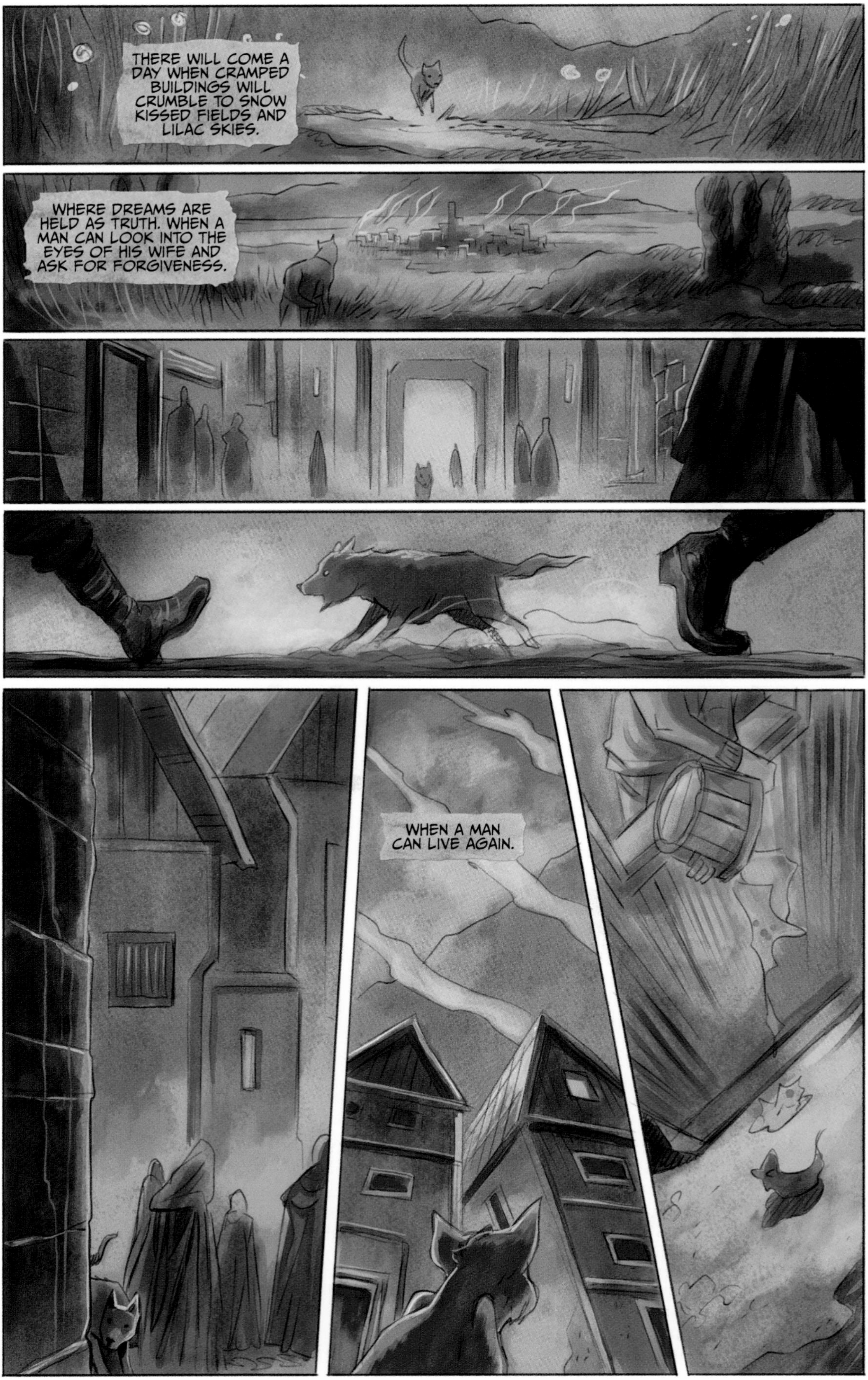
THERE WILL COME A DAY WHEN CRAMPED BUILDINGS WILL CRUMBLE TO SNOW KISSED FIELDS AND LILAC SKIES.
WHERE DREAMS ARE HELD AS TRUTH. WHEN A MAN CAN LOOK INTO THE EYES OF HIS WIFE AND ASK FOR FORGIVENESS.
WHEN A MAN CAN LIVE AGAIN.

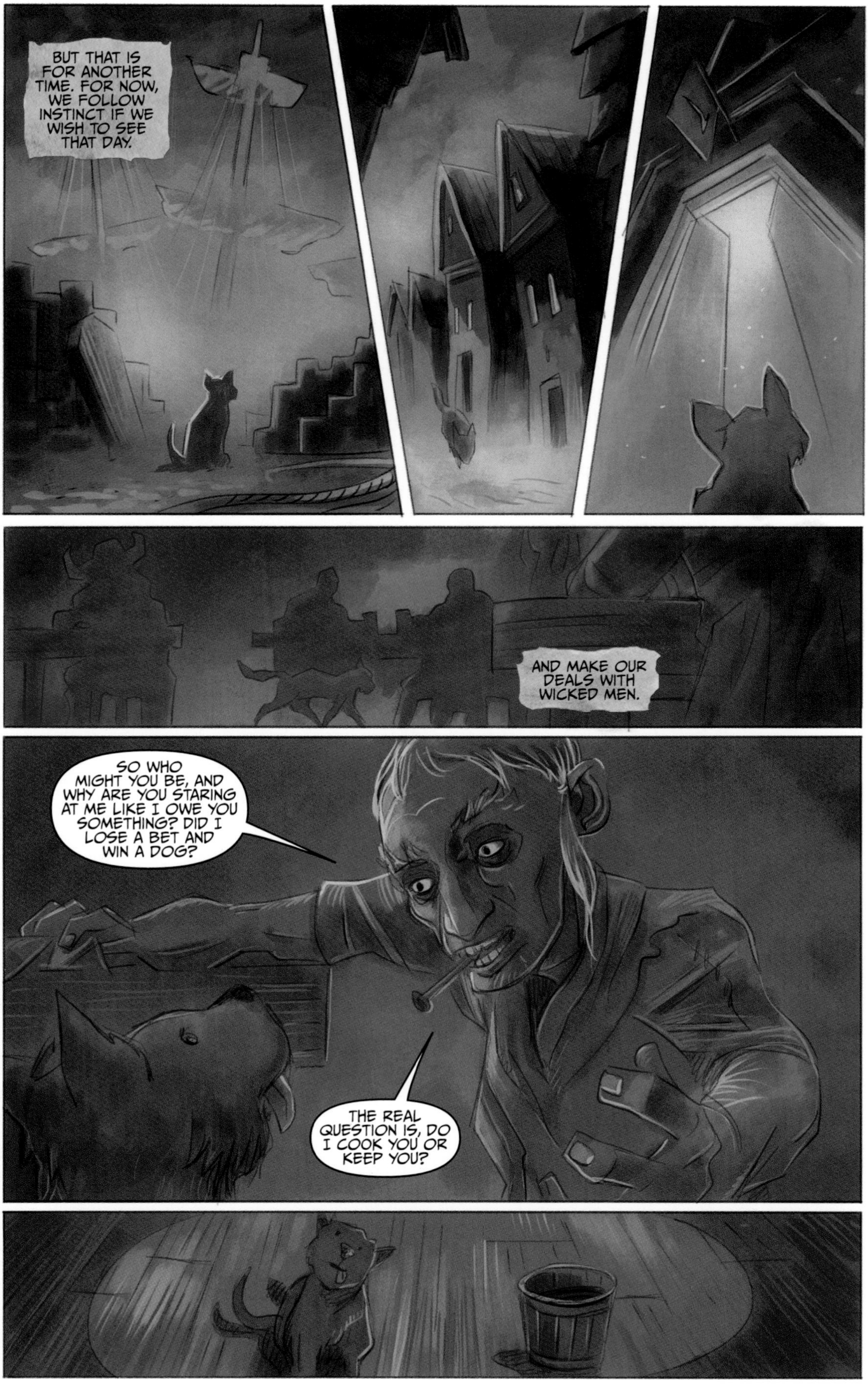
BUT THAT IS FOR ANOTHER TIME. FOR NOW, WE FOLLOW INSTINCT IF WE WISH TO SEE THAT DAY.
AND MAKE OUR DEALS WITH WICKED MEN.
SO WHO MIGHT YOU BE, AND WHY ARE YOU STARING AT ME LIKE I OWE YOU SOMETHING? DID I LOSE A BET AND WIN A DOG?
THE REAL QUESTION IS, DO I COOK YOU OR KEEP YOU?

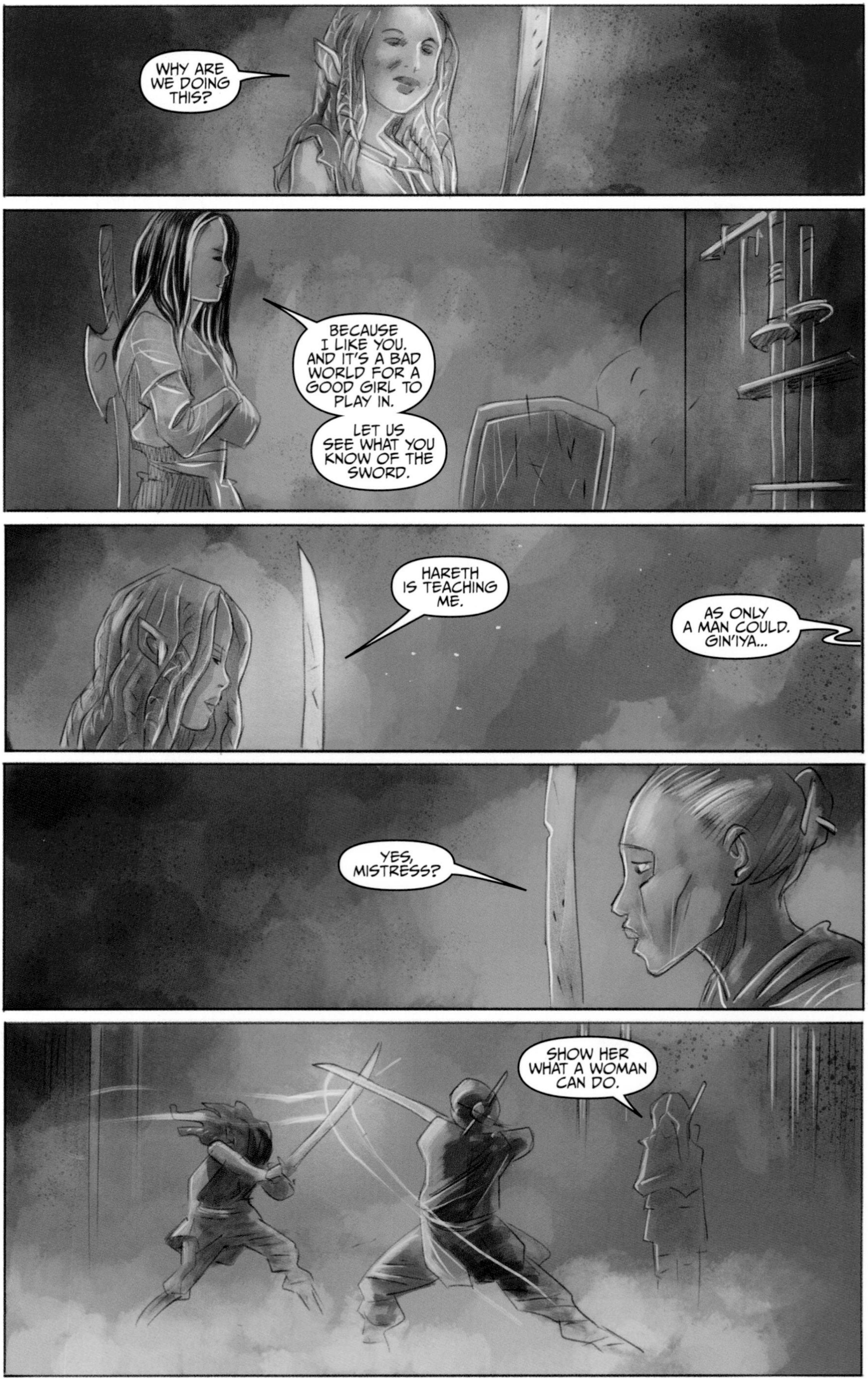
WHY ARE WE DOING THIS?
BECAUSE I LIKE YOU. AND IT'S A BAD WORLD FOR A GOOD GIRL TO PLAY IN.
LET US SEE WHAT YOU KNOW OF THE SWORD.
HARETH IS TEACHING ME.
AS ONLY A MAN COULD. GIN'IYA...
YES, MISTRESS?
SHOW HER WHAT A WOMAN CAN DO.

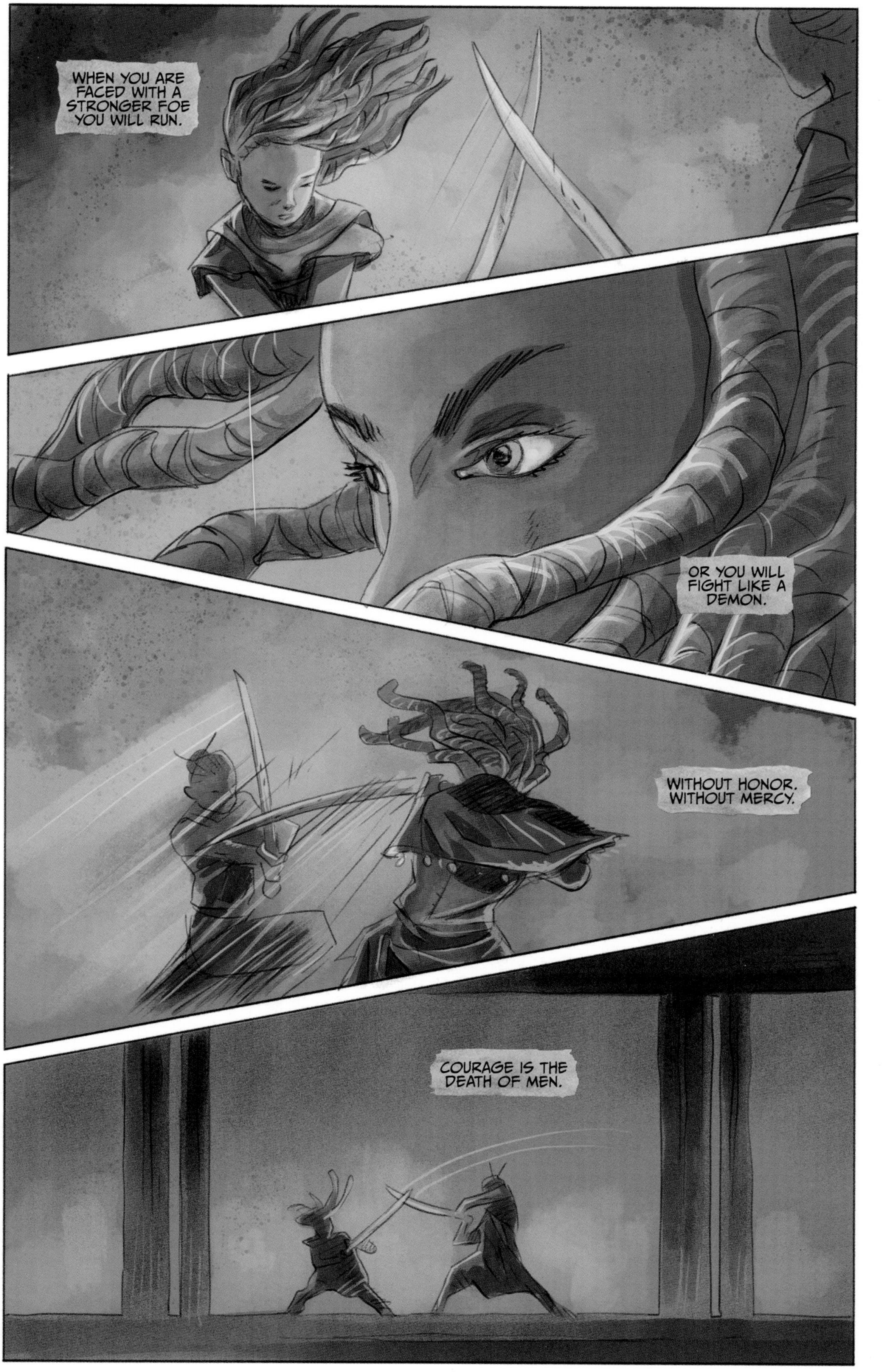
WHEN YOU ARE FACED WITH A STRONGER FOE YOU WILL RUN.
OR YOU WILL FIGHT LIKE A DEMON.
WITHOUT HONOR. WITHOUT MERCY.
COURAGE IS THE DEATH OF MEN.

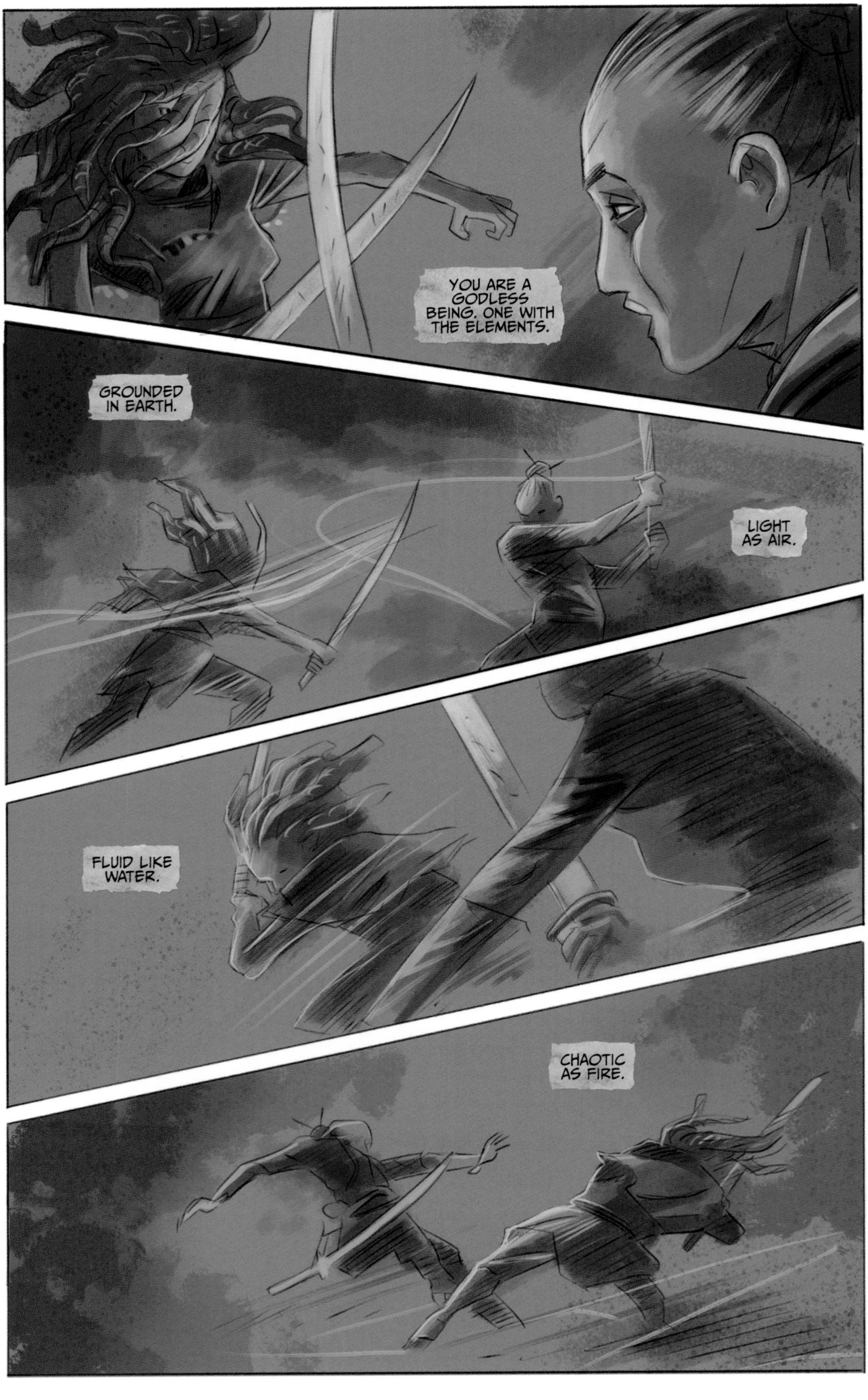
YOU ARE A GODLESS BEING. ONE WITH THE ELEMENTS.
GROUNDED IN EARTH.
LIGHT AS AIR.
FLUID LIKE WATER.
CHAOTIC AS FIRE.

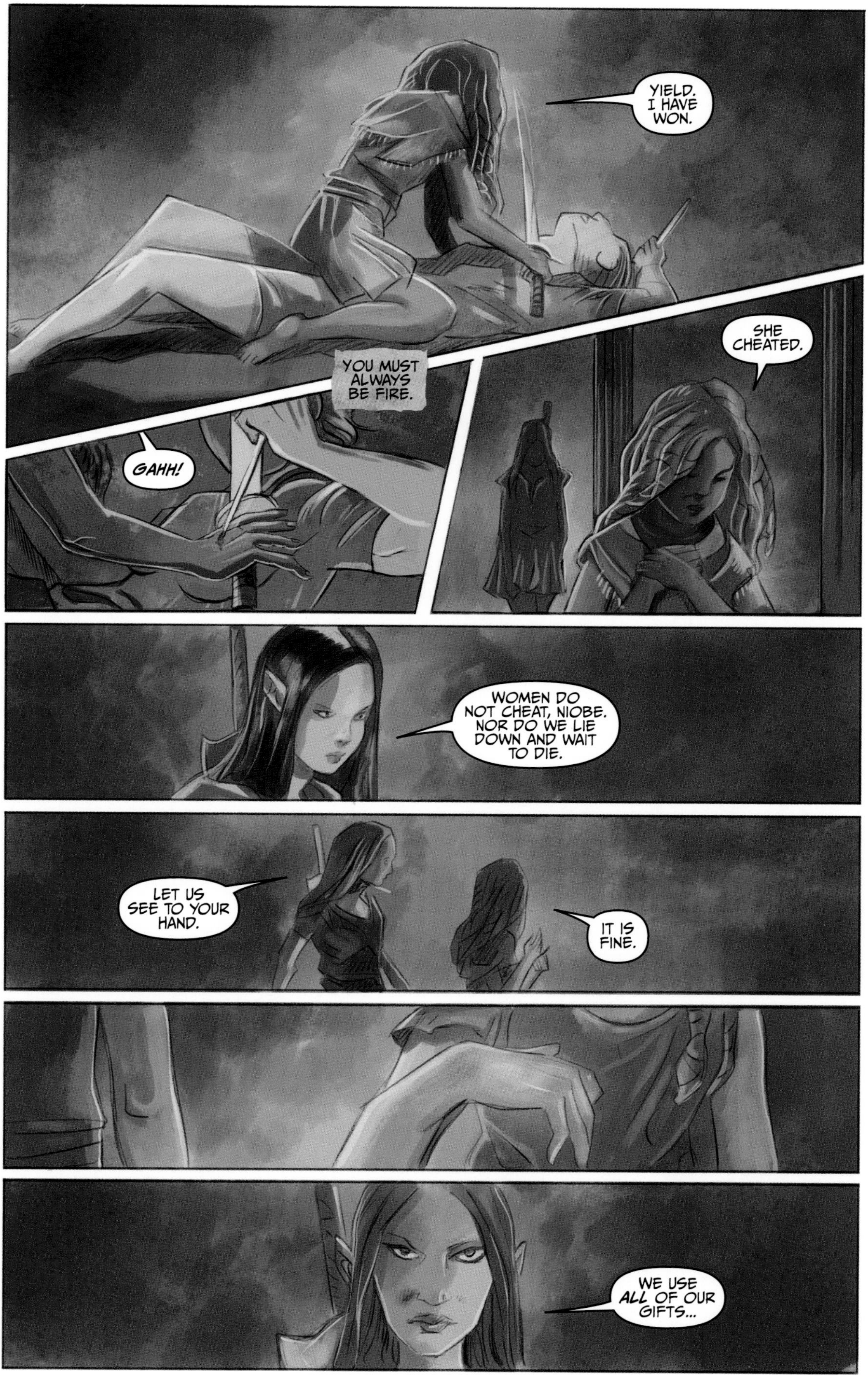
YIELD. I HAVE WON.
YOU MUST ALWAYS BE FIRE.
GAHH!
SHE CHEATED.
WOMEN DO NOT CHEAT, NIOBE. NOR DO WE LIE DOWN AND WAIT TO DIE.
LET US SEE TO YOUR HAND.
IT IS FINE.
WE USE *ALL* OF OUR GIFTS...

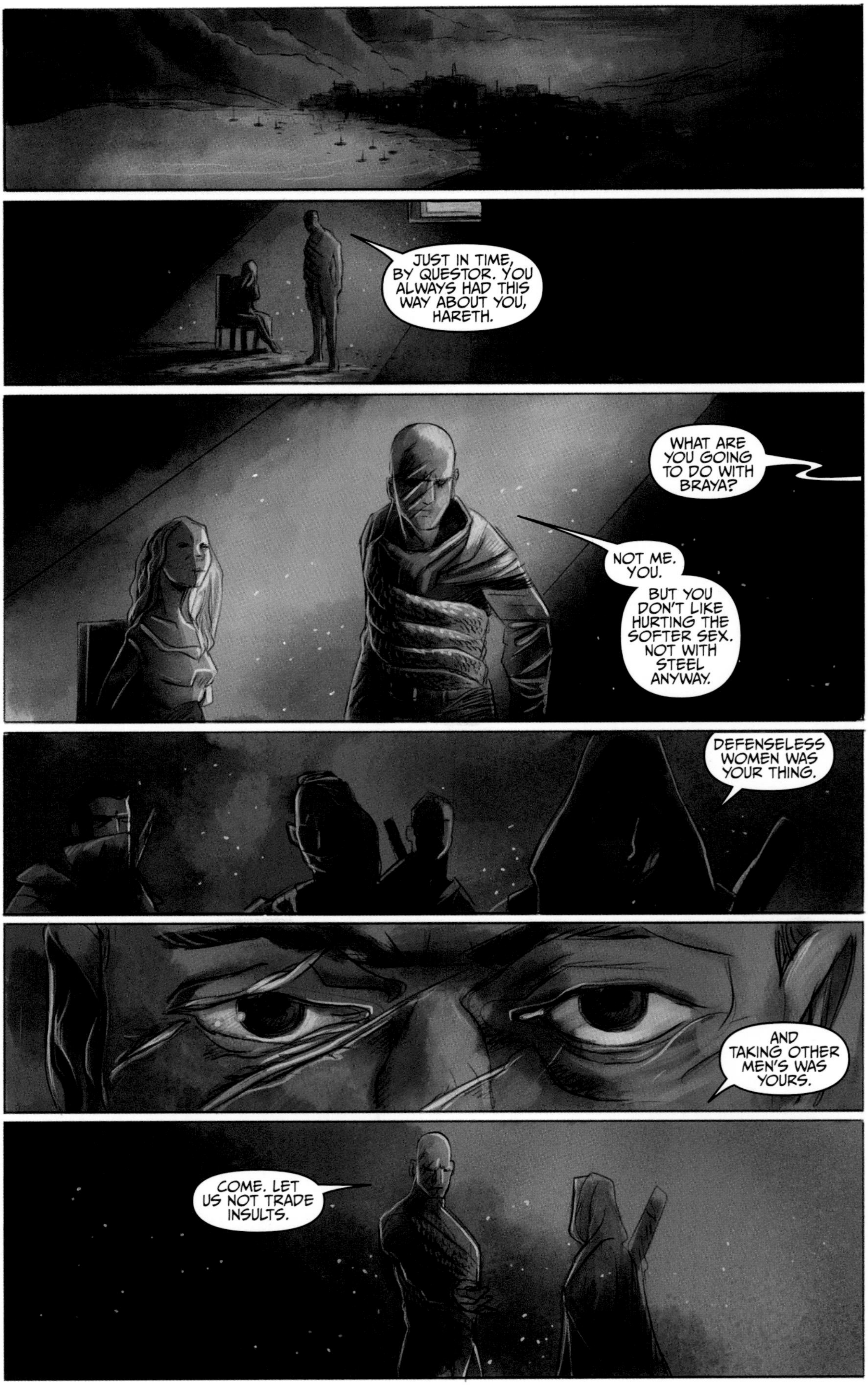
JUST IN TIME, BY QUESTOR. YOU ALWAYS HAD THIS WAY ABOUT YOU, HARETH.
WHAT ARE YOU GOING TO DO WITH BRAYA?
NOT ME. YOU.
BUT YOU DON'T LIKE HURTING THE SOFTER SEX. NOT WITH STEEL ANYWAY.
DEFENSELESS WOMEN WAS YOUR THING.
AND TAKING OTHER MEN'S WAS YOURS.
COME. LET US NOT TRADE INSULTS.

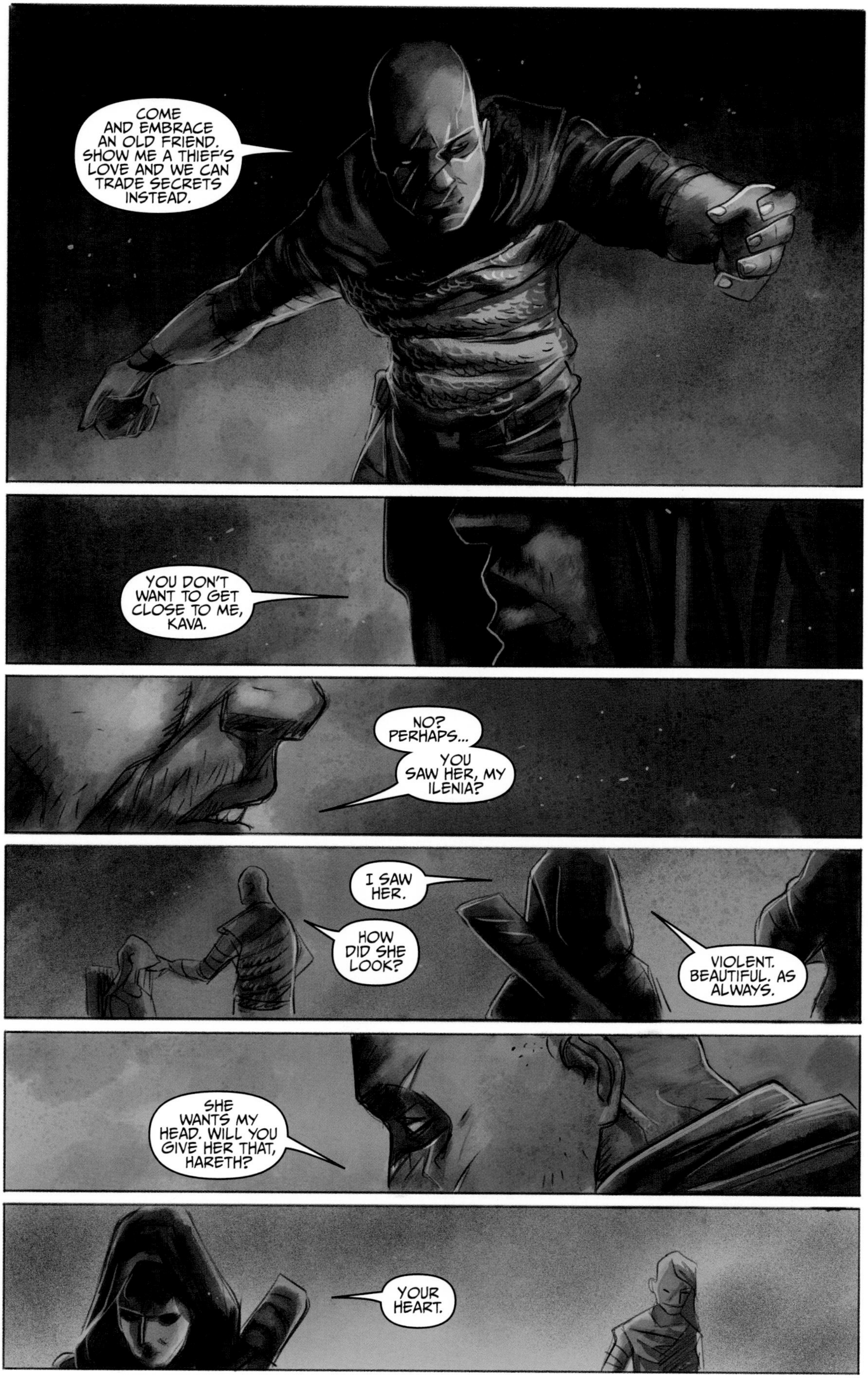
COME AND EMBRACE AN OLD FRIEND. SHOW ME A THIEF'S LOVE AND WE CAN TRADE SECRETS INSTEAD.
YOU DON'T WANT TO GET CLOSE TO ME, KAVA.
NO? PERHAPS...
YOU SAW HER, MY ILENIA?
I SAW HER.
HOW DID SHE LOOK?
VIOLENT. BEAUTIFUL. AS ALWAYS.
SHE WANTS MY HEAD. WILL YOU GIVE HER THAT, HARETH?
YOUR HEART.

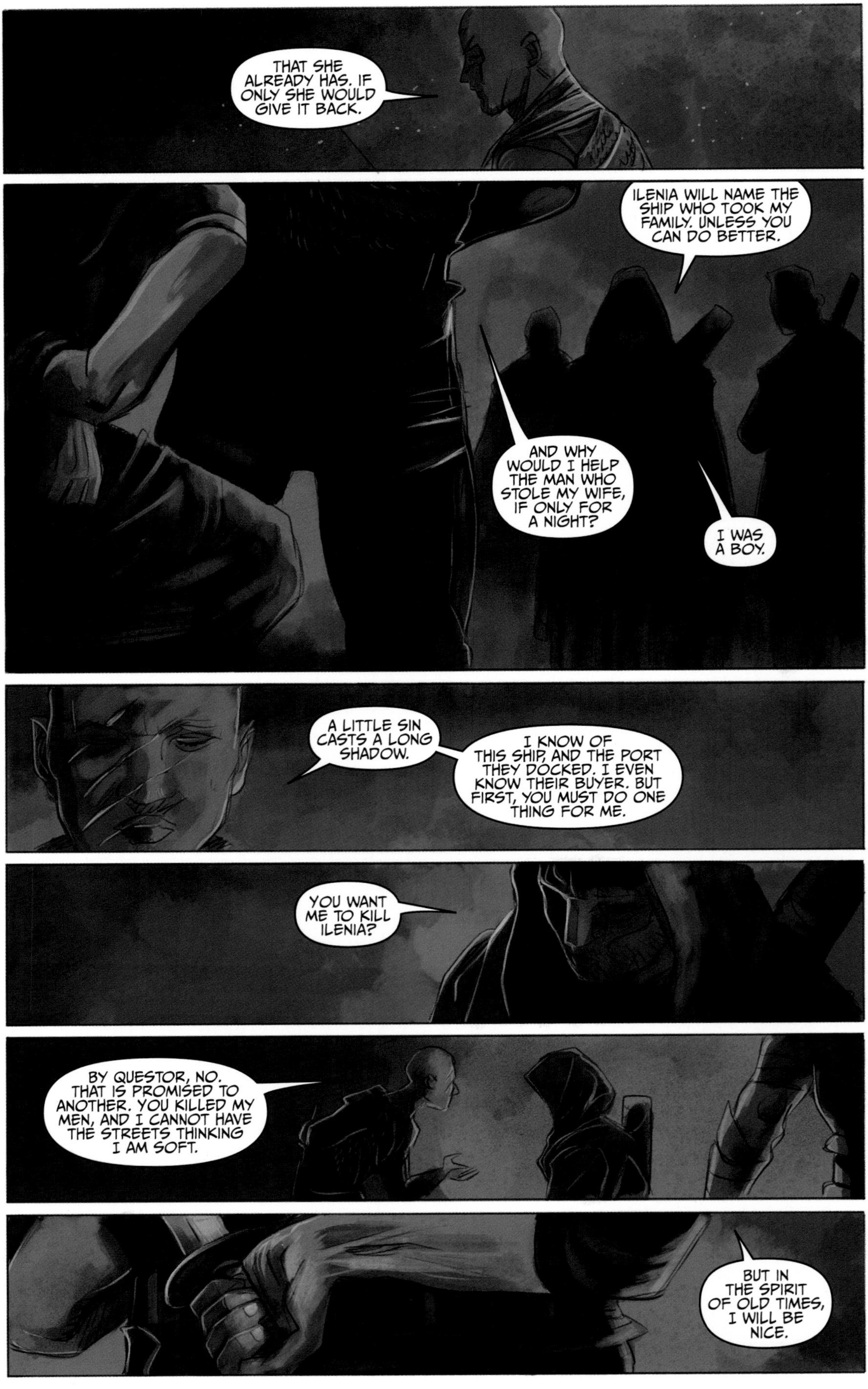
THAT SHE ALREADY HAS. IF ONLY SHE WOULD GIVE IT BACK.
ILENIA WILL NAME THE SHIP WHO TOOK MY FAMILY. UNLESS YOU CAN DO BETTER.
AND WHY WOULD I HELP THE MAN WHO STOLE MY WIFE, IF ONLY FOR A NIGHT?
I WAS A BOY.
A LITTLE SIN CASTS A LONG SHADOW.
I KNOW OF THIS SHIP, AND THE PORT THEY DOCKED. I EVEN KNOW THEIR BUYER. BUT FIRST, YOU MUST DO ONE THING FOR ME.
YOU WANT ME TO KILL ILENIA?
BY QUESTOR, NO. THAT IS PROMISED TO ANOTHER. YOU KILLED MY MEN, AND I CANNOT HAVE THE STREETS THINKING I AM SOFT.
BUT IN THE SPIRIT OF OLD TIMES, I WILL BE NICE.

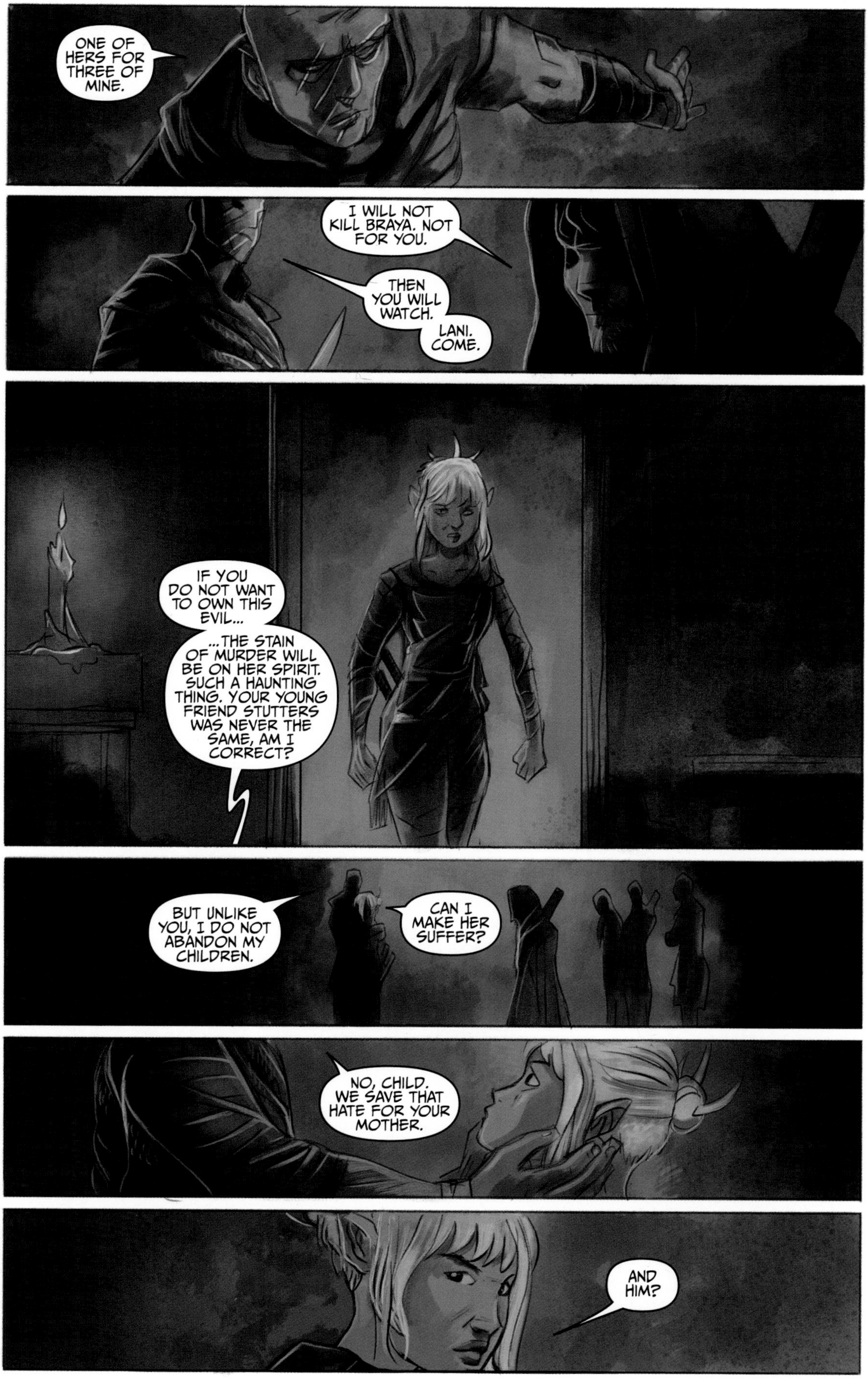

ONE OF HERS FOR THREE OF MINE.
I WILL NOT KILL BRAYA. NOT FOR YOU.
THEN YOU WILL WATCH.
LANI. COME.
IF YOU DO NOT WANT TO OWN THIS EVIL...
...THE STAIN OF MURDER WILL BE ON HER SPIRIT. SUCH A HAUNTING THING. YOUR YOUNG FRIEND STUTTERS WAS NEVER THE SAME, AM I CORRECT?
BUT UNLIKE YOU, I DO NOT ABANDON MY CHILDREN.
CAN I MAKE HER SUFFER?
NO, CHILD. WE SAVE THAT HATE FOR YOUR MOTHER.
AND HIM?

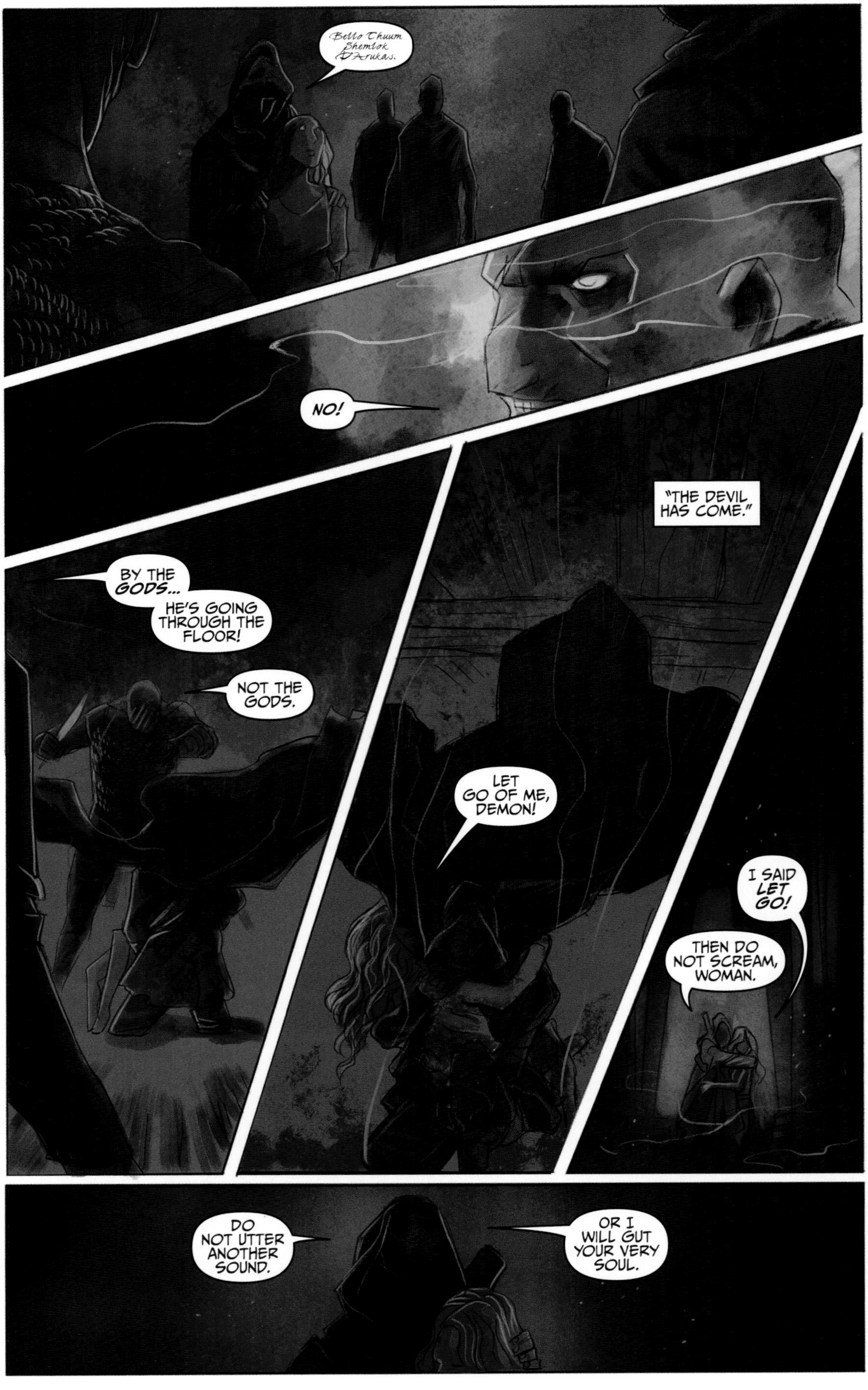
Bello Thuum Shemlok D'Arukas.
NO!
"THE DEVIL HAS COME."
BY THE GODS... HE'S GOING THROUGH THE FLOOR!
NOT THE GODS.
LET GO OF ME, DEMON!
I SAID LET GO!
THEN DO NOT SCREAM, WOMAN.
DO NOT UTTER ANOTHER SOUND.
OR I WILL GUT YOUR VERY SOUL.

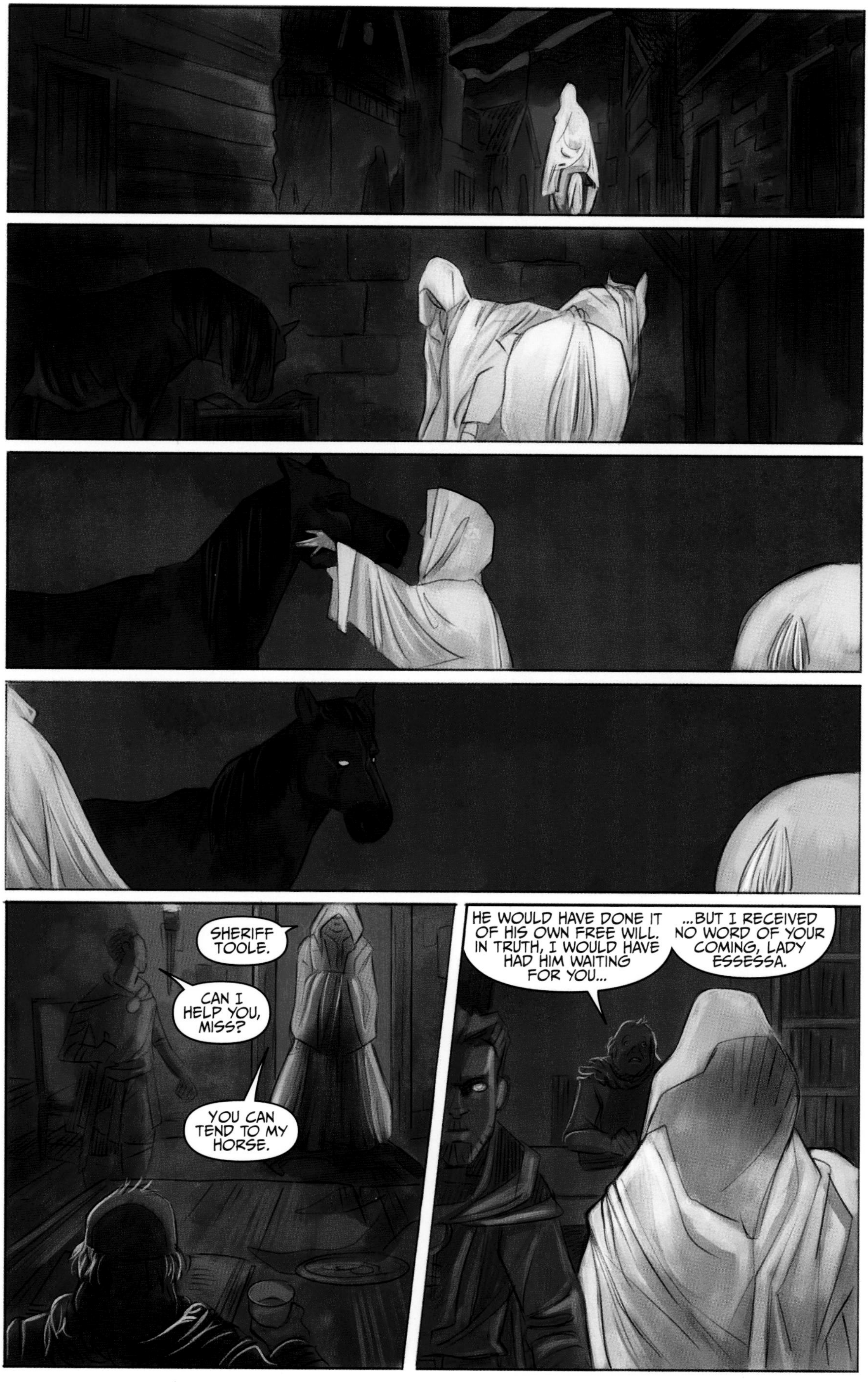
SHERIFF TOOLE.
CAN I HELP YOU, MISS?
YOU CAN TEND TO MY HORSE.
HE WOULD HAVE DONE IT OF HIS OWN FREE WILL. IN TRUTH, I WOULD HAVE HAD HIM WAITING FOR YOU...
...BUT I RECEIVED NO WORD OF YOUR COMING, LADY ESSESSA.

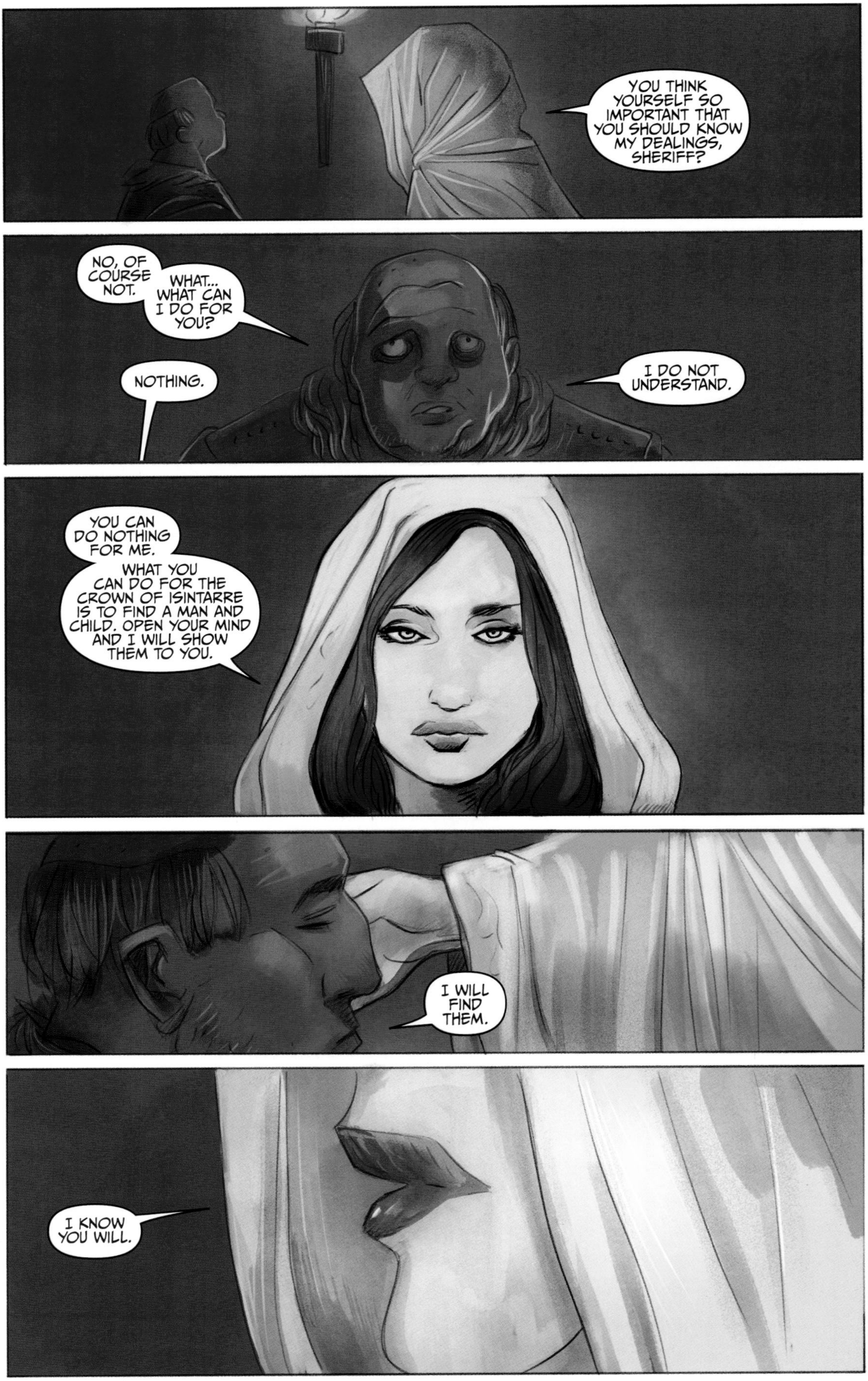
YOU THINK YOURSELF SO IMPORTANT THAT YOU SHOULD KNOW MY DEALINGS, SHERIFF?
NO, OF COURSE NOT.
WHAT... WHAT CAN I DO FOR YOU?
NOTHING.
I DO NOT UNDERSTAND.
YOU CAN DO NOTHING FOR ME.
WHAT YOU CAN DO FOR THE CROWN OF ISINTARRE IS TO FIND A MAN AND CHILD. OPEN YOUR MIND AND I WILL SHOW THEM TO YOU.
I WILL FIND THEM.
I KNOW YOU WILL.

Faith. For many of us, it is the air we breathe. It is how we live and how we die. Our world is governed by faith. It is a belief in ourselves, our fellow beings, and/or a higher power. It is a maze, a map to a foundation of principles we are so desperate to cling to, simply to be better human beings. It is the guide that divides us and makes us righteous.

Be wary of the teacher that screams the loudest, assuring that his path is the best. The shepherd who is only concerned with unlocking the maze's puzzle first is blinded from the journey and the truth – that although his road may be different from yours or mine or the next, the heart of the maze is still the same.

It wasn't the first time Niobe heard the voice, but it had been some time, many years in fact. The first time was on the flight to Oasis, when she was a child hunted by a dreaded Grachukk war chief, the Jade Lord, Morka Moa. The voice was calm, motherly, and yet it spoke from within. It had led the young half-elf girl, running through the jungles of Ugoma and onto the path to a town that would hide her among a haven of killers and thieves.

And now it had returned, stronger than before, like a concerned parent who had finally seen their child spread her wings and leave the nest. It would not hold her hand like before, but it would heal her wounds. All Niobe had to do was listen, and pray.

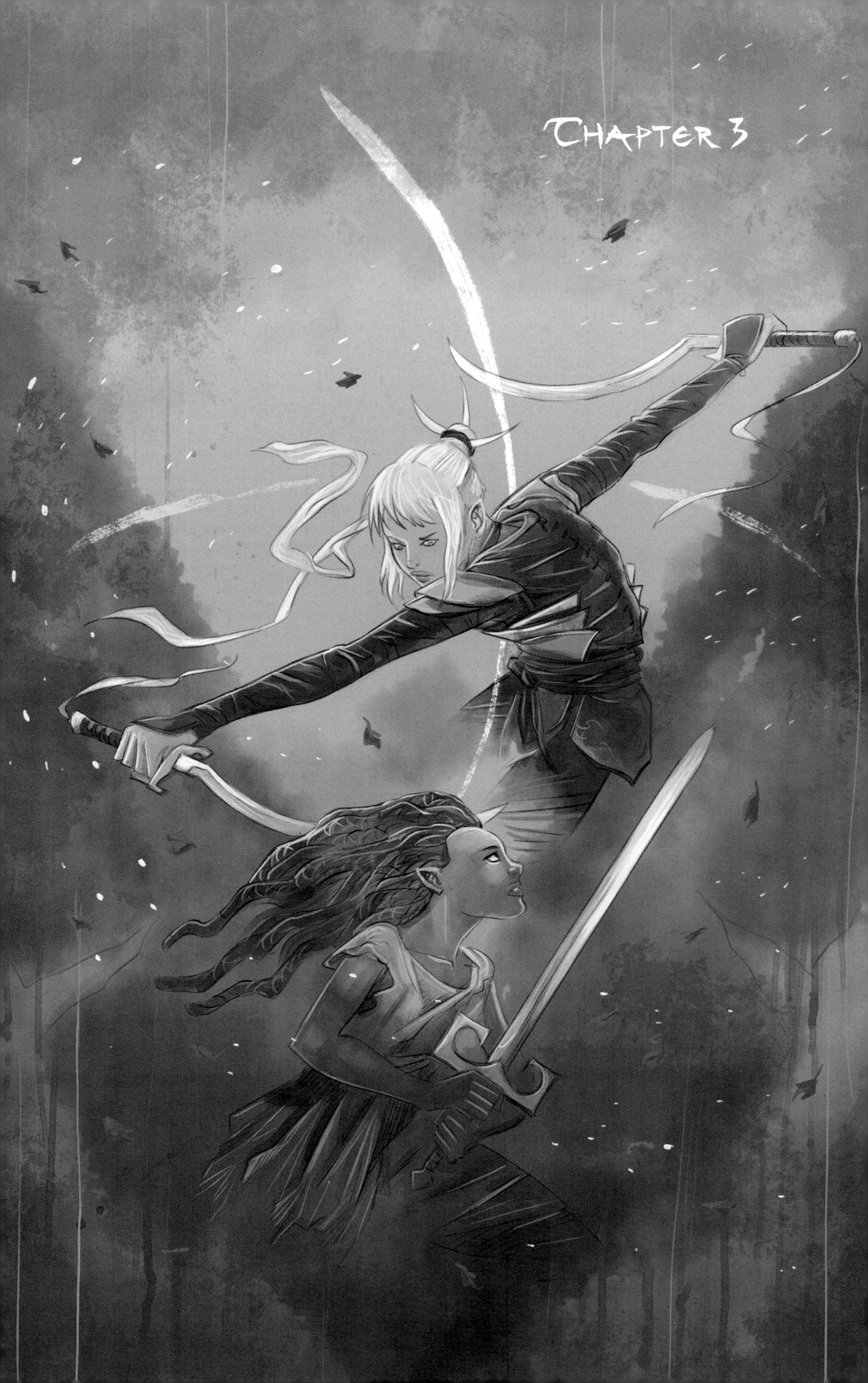
Chapter 3

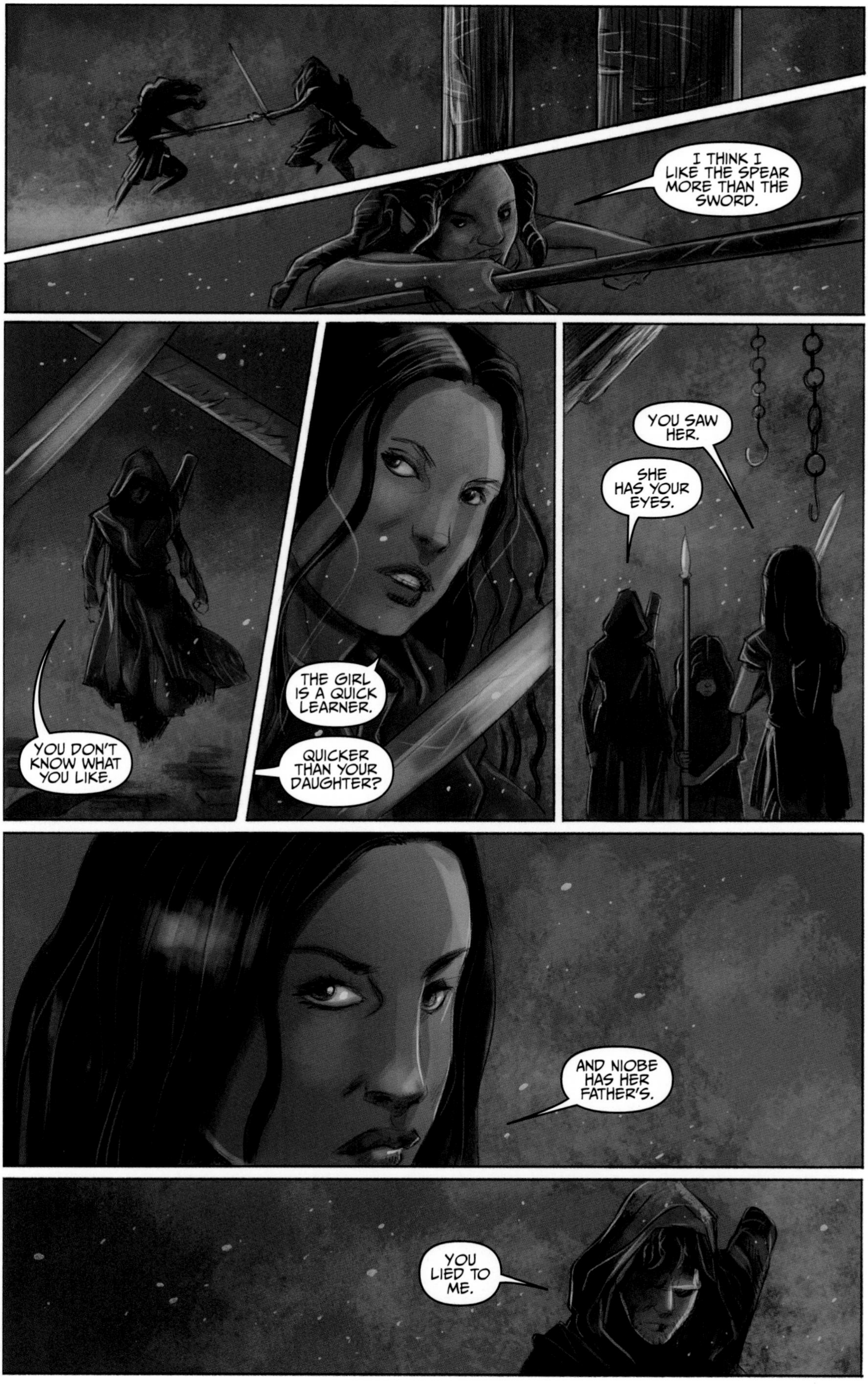
I THINK I LIKE THE SPEAR MORE THAN THE SWORD.
YOU DON'T KNOW WHAT YOU LIKE.
THE GIRL IS A QUICK LEARNER.
QUICKER THAN YOUR DAUGHTER?
YOU SAW HER.
SHE HAS YOUR EYES.
AND NIOBE HAS HER FATHER'S.
YOU LIED TO ME.

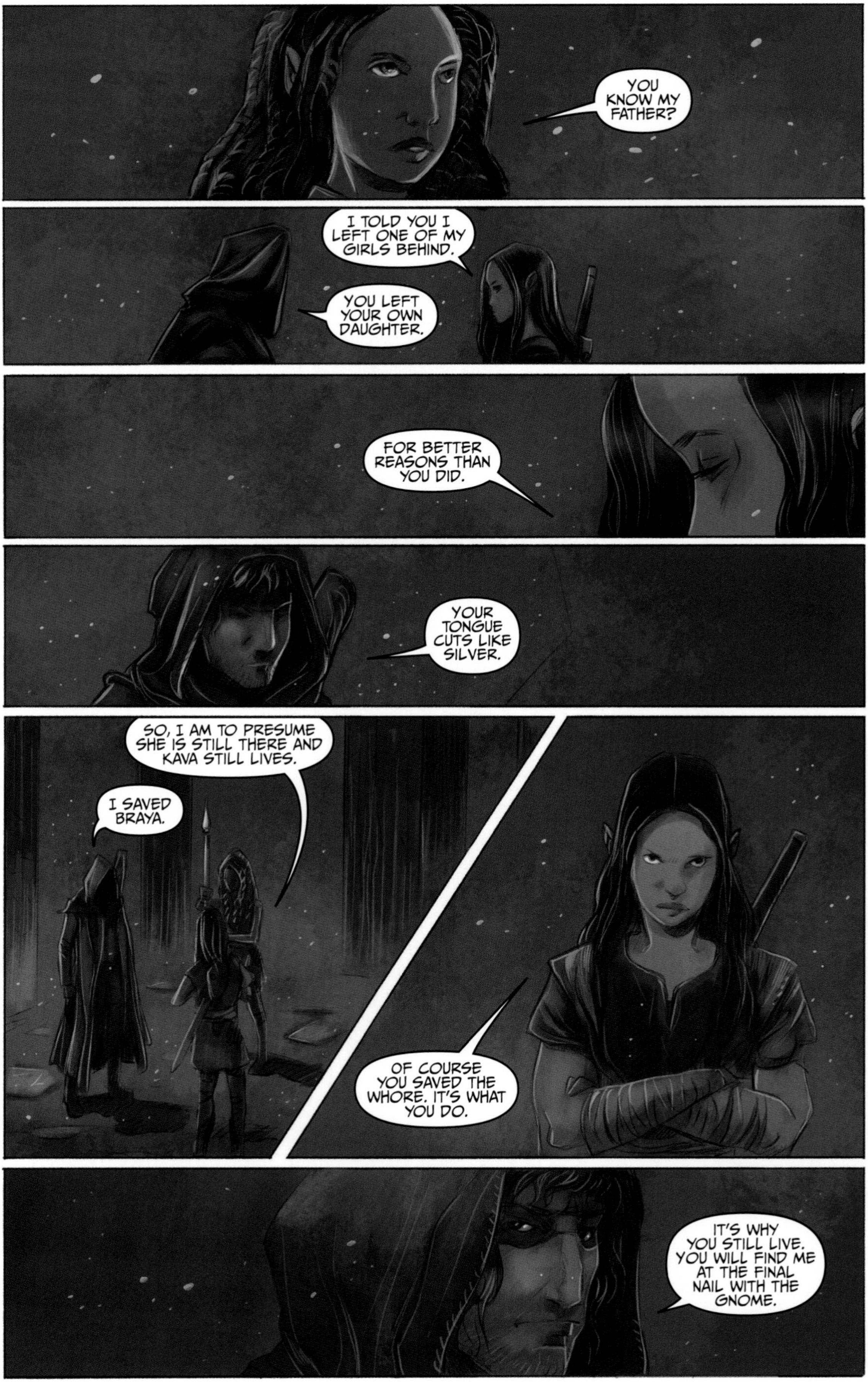
YOU KNOW MY FATHER?
I TOLD YOU I LEFT ONE OF MY GIRLS BEHIND.
YOU LEFT YOUR OWN DAUGHTER.
FOR BETTER REASONS THAN YOU DID.
YOUR TONGUE CUTS LIKE SILVER.
SO, I AM TO PRESUME SHE IS STILL THERE AND KAVA STILL LIVES.
I SAVED BRAYA.
OF COURSE YOU SAVED THE WHORE. IT'S WHAT YOU DO.
IT'S WHY YOU STILL LIVE. YOU WILL FIND ME AT THE FINAL NAIL WITH THE GNOME.

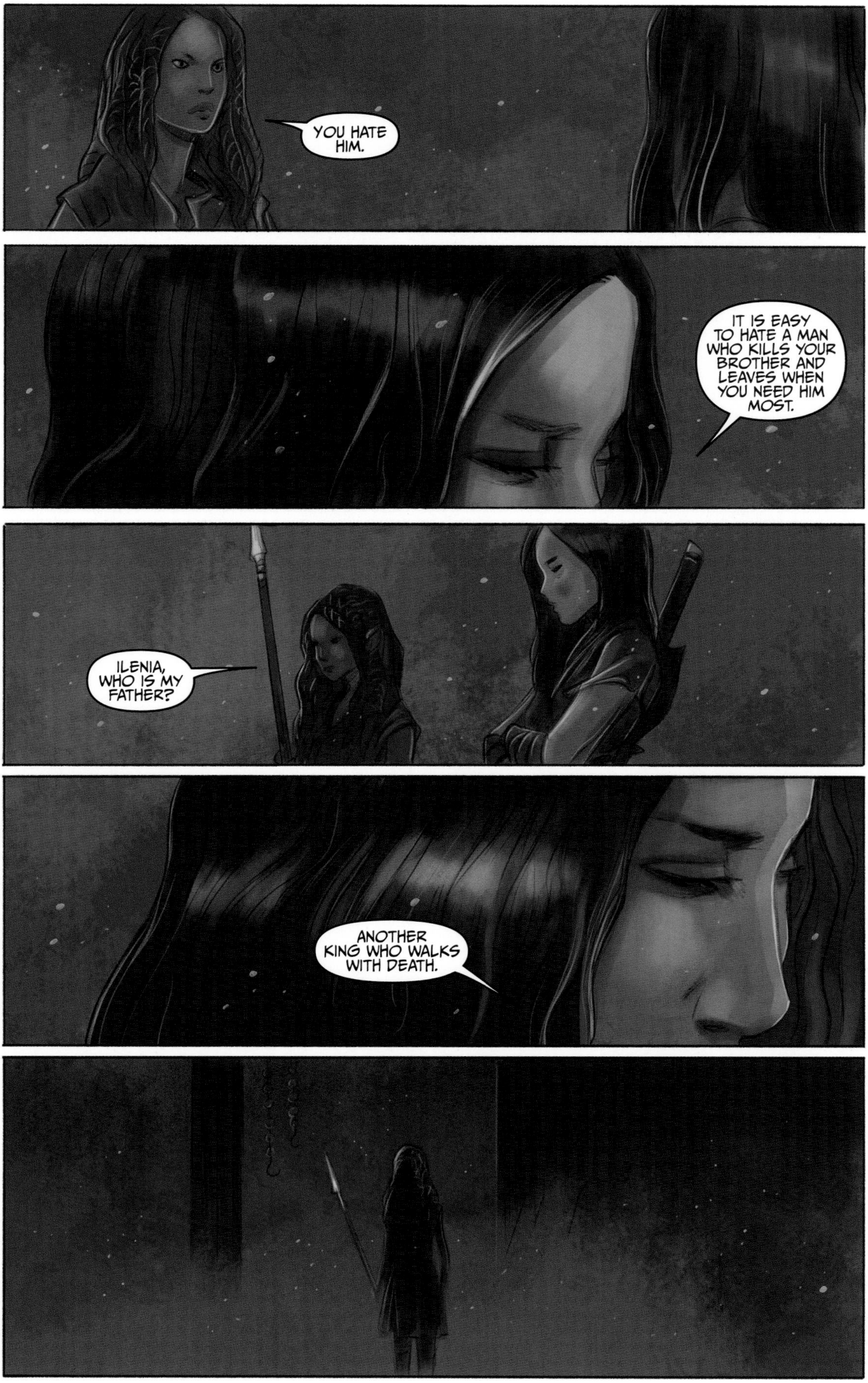
YOU HATE HIM.
IT IS EASY TO HATE A MAN WHO KILLS YOUR BROTHER AND LEAVES WHEN YOU NEED HIM MOST.
ILENIA, WHO IS MY FATHER?
ANOTHER KING WHO WALKS WITH DEATH.

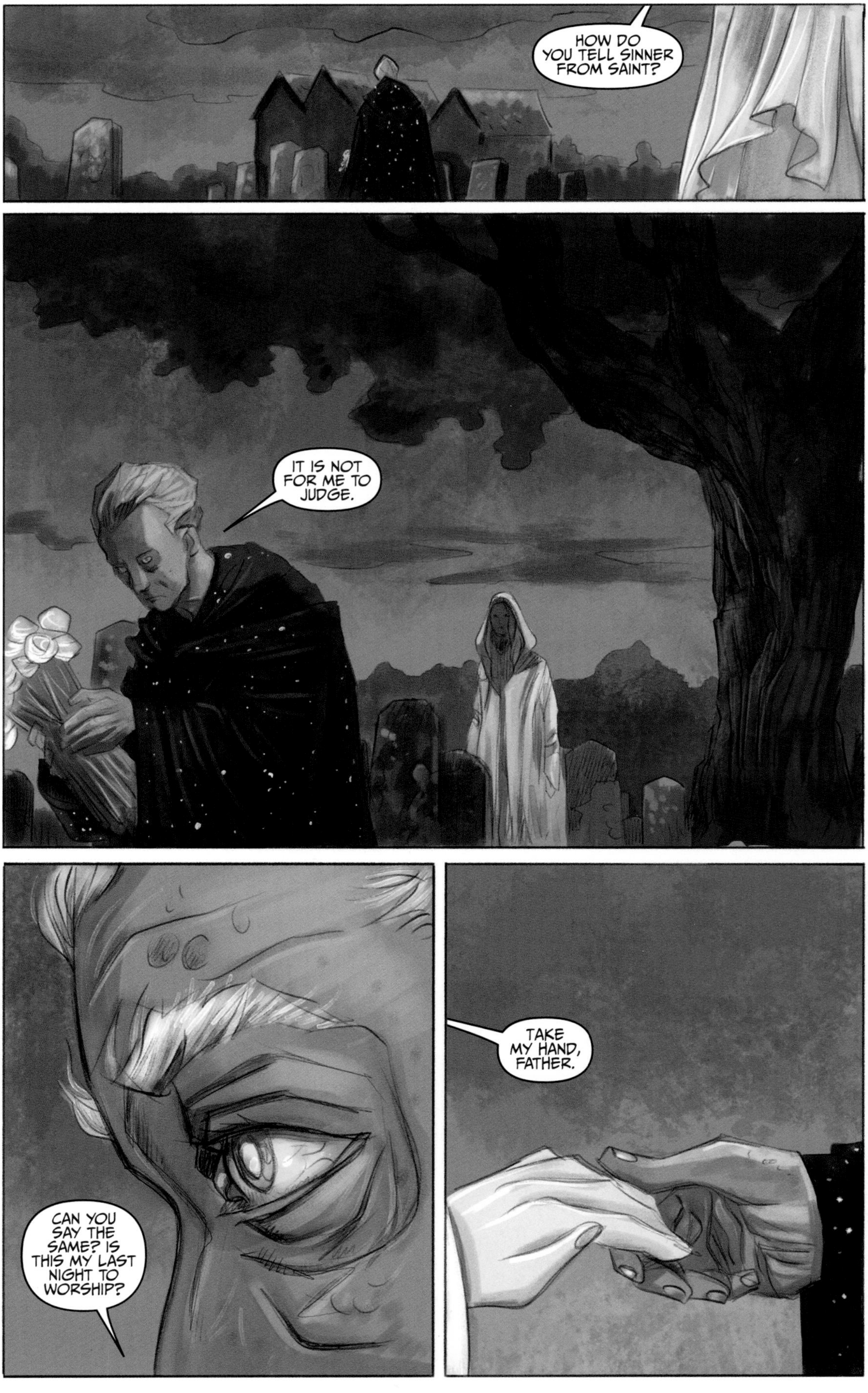
HOW DO YOU TELL SINNER FROM SAINT?
IT IS NOT FOR ME TO JUDGE.
CAN YOU SAY THE SAME? IS THIS MY LAST NIGHT TO WORSHIP?
TAKE MY HAND, FATHER.

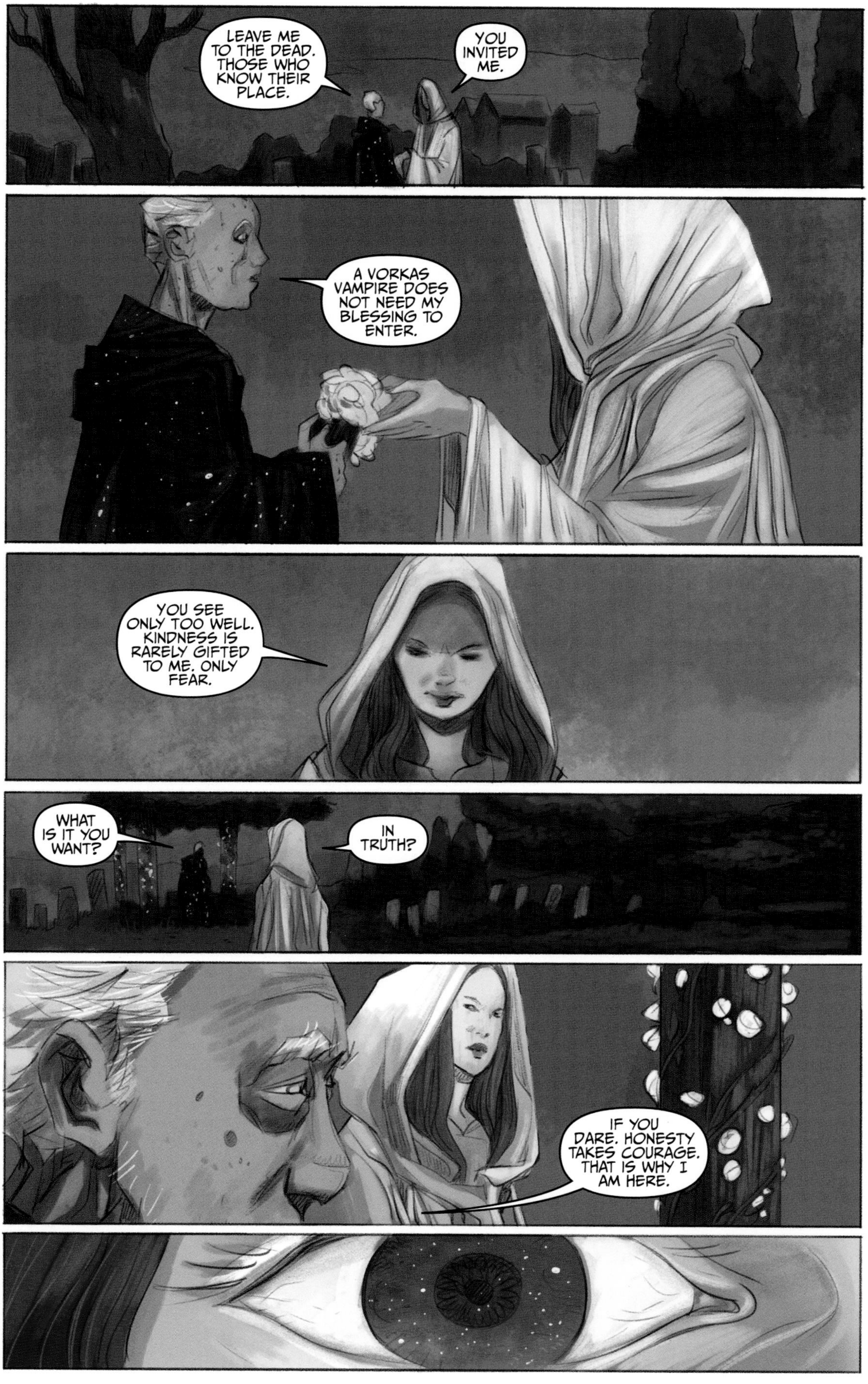
LEAVE ME TO THE DEAD. THOSE WHO KNOW THEIR PLACE.
YOU INVITED ME.
A VORKAS VAMPIRE DOES NOT NEED MY BLESSING TO ENTER.
YOU SEE ONLY TOO WELL. KINDNESS IS RARELY GIFTED TO ME. ONLY FEAR.
WHAT IS IT YOU WANT?
IN TRUTH?
IF YOU DARE. HONESTY TAKES COURAGE. THAT IS WHY I AM HERE.

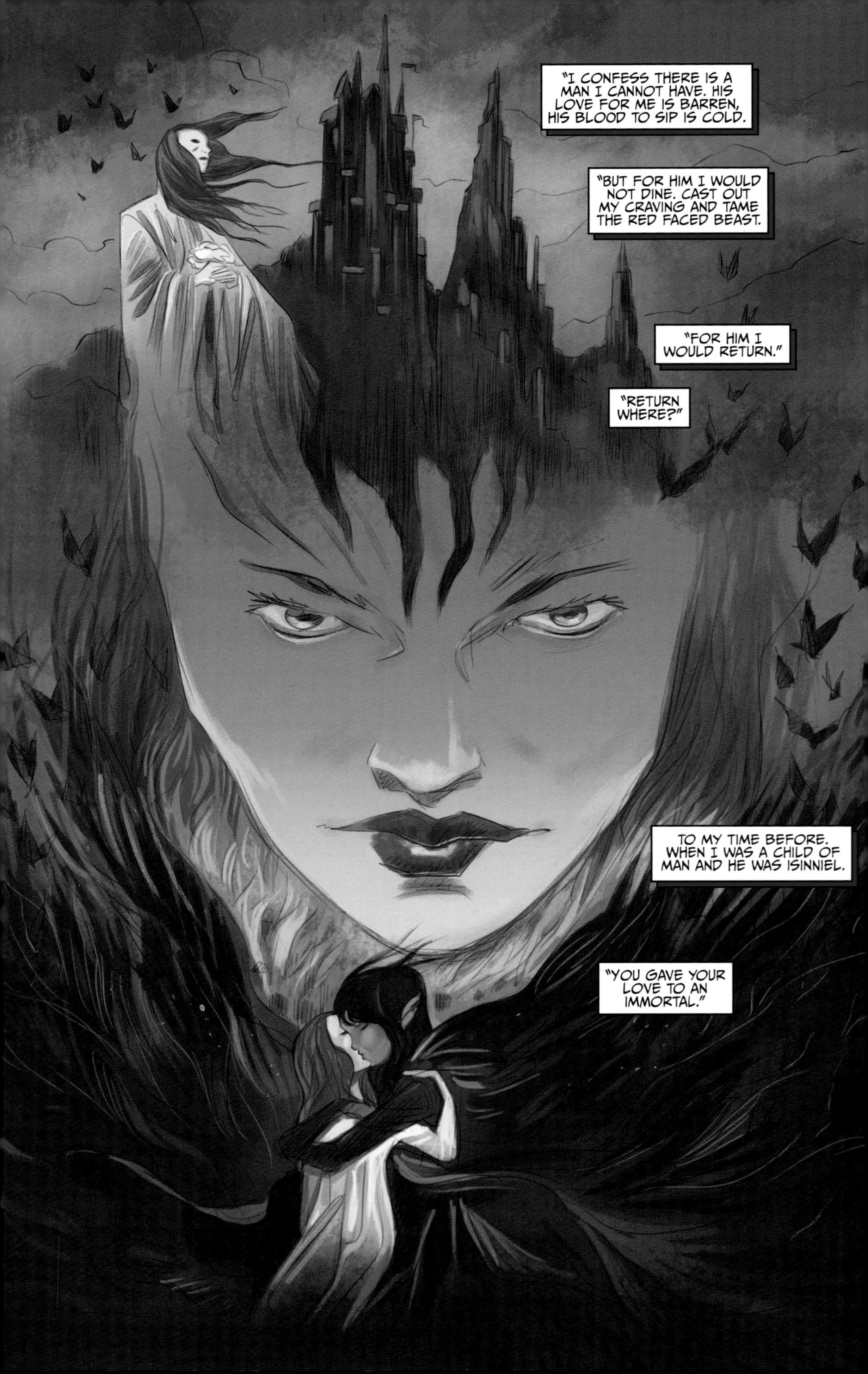
"I CONFESS THERE IS A MAN I CANNOT HAVE. HIS LOVE FOR ME IS BARREN, HIS BLOOD TO SIP IS COLD.
"BUT FOR HIM I WOULD NOT DINE. CAST OUT MY CRAVING AND TAME THE RED FACED BEAST.
"FOR HIM I WOULD RETURN."
"RETURN WHERE?"
TO MY TIME BEFORE. WHEN I WAS A CHILD OF MAN AND HE WAS ISINNIEL.
"YOU GAVE YOUR LOVE TO AN IMMORTAL."

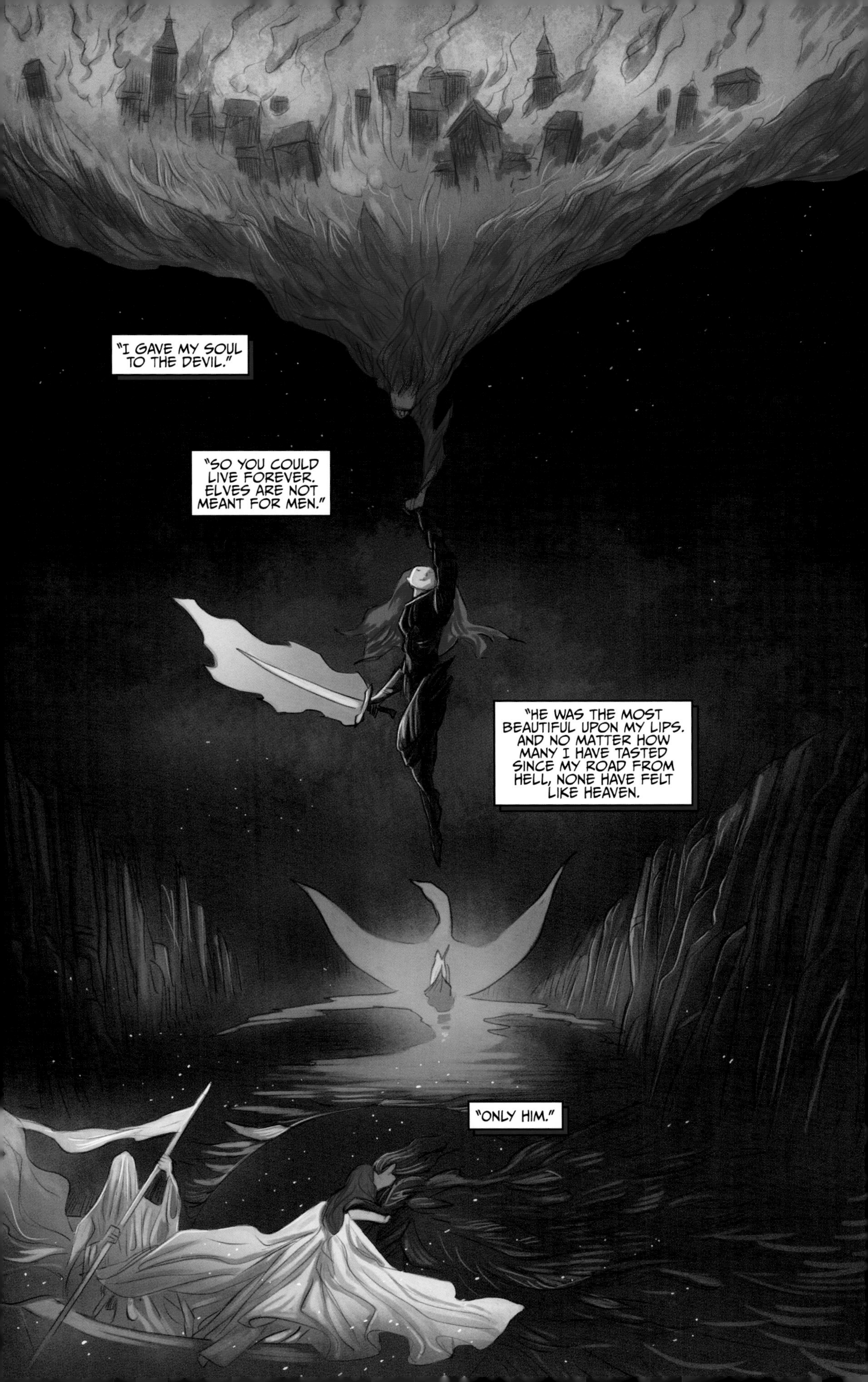
"I GAVE MY SOUL TO THE DEVIL."
"SO YOU COULD LIVE FOREVER. ELVES ARE NOT MEANT FOR MEN."
"HE WAS THE MOST BEAUTIFUL UPON MY LIPS. AND NO MATTER HOW MANY I HAVE TASTED SINCE MY ROAD FROM HELL, NONE HAVE FELT LIKE HEAVEN.
"ONLY HIM."

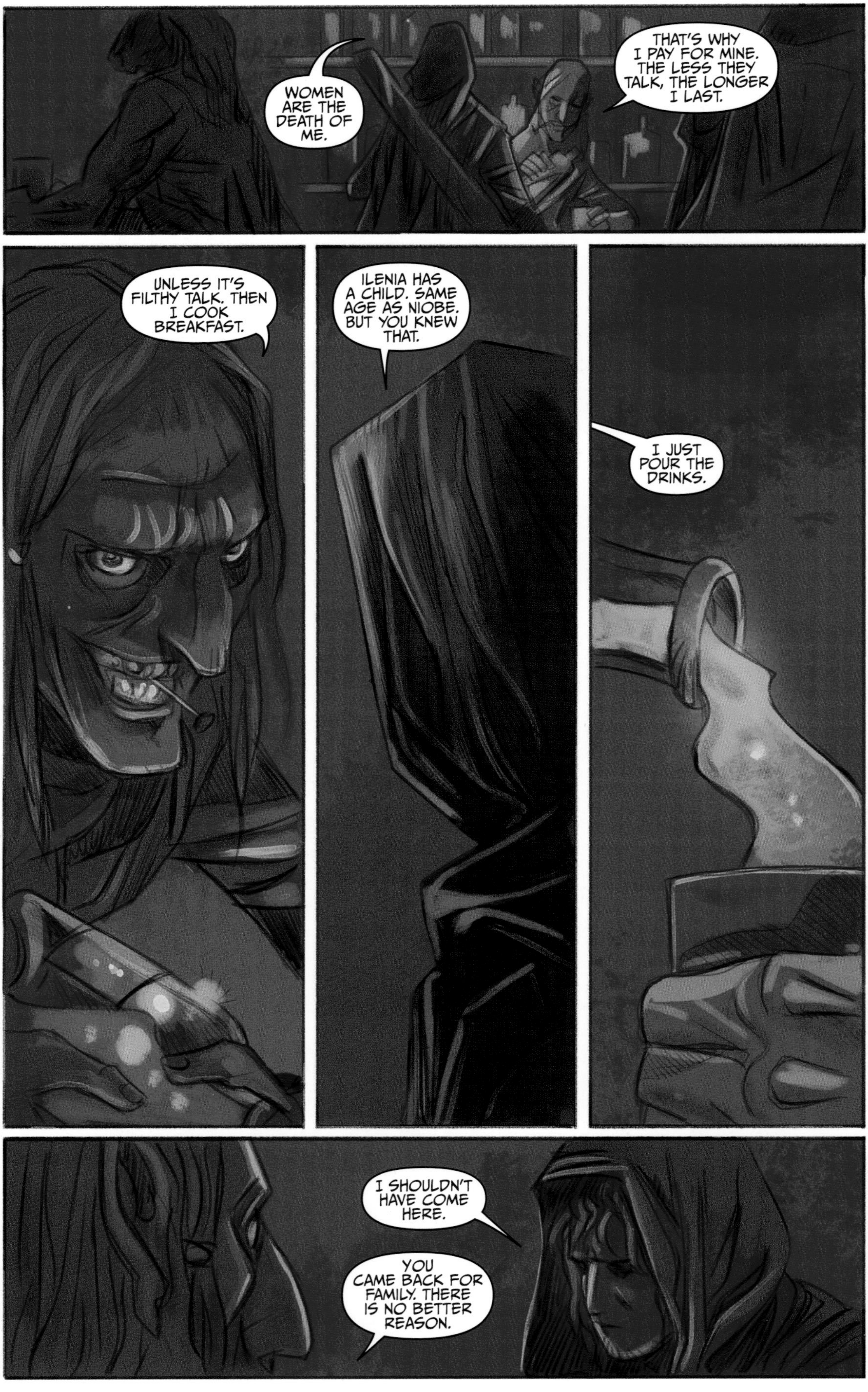
WOMEN ARE THE DEATH OF ME.
THAT'S WHY I PAY FOR MINE. THE LESS THEY TALK, THE LONGER I LAST.
UNLESS IT'S FILTHY TALK. THEN I COOK BREAKFAST.
ILENIA HAS A CHILD. SAME AGE AS NIOBE. BUT YOU KNEW THAT.
I JUST POUR THE DRINKS.
I SHOULDN'T HAVE COME HERE.
YOU CAME BACK FOR FAMILY. THERE IS NO BETTER REASON.

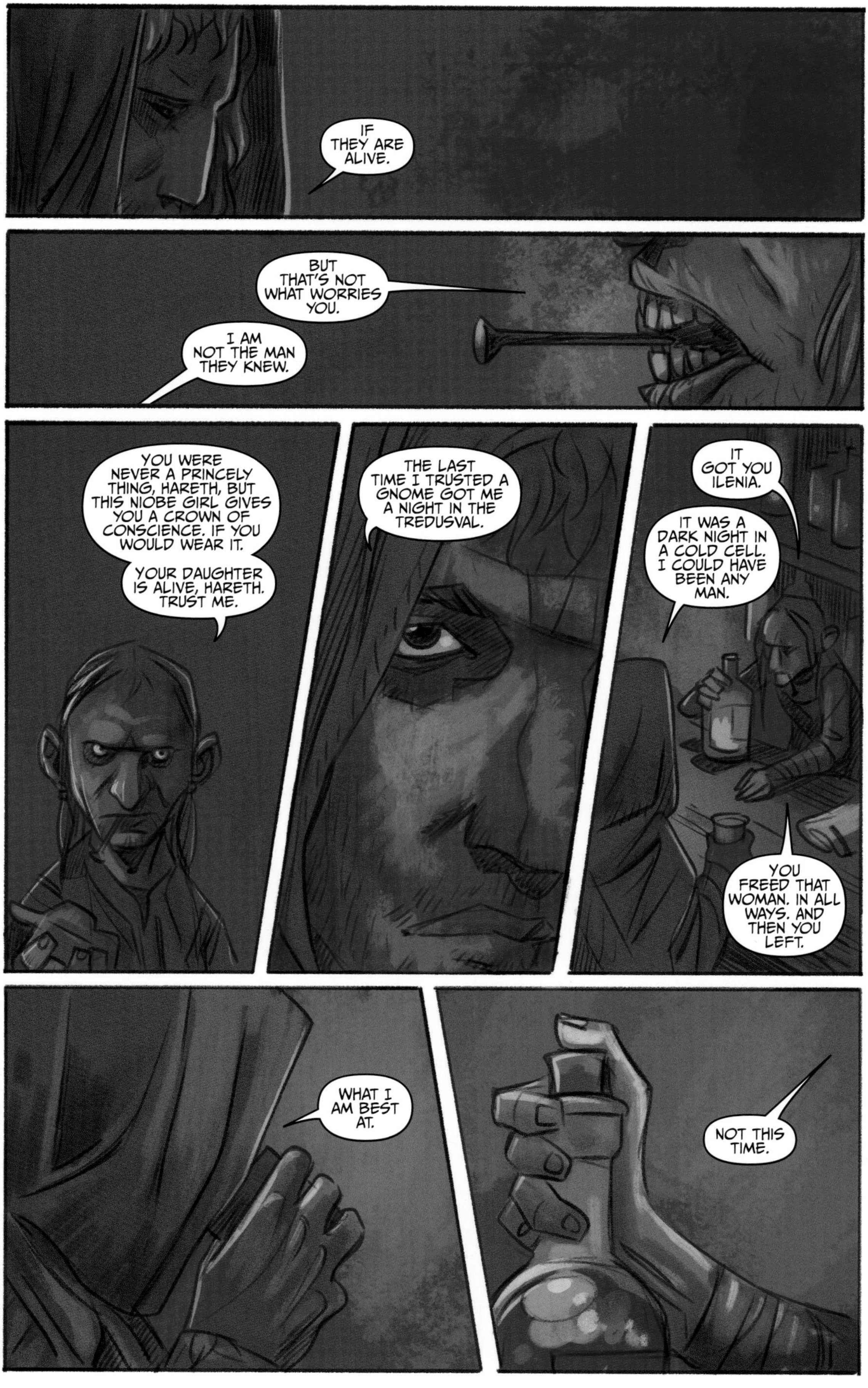
IF THEY ARE ALIVE.
BUT THAT'S NOT WHAT WORRIES YOU.
I AM NOT THE MAN THEY KNEW.
YOU WERE NEVER A PRINCELY THING, HARETH, BUT THIS NIOBE GIRL GIVES YOU A CROWN OF CONSCIENCE. IF YOU WOULD WEAR IT.
YOUR DAUGHTER IS ALIVE, HARETH. TRUST ME.
THE LAST TIME I TRUSTED A GNOME GOT ME A NIGHT IN THE TREDUSVAL.
IT GOT YOU ILENIA.
IT WAS A DARK NIGHT IN A COLD CELL. I COULD HAVE BEEN ANY MAN.
YOU FREED THAT WOMAN. IN ALL WAYS. AND THEN YOU LEFT.
WHAT I AM BEST AT.
NOT THIS TIME.

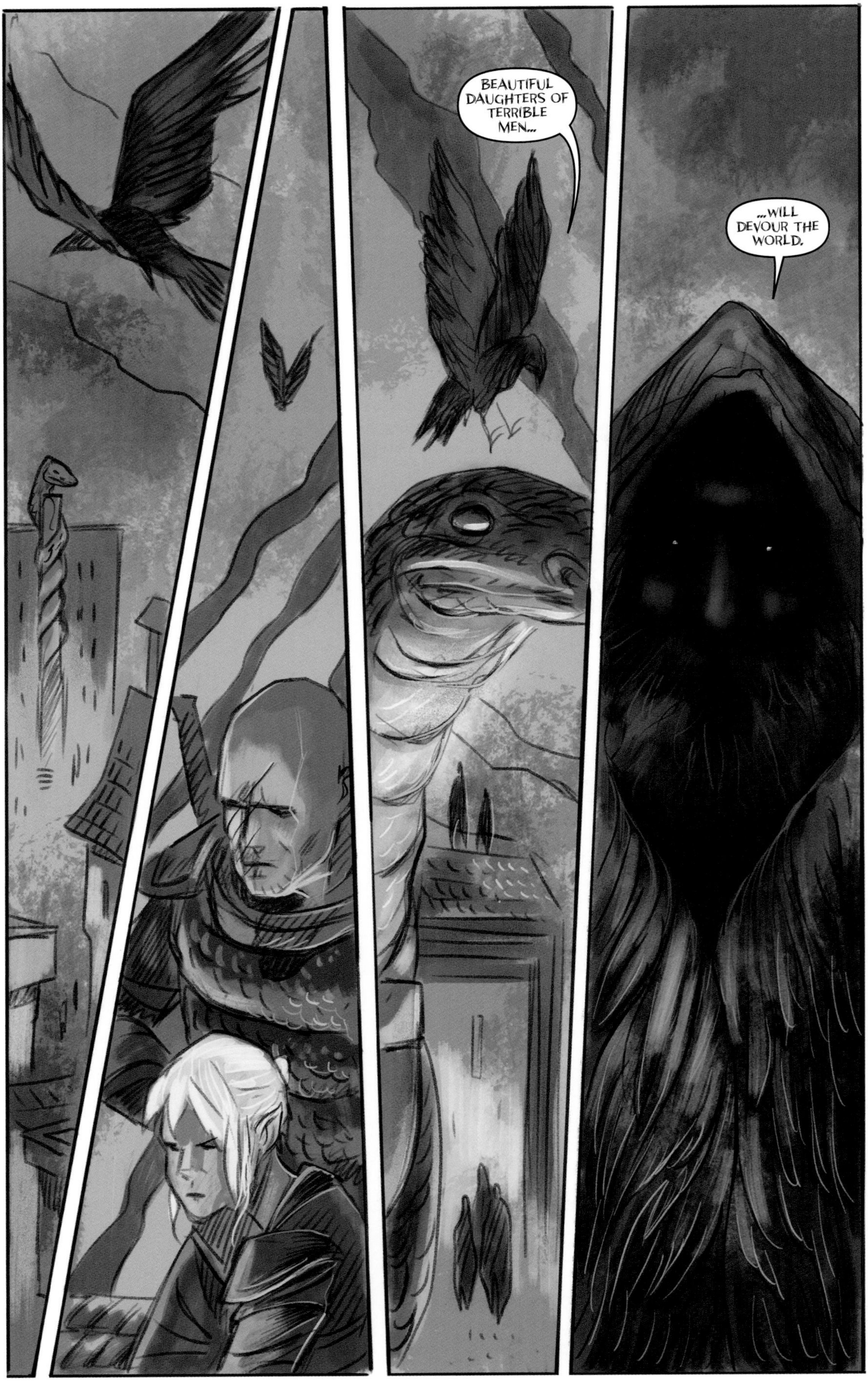
BEAUTIFUL DAUGHTERS OF TERRIBLE MEN...
...WILL DEVOUR THE WORLD.

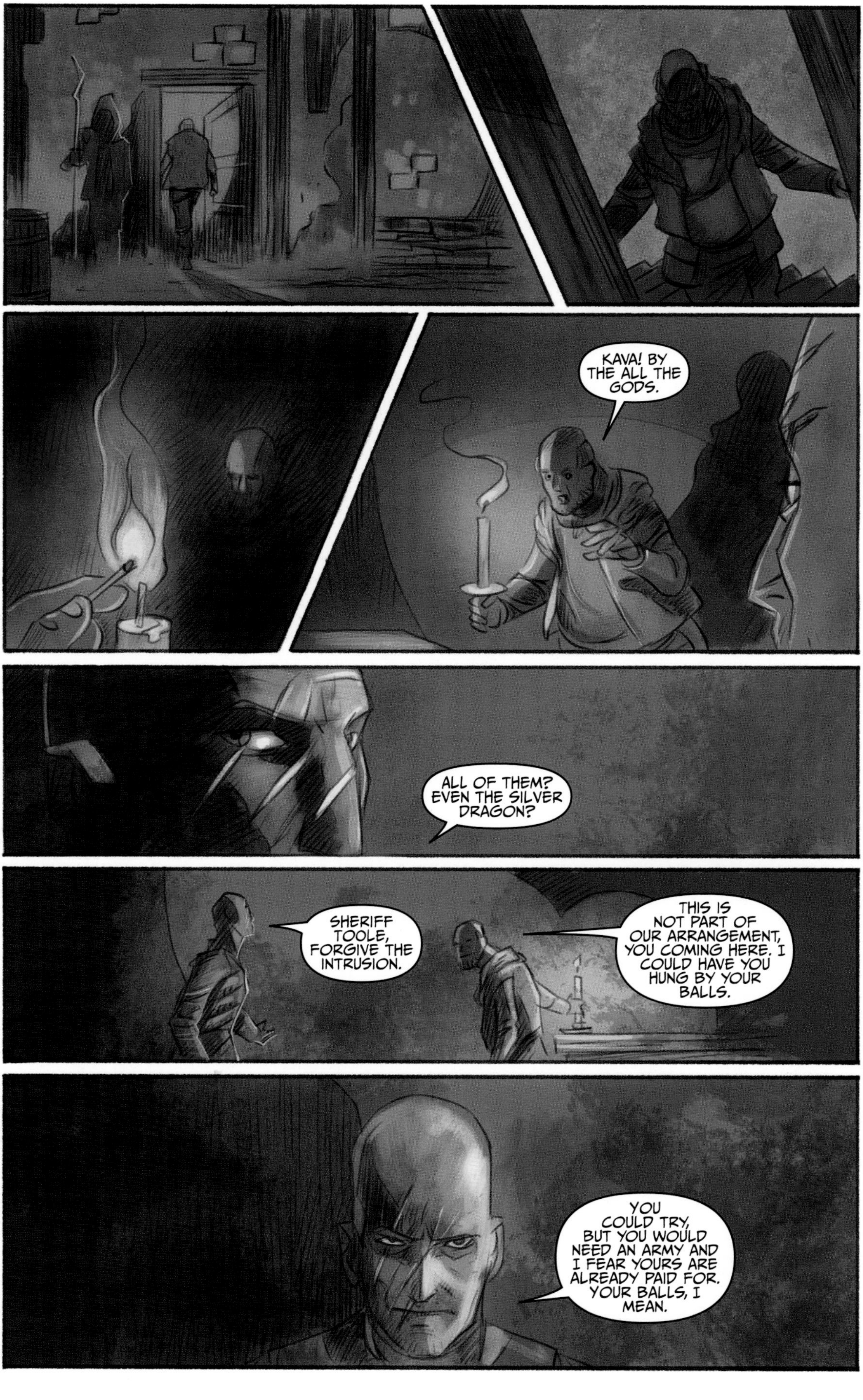
KAVA! BY THE ALL THE GODS.
ALL OF THEM? EVEN THE SILVER DRAGON?
SHERIFF TOOLE, FORGIVE THE INTRUSION.
THIS IS NOT PART OF OUR ARRANGEMENT, YOU COMING HERE. I COULD HAVE YOU HUNG BY YOUR BALLS.
YOU COULD TRY, BUT YOU WOULD NEED AN ARMY AND I FEAR YOURS ARE ALREADY PAID FOR. YOUR BALLS, I MEAN.

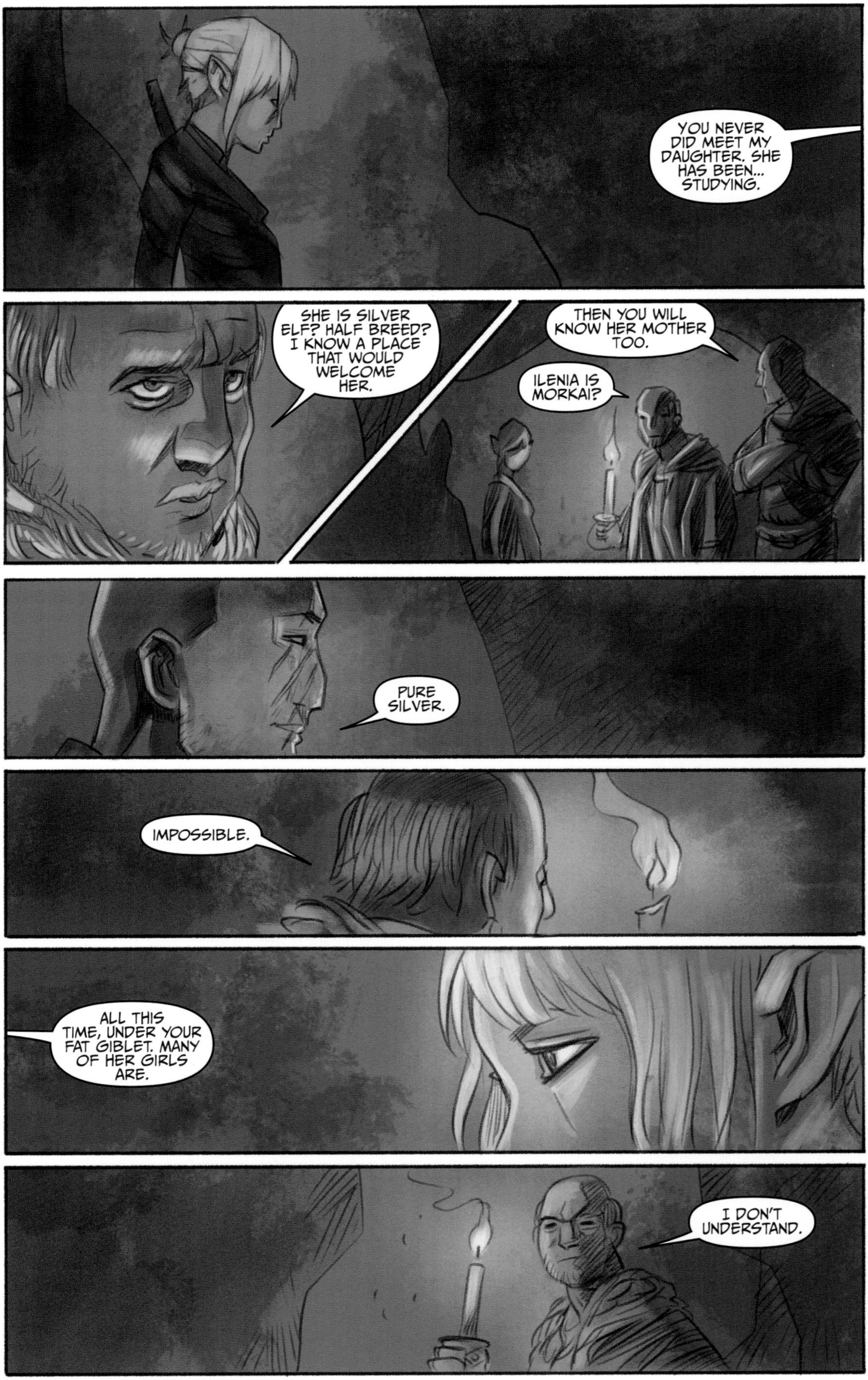
YOU NEVER DID MEET MY DAUGHTER. SHE HAS BEEN... STUDYING.
SHE IS SILVER ELF? HALF BREED? I KNOW A PLACE THAT WOULD WELCOME HER.
THEN YOU WILL KNOW HER MOTHER TOO.
ILENIA IS MORKAI?
PURE SILVER.
IMPOSSIBLE.
ALL THIS TIME, UNDER YOUR FAT GIBLET. MANY OF HER GIRLS ARE.
I DON'T UNDERSTAND.

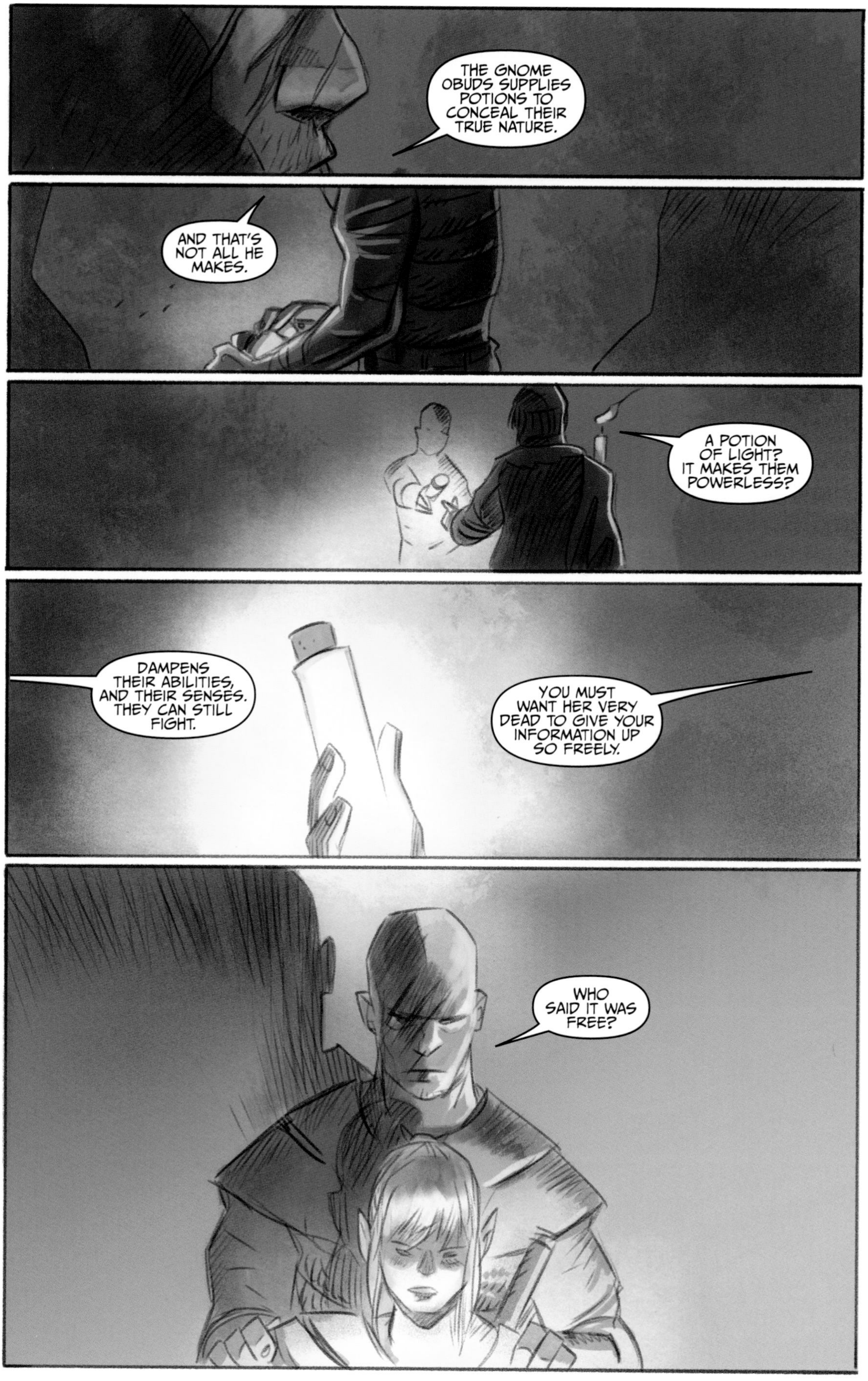
THE GNOME OBUDS SUPPLIES POTIONS TO CONCEAL THEIR TRUE NATURE.
AND THAT'S NOT ALL HE MAKES.
A POTION OF LIGHT? IT MAKES THEM POWERLESS?
DAMPENS THEIR ABILITIES, AND THEIR SENSES. THEY CAN STILL FIGHT.
YOU MUST WANT HER VERY DEAD TO GIVE YOUR INFORMATION UP SO FREELY.
WHO SAID IT WAS FREE?

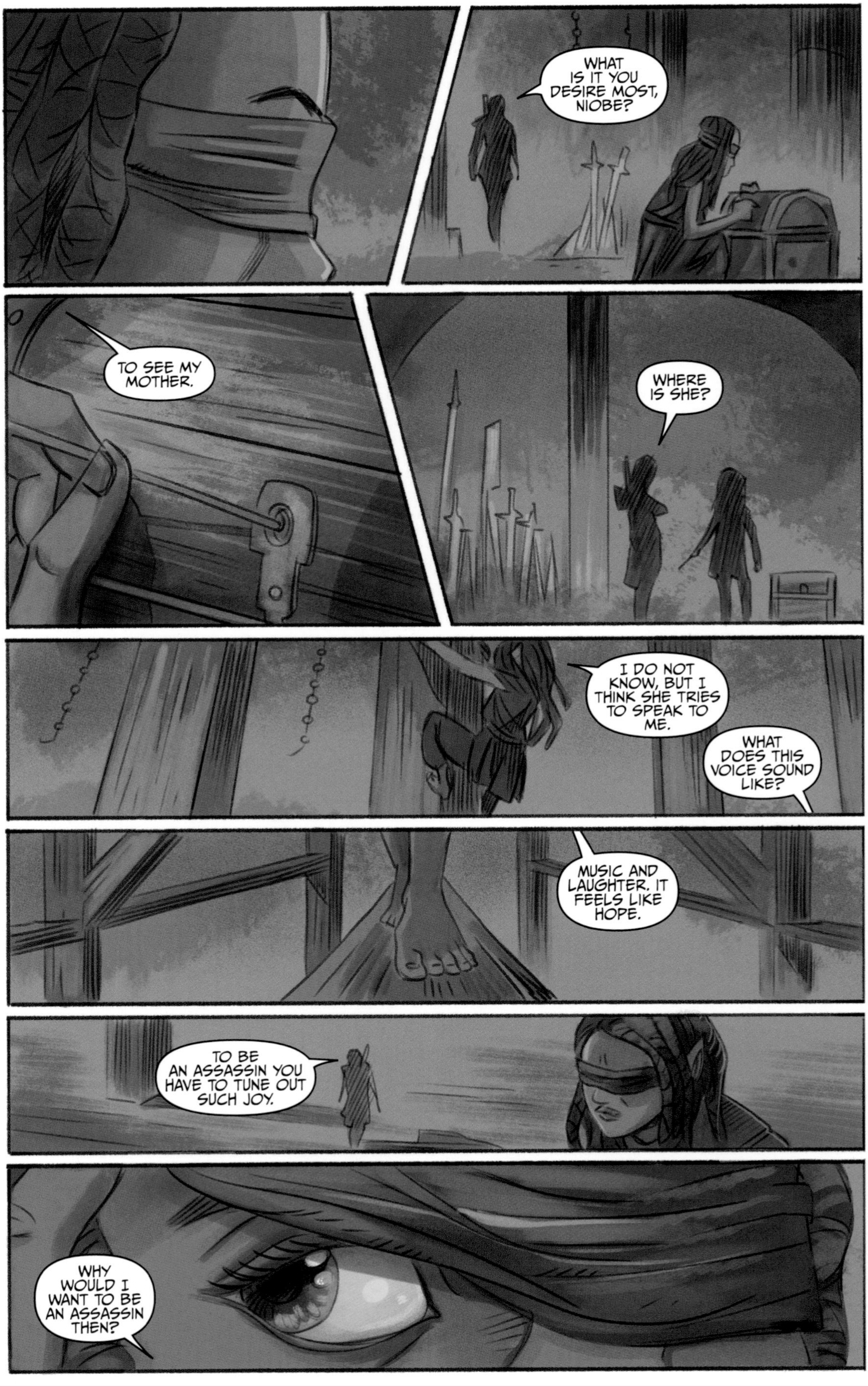
WHAT IS IT YOU DESIRE MOST, NIOBE?
TO SEE MY MOTHER.
WHERE IS SHE?
I DO NOT KNOW, BUT I THINK SHE TRIES TO SPEAK TO ME.
WHAT DOES THIS VOICE SOUND LIKE?
MUSIC AND LAUGHTER. IT FEELS LIKE HOPE.
TO BE AN ASSASSIN YOU HAVE TO TUNE OUT SUCH JOY.
WHY WOULD I WANT TO BE AN ASSASSIN THEN?

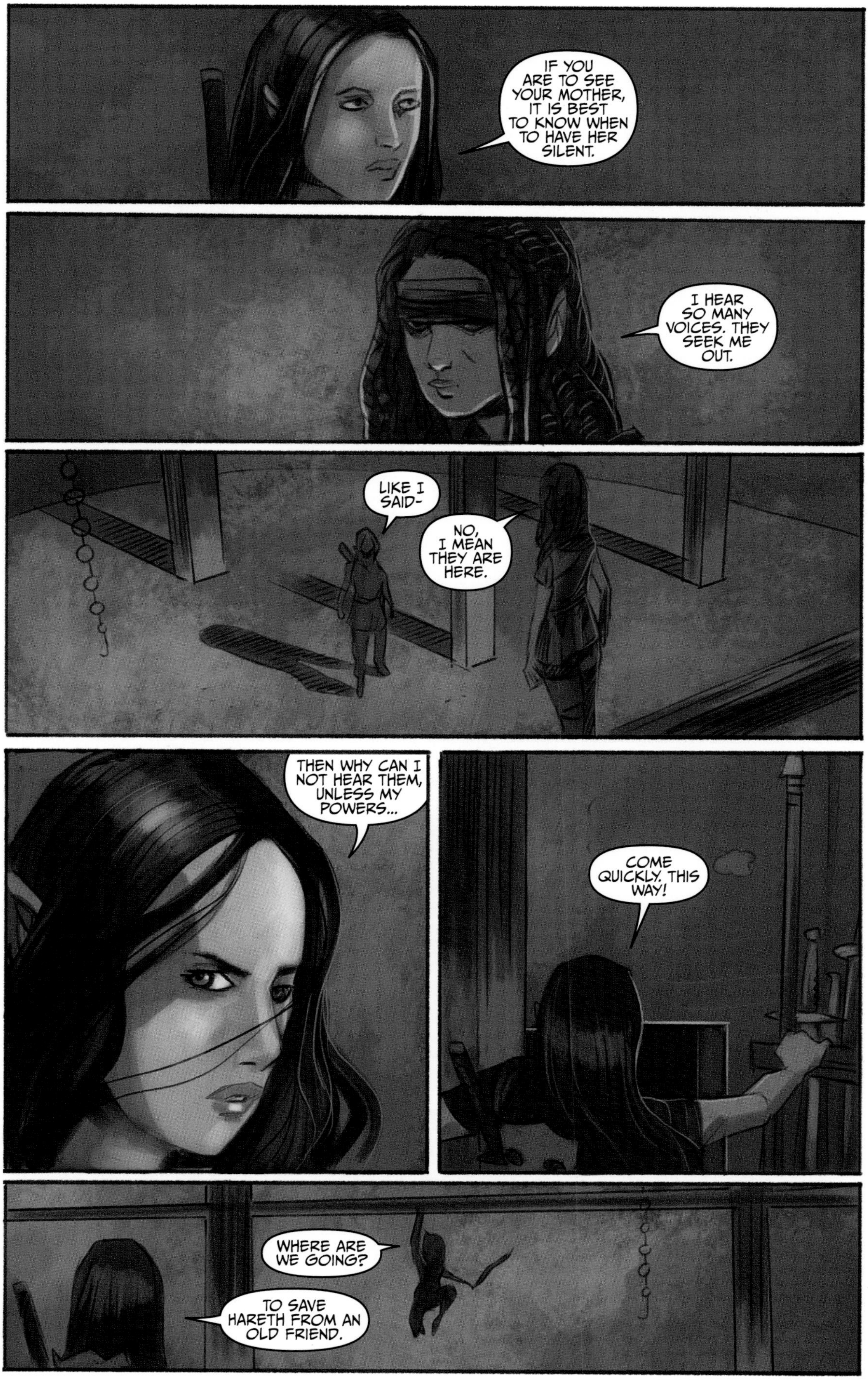
IF YOU ARE TO SEE YOUR MOTHER, IT IS BEST TO KNOW WHEN TO HAVE HER SILENT.
I HEAR SO MANY VOICES. THEY SEEK ME OUT.
LIKE I SAID-
NO, I MEAN THEY ARE HERE.
THEN WHY CAN I NOT HEAR THEM, UNLESS MY POWERS...
COME QUICKLY. THIS WAY!
WHERE ARE WE GOING?
TO SAVE HARETH FROM AN OLD FRIEND.

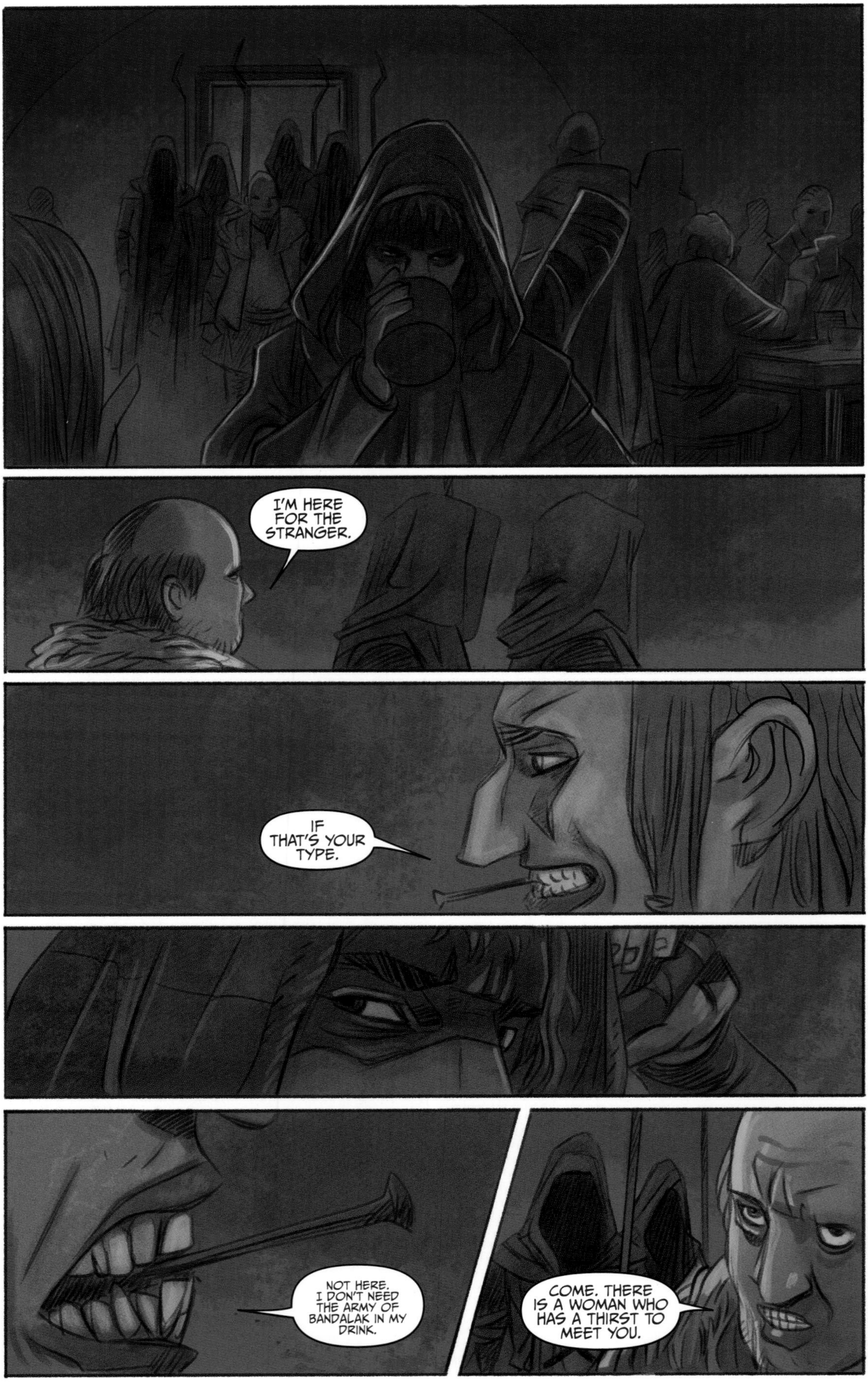
I'M HERE FOR THE STRANGER.
IF THAT'S YOUR TYPE.
NOT HERE. I DON'T NEED THE ARMY OF BANDALAK IN MY DRINK.
COME. THERE IS A WOMAN WHO HAS A THIRST TO MEET YOU.

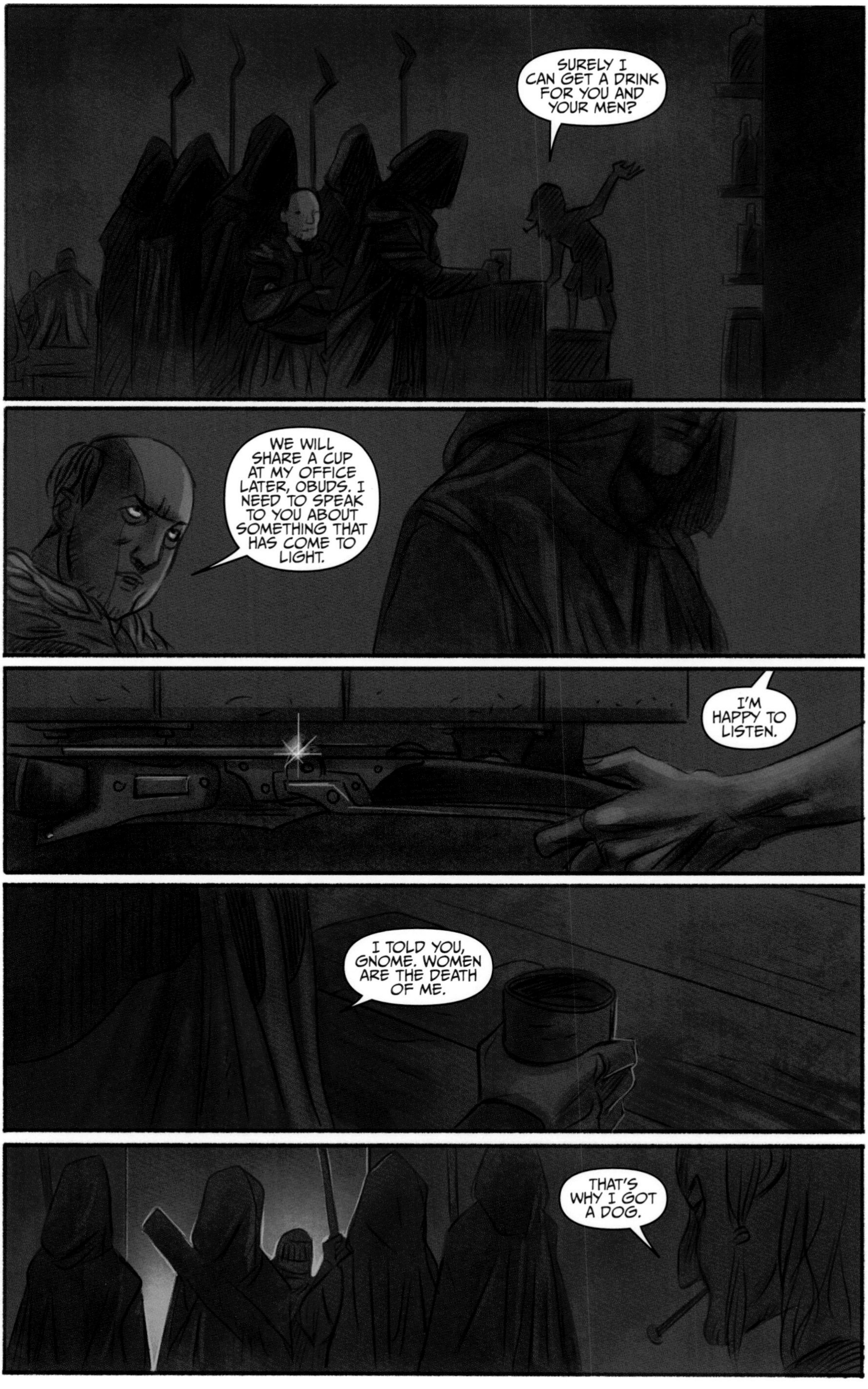
SURELY I CAN GET A DRINK FOR YOU AND YOUR MEN?
WE WILL SHARE A CUP AT MY OFFICE LATER, OBUDS. I NEED TO SPEAK TO YOU ABOUT SOMETHING THAT HAS COME TO LIGHT.
I'M HAPPY TO LISTEN.
I TOLD YOU, GNOME. WOMEN ARE THE DEATH OF ME.
THAT'S WHY I GOT A DOG.

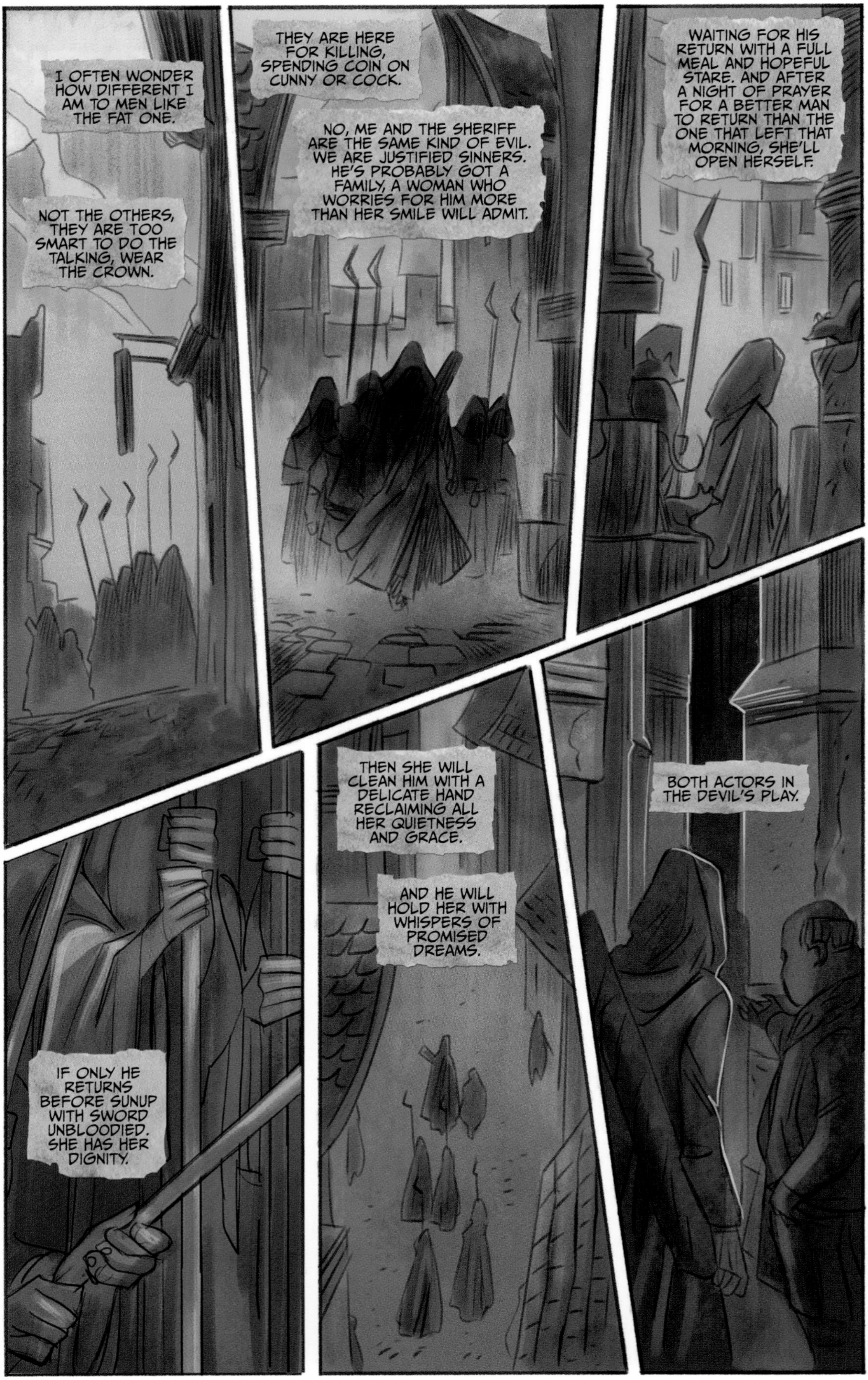
I OFTEN WONDER HOW DIFFERENT I AM TO MEN LIKE THE FAT ONE.
NOT THE OTHERS, THEY ARE TOO SMART TO DO THE TALKING, WEAR THE CROWN.
THEY ARE HERE FOR KILLING, SPENDING COIN ON CUNNY OR COCK.
NO, ME AND THE SHERIFF ARE THE SAME KIND OF EVIL. WE ARE JUSTIFIED SINNERS. HE'S PROBABLY GOT A FAMILY, A WOMAN WHO WORRIES FOR HIM MORE THAN HER SMILE WILL ADMIT.
WAITING FOR HIS RETURN WITH A FULL MEAL AND HOPEFUL STARE. AND AFTER A NIGHT OF PRAYER FOR A BETTER MAN TO RETURN THAN THE ONE THAT LEFT THAT MORNING, SHE'LL OPEN HERSELF.
IF ONLY HE RETURNS BEFORE SUNUP WITH SWORD UNBLOODIED. SHE HAS HER DIGNITY.
THEN SHE WILL CLEAN HIM WITH A DELICATE HAND RECLAIMING ALL HER QUIETNESS AND GRACE.
AND HE WILL HOLD HER WITH WHISPERS OF PROMISED DREAMS.
BOTH ACTORS IN THE DEVIL'S PLAY.

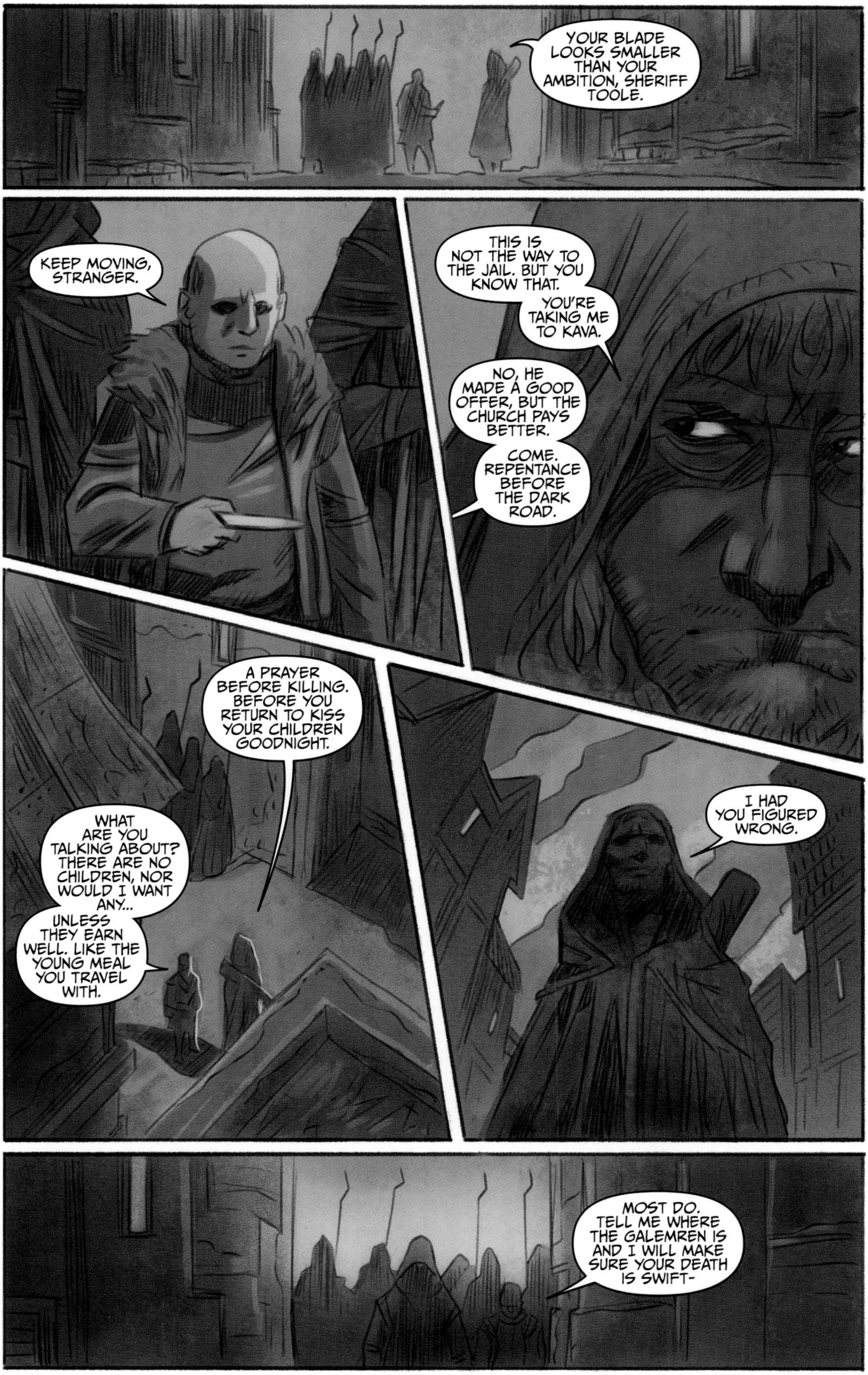
YOUR BLADE LOOKS SMALLER THAN YOUR AMBITION, SHERIFF TOOLE.
KEEP MOVING, STRANGER.
THIS IS NOT THE WAY TO THE JAIL. BUT YOU KNOW THAT.
YOU'RE TAKING ME TO KAVA.
NO, HE MADE A GOOD OFFER, BUT THE CHURCH PAYS BETTER.
COME. REPENTANCE BEFORE THE DARK ROAD.
A PRAYER BEFORE KILLING. BEFORE YOU RETURN TO KISS YOUR CHILDREN GOODNIGHT.
WHAT ARE YOU TALKING ABOUT? THERE ARE NO CHILDREN, NOR WOULD I WANT ANY...
UNLESS THEY EARN WELL. LIKE THE YOUNG MEAL YOU TRAVEL WITH.
I HAD YOU FIGURED WRONG.
MOST DO. TELL ME WHERE THE GALEMREN IS AND I WILL MAKE SURE YOUR DEATH IS SWIFT-

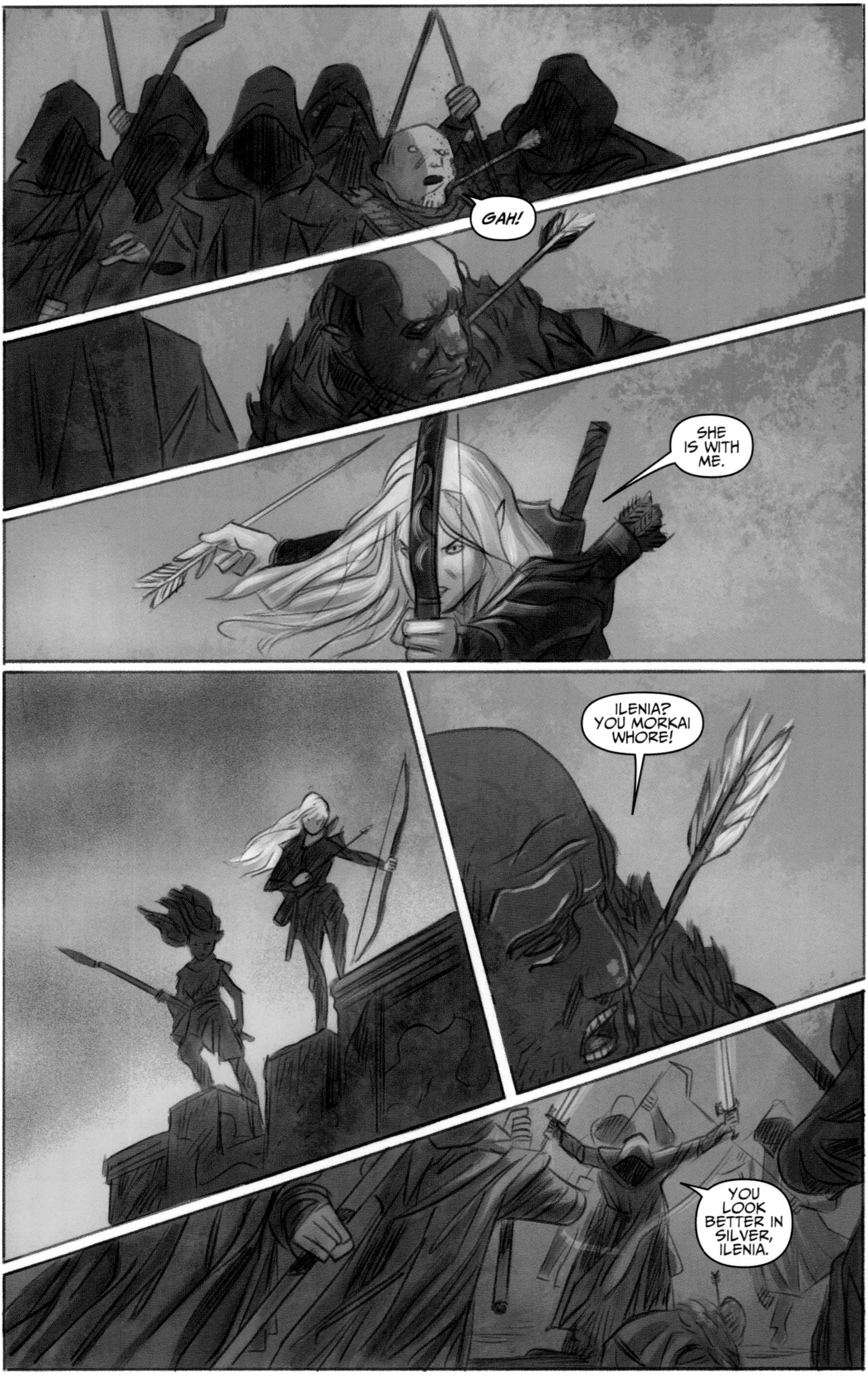
GAH!
SHE IS WITH ME.
ILENIA? YOU MORKAI WHORE!
YOU LOOK BETTER IN SILVER, ILENIA.

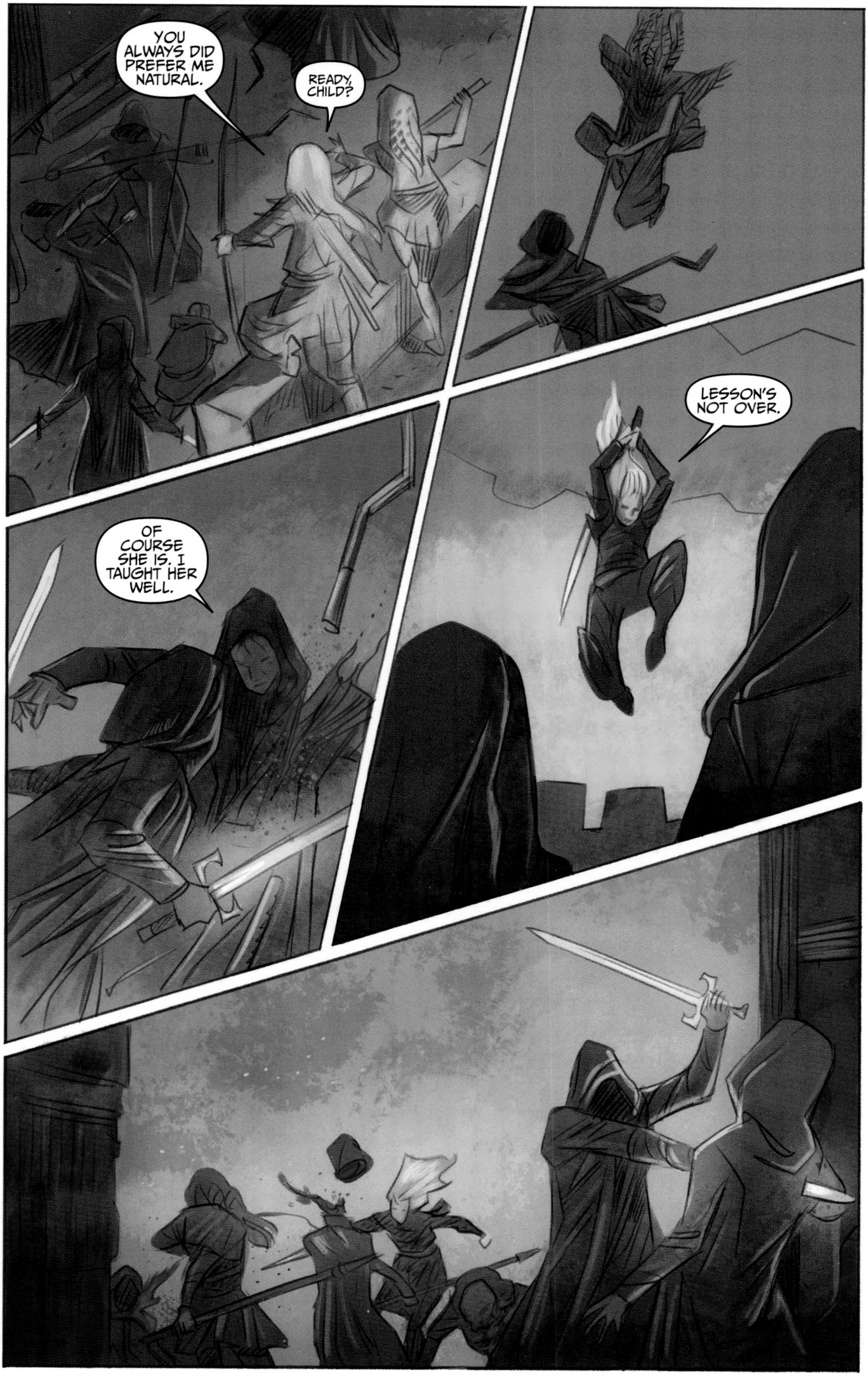
YOU ALWAYS DID PREFER ME NATURAL.
READY, CHILD?
LESSON'S NOT OVER.
OF COURSE SHE IS. I TAUGHT HER WELL.

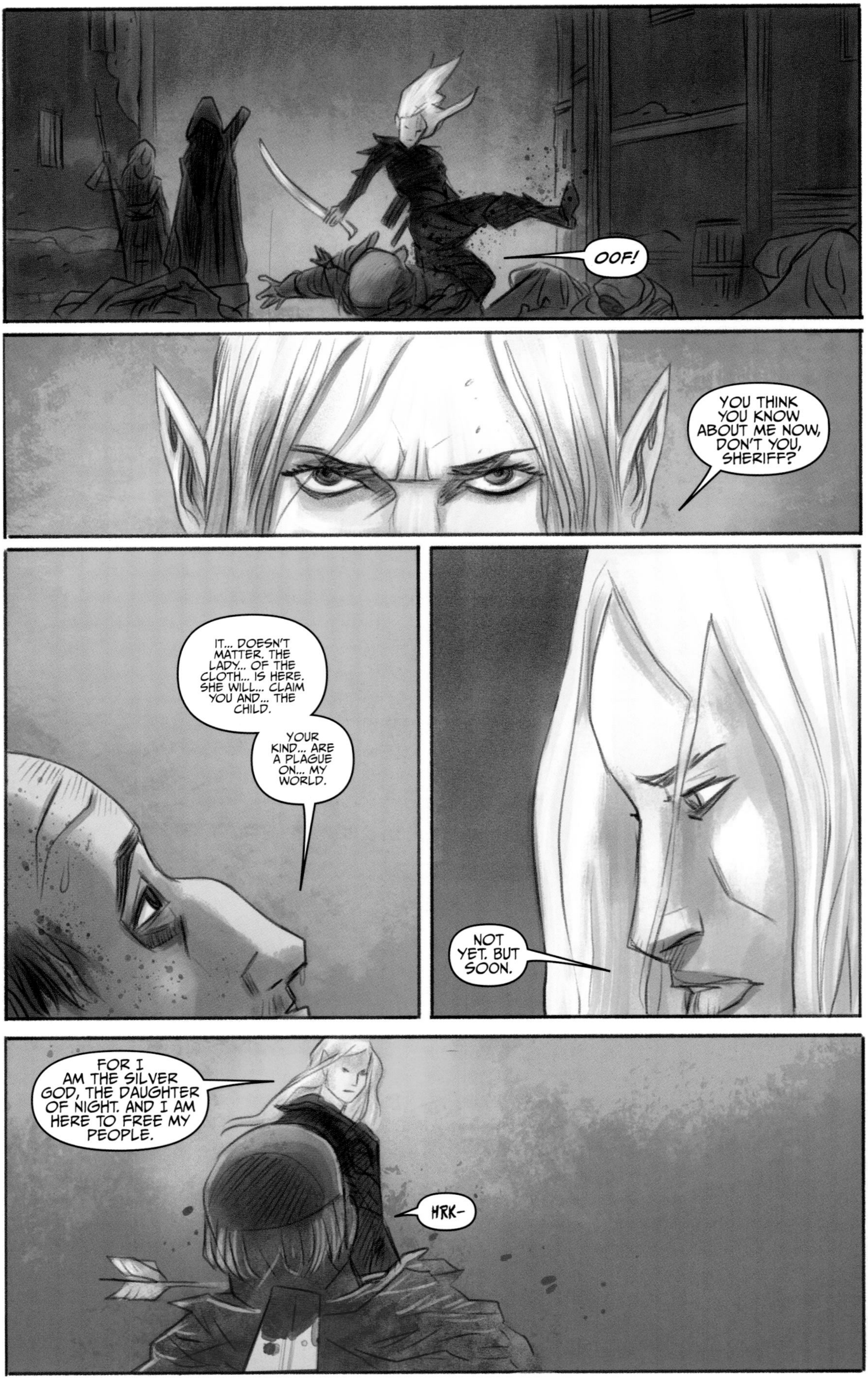
OOF!
YOU THINK YOU KNOW ABOUT ME NOW, DON'T YOU, SHERIFF?
IT... DOESN'T MATTER. THE LADY... OF THE CLOTH... IS HERE. SHE WILL... CLAIM YOU AND... THE CHILD.
YOUR KIND... ARE A PLAGUE ON... MY WORLD.
NOT YET. BUT SOON.
FOR I AM THE SILVER GOD, THE DAUGHTER OF NIGHT. AND I AM HERE TO FREE MY PEOPLE.
HRK-

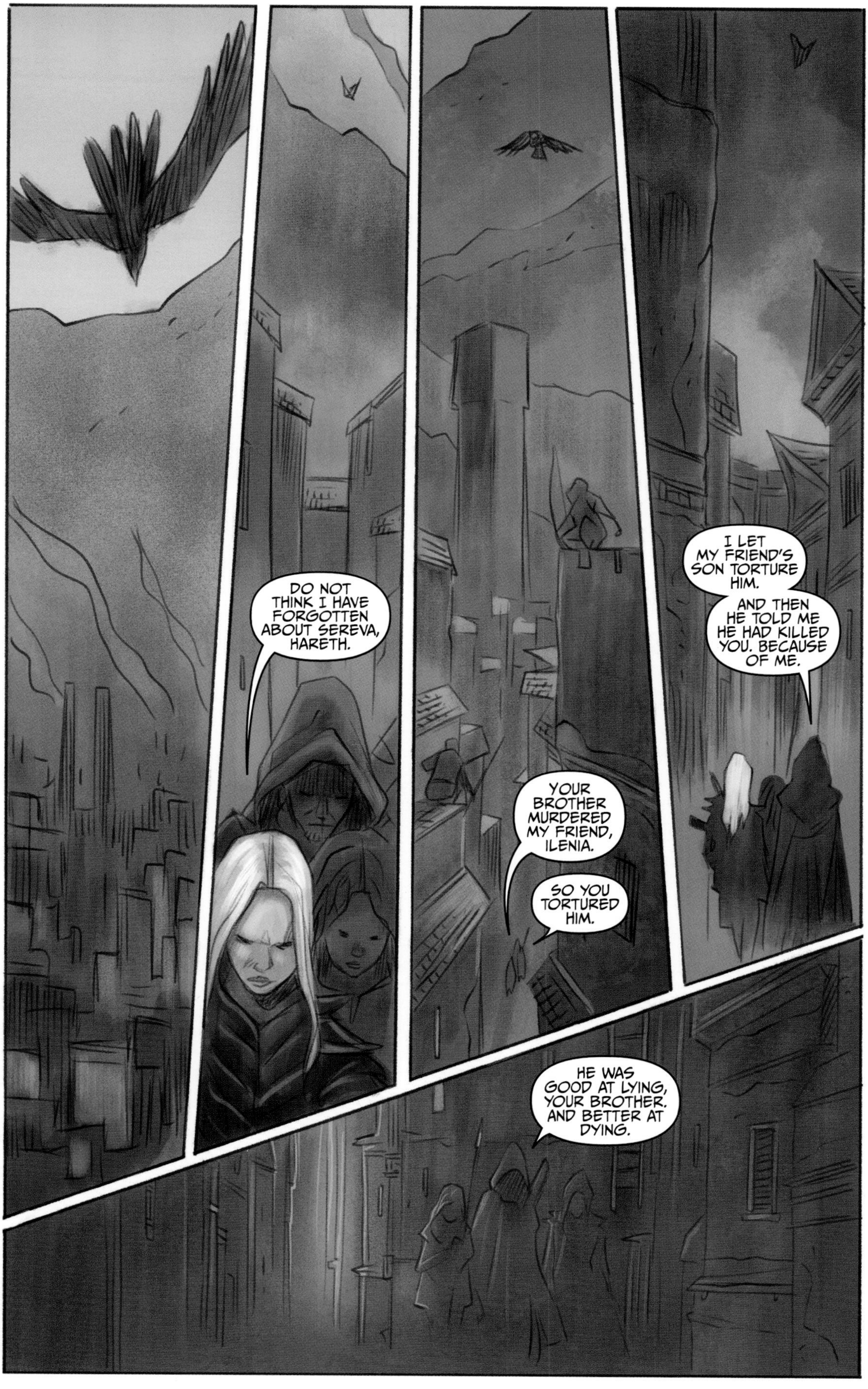
DO NOT THINK I HAVE FORGOTTEN ABOUT SEREVA, HARETH.
YOUR BROTHER MURDERED MY FRIEND, ILENIA.
SO YOU TORTURED HIM.
I LET MY FRIEND'S SON TORTURE HIM.
AND THEN HE TOLD ME HE HAD KILLED YOU. BECAUSE OF ME.
HE WAS GOOD AT LYING, YOUR BROTHER. AND BETTER AT DYING.

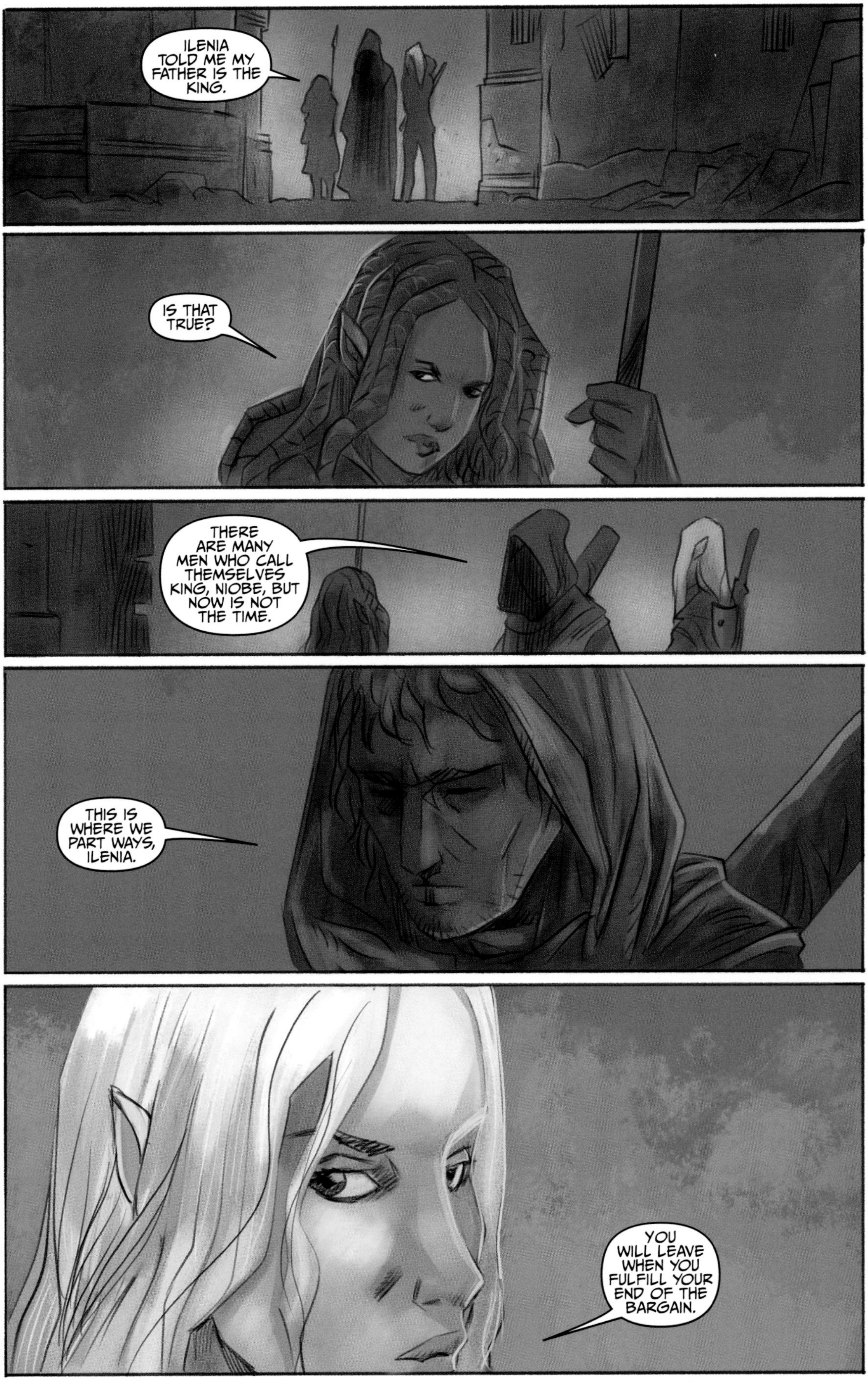
ILENIA TOLD ME MY FATHER IS THE KING.
IS THAT TRUE?
THERE ARE MANY MEN WHO CALL THEMSELVES KING, NIOBE, BUT NOW IS NOT THE TIME.
THIS IS WHERE WE PART WAYS, ILENIA.
YOU WILL LEAVE WHEN YOU FULFILL YOUR END OF THE BARGAIN.

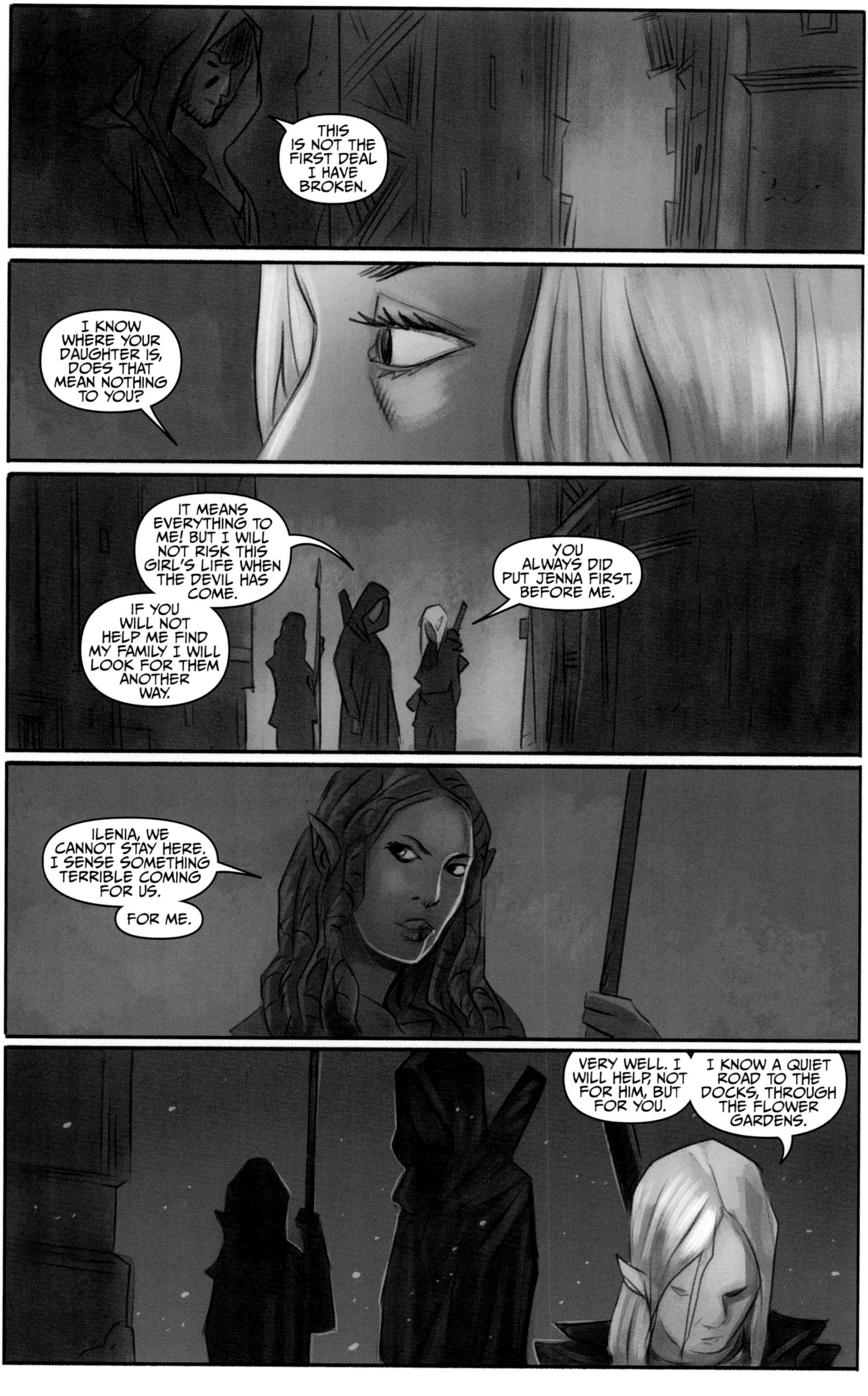
THIS IS NOT THE FIRST DEAL I HAVE BROKEN.
I KNOW WHERE YOUR DAUGHTER IS, DOES THAT MEAN NOTHING TO YOU?
IT MEANS EVERYTHING TO ME! BUT I WILL NOT RISK THIS GIRL'S LIFE WHEN THE DEVIL HAS COME.
IF YOU WILL NOT HELP ME FIND MY FAMILY I WILL LOOK FOR THEM ANOTHER WAY.
YOU ALWAYS DID PUT JENNA FIRST. BEFORE ME.
ILENIA, WE CANNOT STAY HERE. I SENSE SOMETHING TERRIBLE COMING FOR US.
FOR ME.
VERY WELL. I WILL HELP, NOT FOR HIM, BUT FOR YOU.
I KNOW A QUIET ROAD TO THE DOCKS, THROUGH THE FLOWER GARDENS.

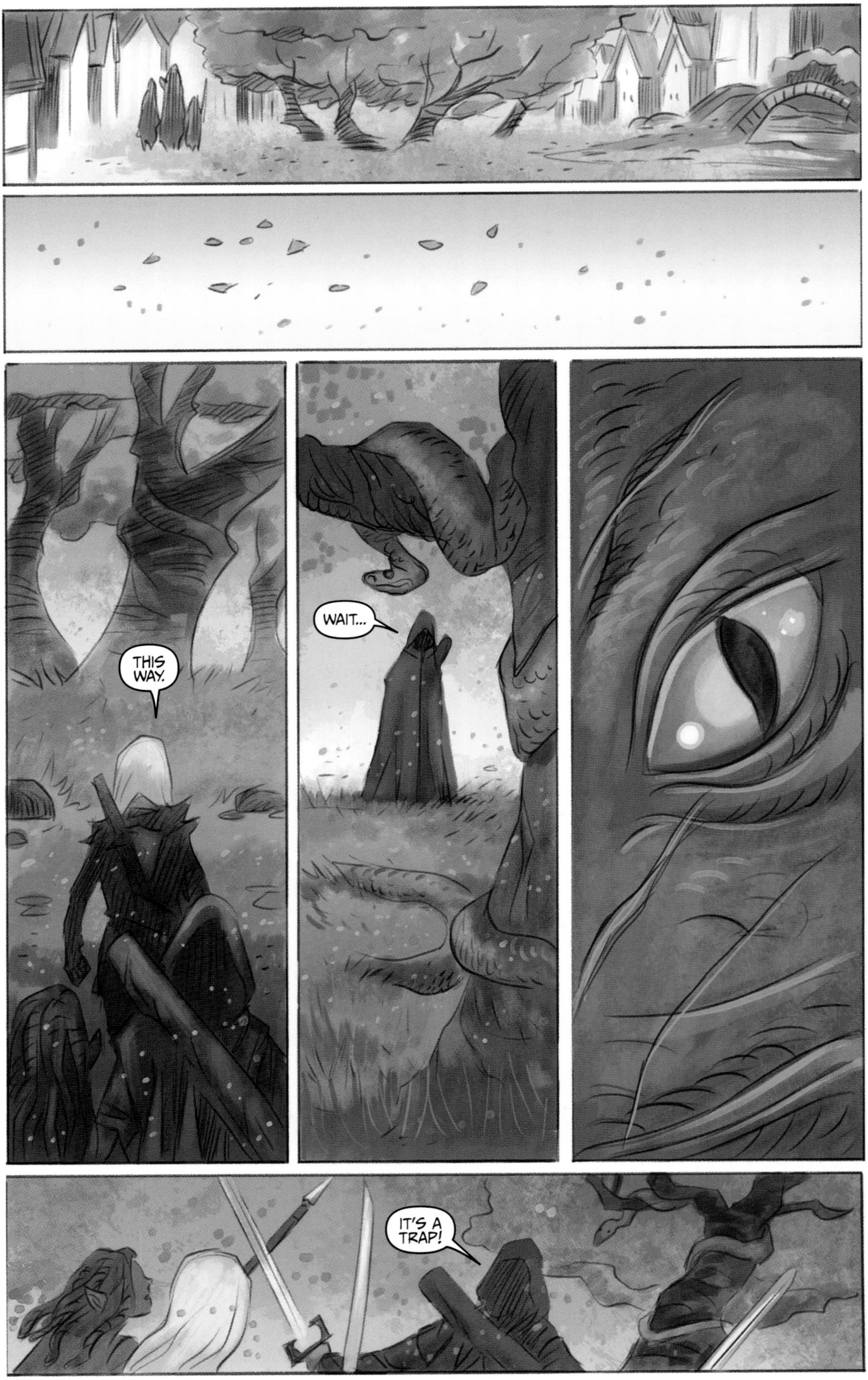
THIS WAY.
WAIT...
IT'S A TRAP!

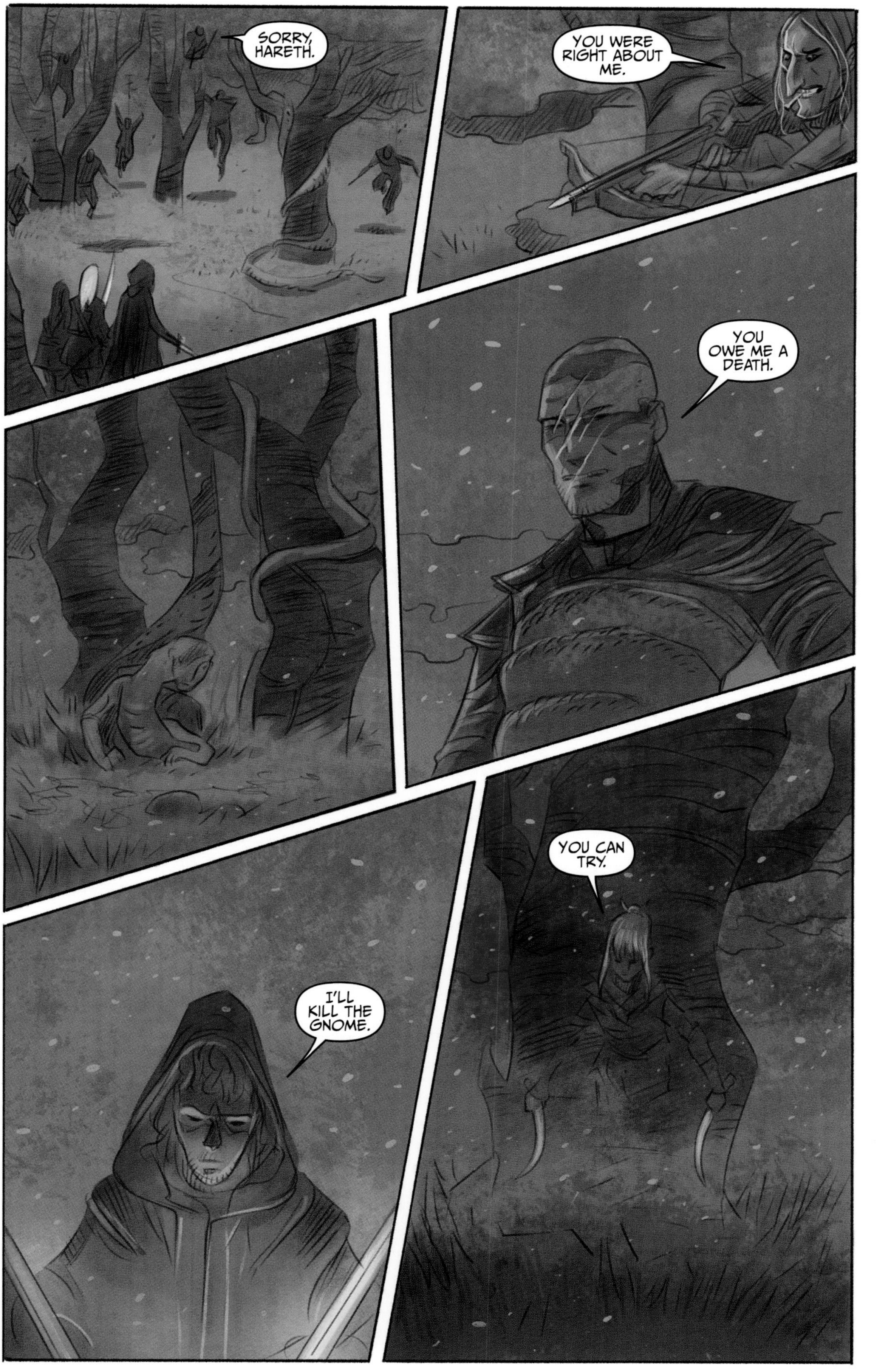
SORRY, HARETH.
YOU WERE RIGHT ABOUT ME.
YOU OWE ME A DEATH.
YOU CAN TRY.
I'LL KILL THE GNOME.

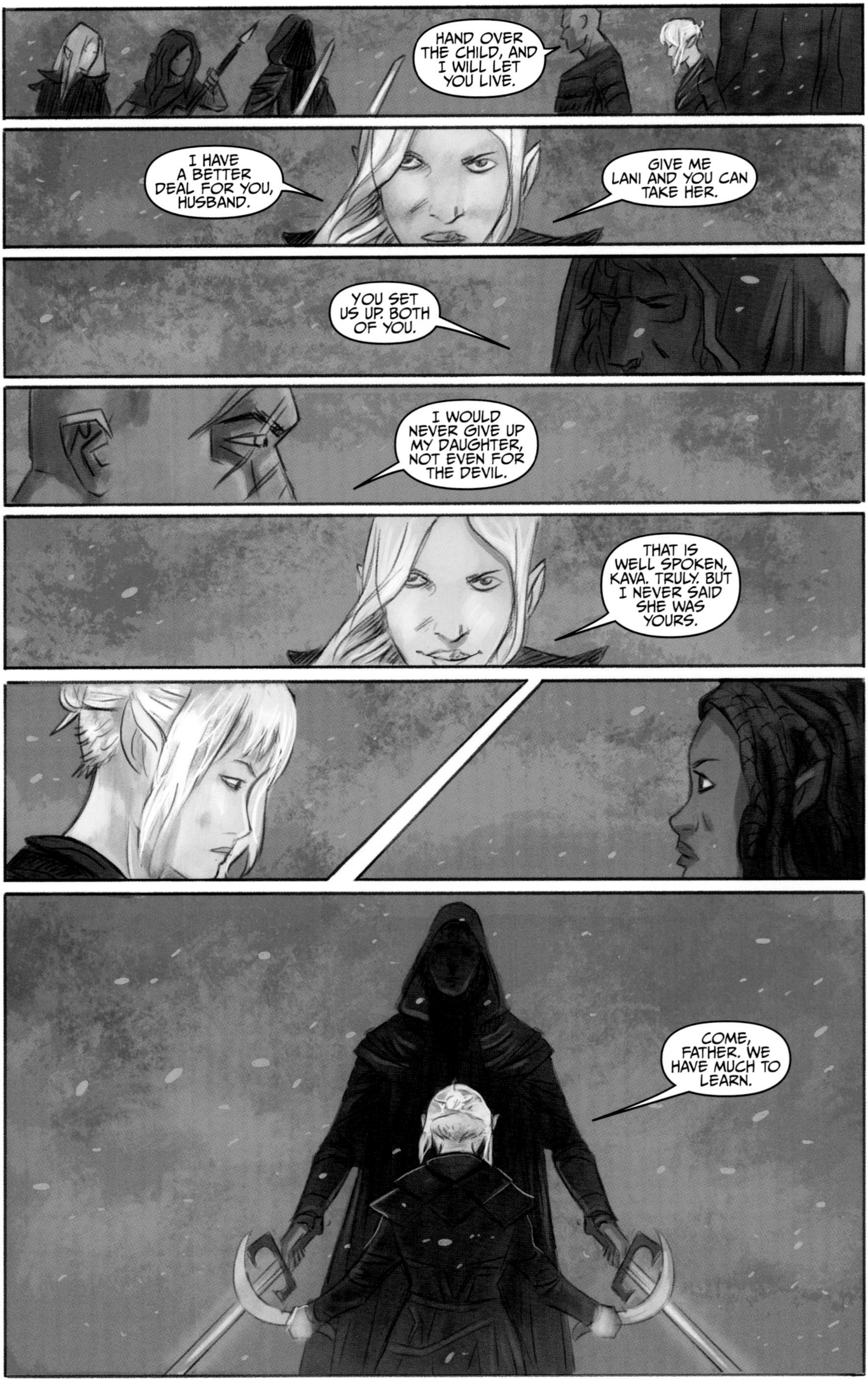
HAND OVER THE CHILD, AND I WILL LET YOU LIVE.
I HAVE A BETTER DEAL FOR YOU, HUSBAND.
GIVE ME LANI AND YOU CAN TAKE HER.
YOU SET US UP. BOTH OF YOU.
I WOULD NEVER GIVE UP MY DAUGHTER, NOT EVEN FOR THE DEVIL.
THAT IS WELL SPOKEN, KAVA. TRULY. BUT I NEVER SAID SHE WAS YOURS.
COME, FATHER. WE HAVE MUCH TO LEARN.

Hello Stranger

Trust. Every day we put our trust in friends and family, in our lovers, and in our leaders. But we are often betrayed. By those we love, who have given their word, or shaken hands. How often have you taped your heart together? And how many times have you lied to protect your own? On a journey of broken promises are you forever changed, affecting each new relationship? Or are you consumed by a need for retaliation? Vengeance is a seed of cancer, spreading from spirit to song. Put down the sword and put trust in yourself to be better than the day before. As much as some do not deserve your kindness, as a girl once told me, take a deep breath and let it go (and trust)... "A little sin casts a long shadow."

The broken man's world had fallen around him. His remaining hope in tomorrow stood on one foot upon a razor thin jagged spire. One misstep would send him falling into a chasm of despair and shattered dreams. He stood statue still under the strain of changing weather, from beating sun to torrential rain, depleting his reserves, and resolve. An internal terror paralyzed him from moving, from leaping to the next outcropping of rock. It wasn't his fear of falling to his death that held him; it was his fear of life.

And so she came, through the tomb silent void as more than an angel or woman to worship. She was a golden line of light cast from an unseen place, an outstretched hand, a friend, telling him it was okay to move... to move on. And be more than a ghost.

He left the shadow behind.

It would creep up on him from time to time. But he would see it coming, thanks to her, and leap.

Chapter 9

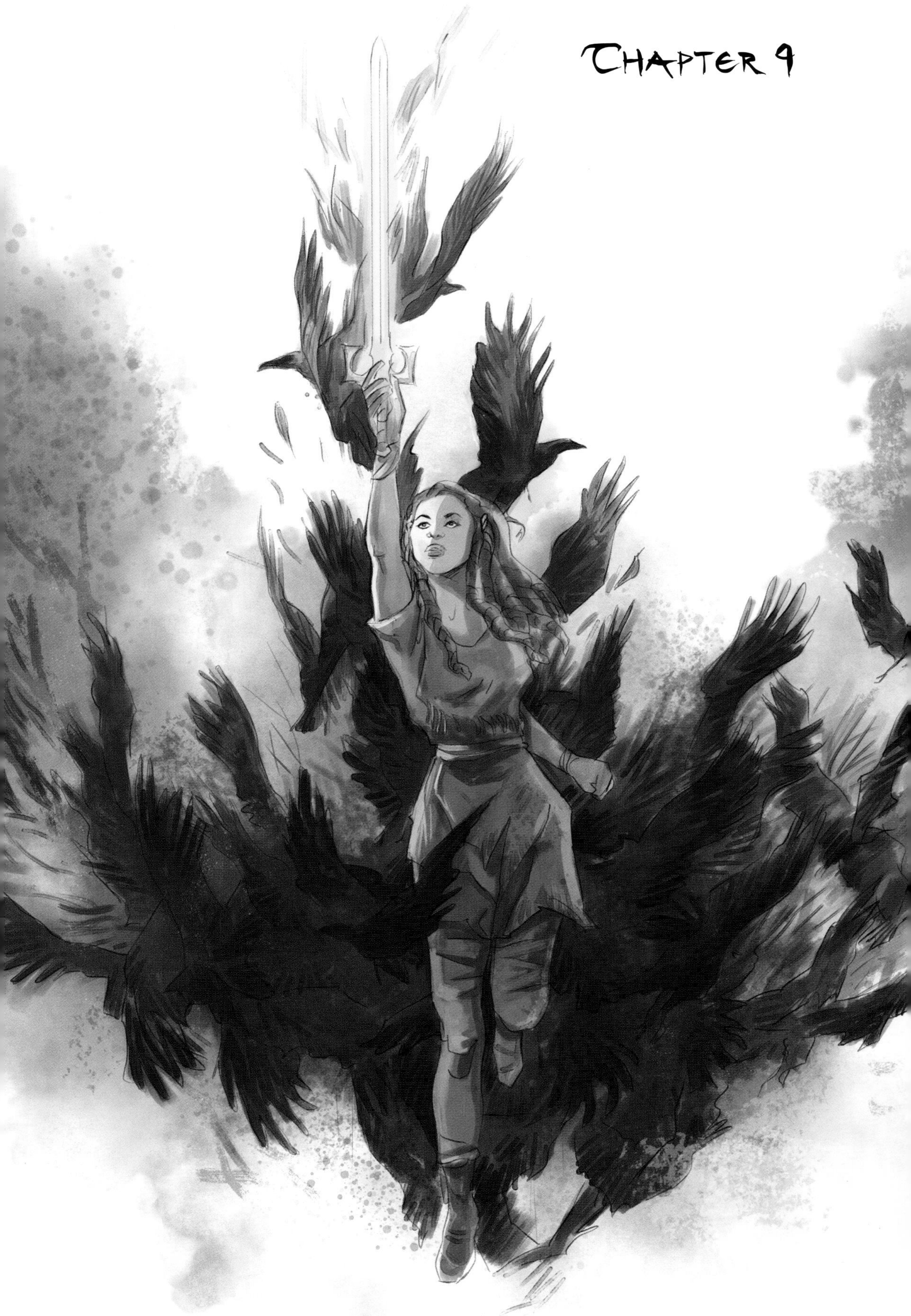

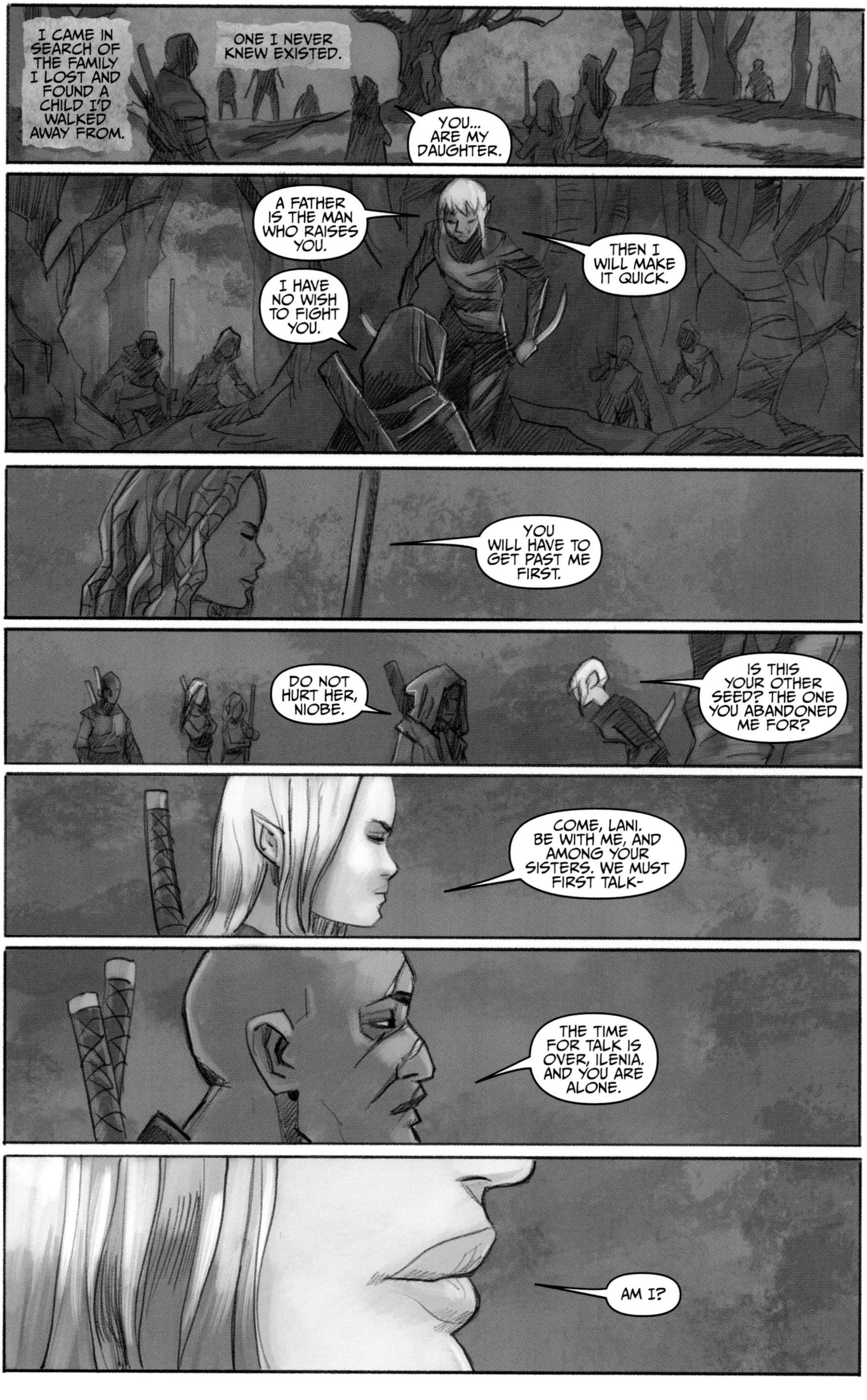
I CAME IN SEARCH OF THE FAMILY I LOST AND FOUND A CHILD I'D WALKED AWAY FROM.
ONE I NEVER KNEW EXISTED.
YOU... ARE MY DAUGHTER.
A FATHER IS THE MAN WHO RAISES YOU.
THEN I WILL MAKE IT QUICK.
I HAVE NO WISH TO FIGHT YOU.
YOU WILL HAVE TO GET PAST ME FIRST.
DO NOT HURT HER, NIOBE.
IS THIS YOUR OTHER SEED? THE ONE YOU ABANDONED ME FOR?
COME, LANI. BE WITH ME, AND AMONG YOUR SISTERS. WE MUST FIRST TALK-
THE TIME FOR TALK IS OVER, ILENIA. AND YOU ARE ALONE.
AM I?

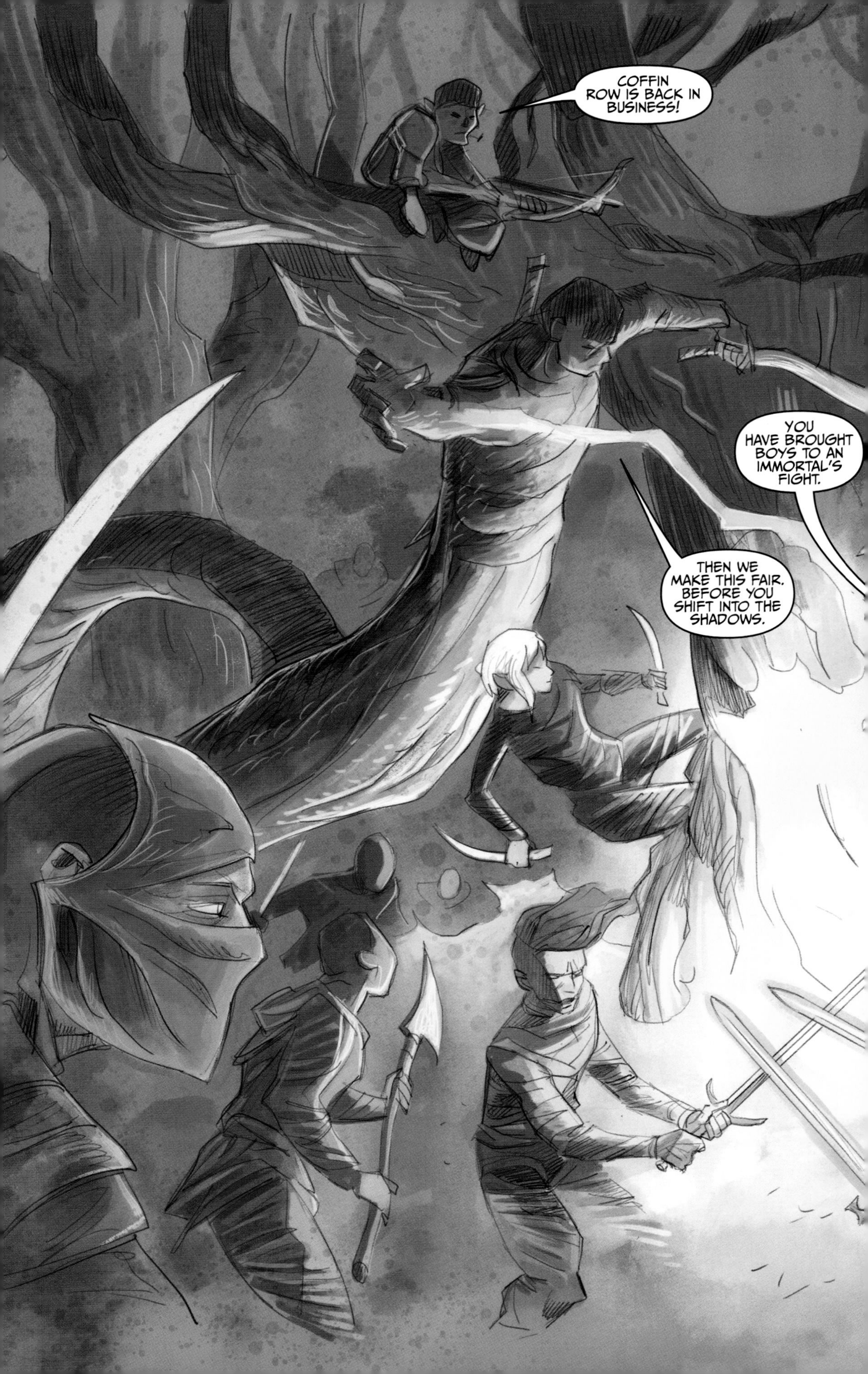
COFFIN ROW IS BACK IN BUSINESS!
YOU HAVE BROUGHT BOYS TO AN IMMORTAL'S FIGHT.
THEN WE MAKE THIS FAIR. BEFORE YOU SHIFT INTO THE SHADOWS.

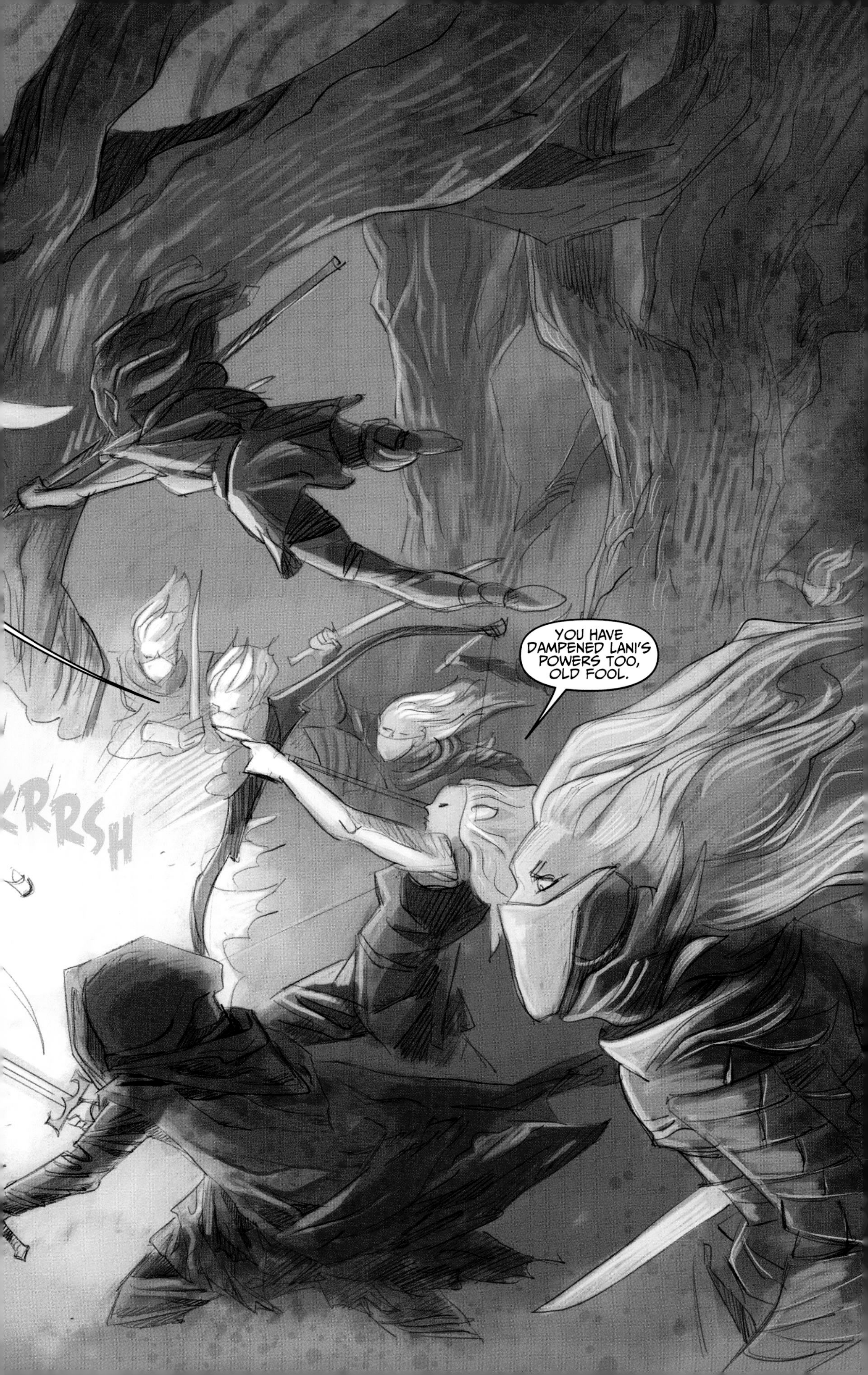
YOU HAVE DAMPENED LANI'S POWERS TOO, OLD FOOL.

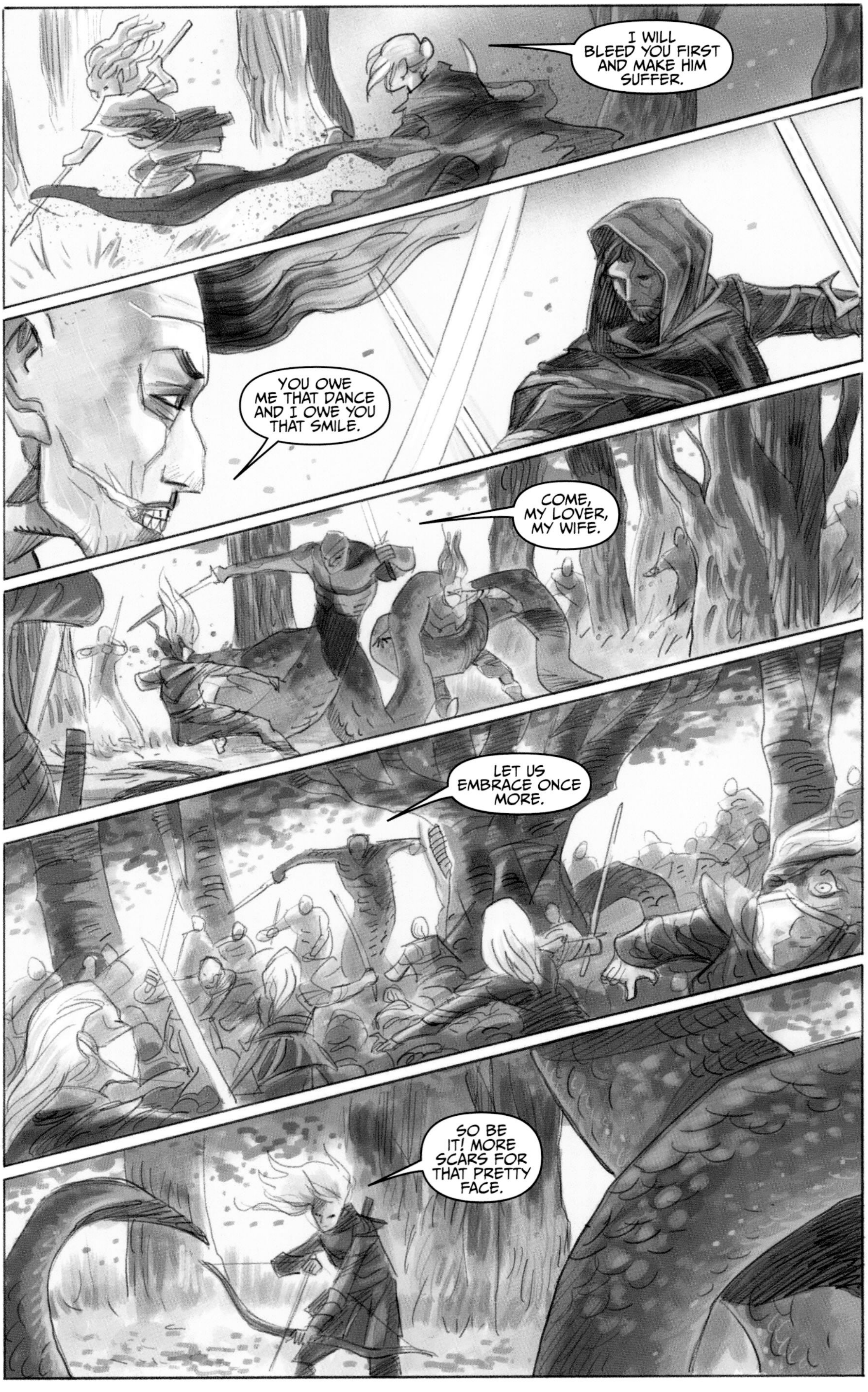
I WILL BLEED YOU FIRST AND MAKE HIM SUFFER.
YOU OWE ME THAT DANCE AND I OWE YOU THAT SMILE.
COME, MY LOVER, MY WIFE.
LET US EMBRACE ONCE MORE.
SO BE IT! MORE SCARS FOR THAT PRETTY FACE.

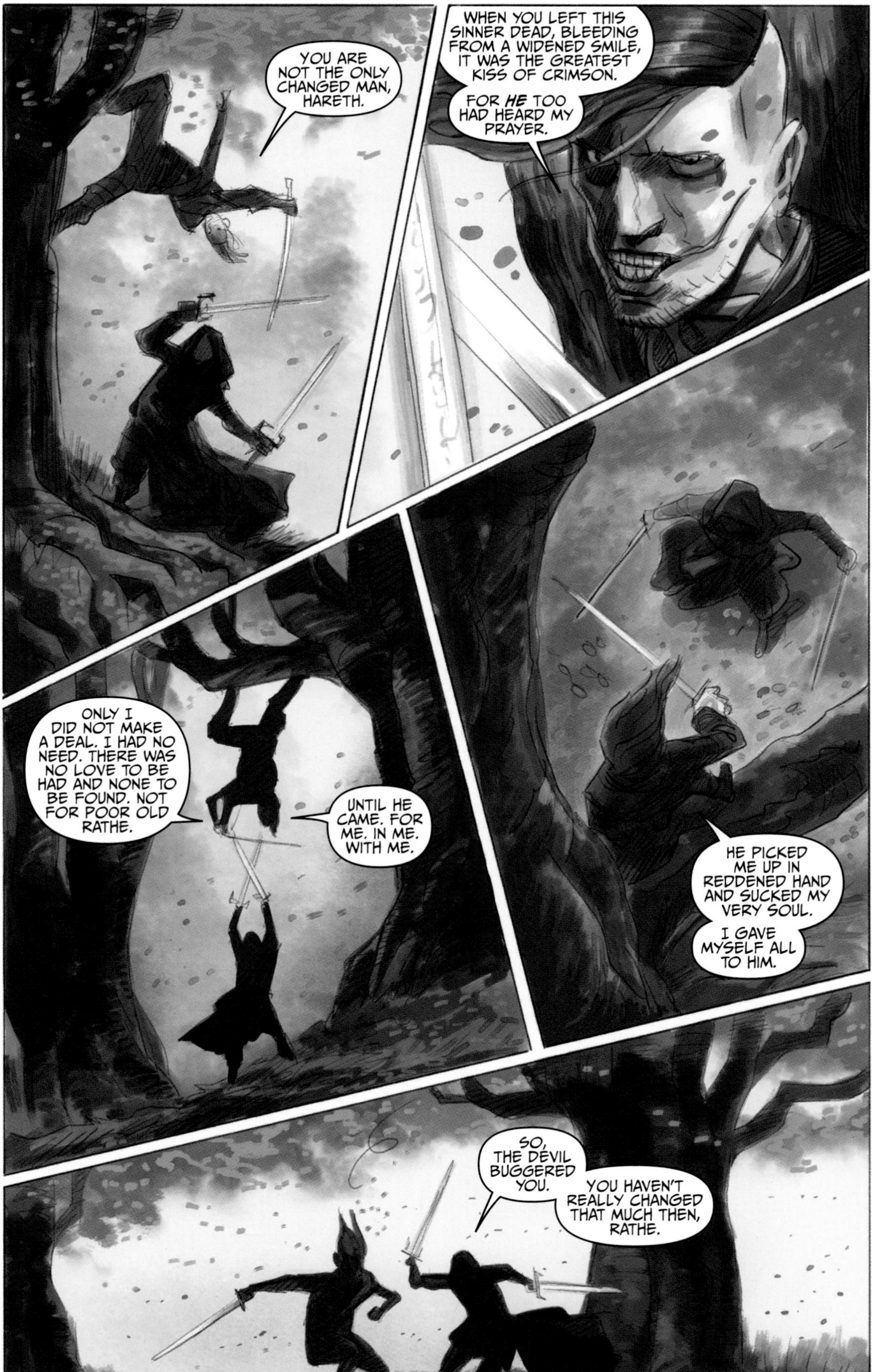
YOU ARE NOT THE ONLY CHANGED MAN, HARETH.
WHEN YOU LEFT THIS SINNER DEAD, BLEEDING FROM A WIDENED SMILE, IT WAS THE GREATEST KISS OF CRIMSON.
FOR *HE* TOO HAD HEARD MY PRAYER.
ONLY I DID NOT MAKE A DEAL. I HAD NO NEED. THERE WAS NO LOVE TO BE HAD AND NONE TO BE FOUND. NOT FOR POOR OLD RATHE.
UNTIL HE CAME. FOR ME. IN ME. WITH ME.
HE PICKED ME UP IN REDDENED HAND AND SUCKED MY VERY SOUL.
I GAVE MYSELF ALL TO HIM.
SO, THE DEVIL BUGGERED YOU.
YOU HAVEN'T REALLY CHANGED THAT MUCH THEN, RATHE.

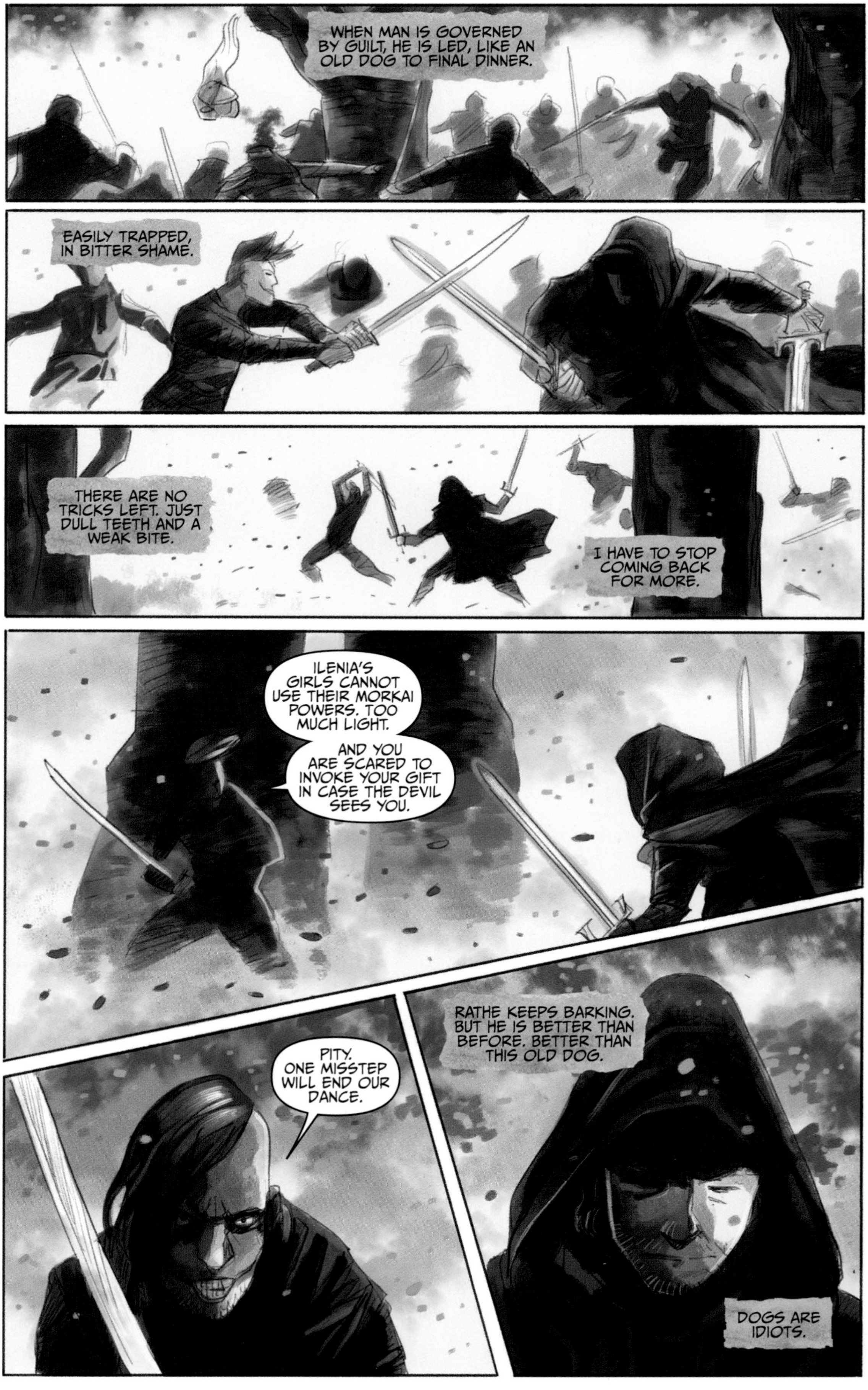
WHEN MAN IS GOVERNED BY GUILT, HE IS LED, LIKE AN OLD DOG TO FINAL DINNER.
EASILY TRAPPED, IN BITTER SHAME.
THERE ARE NO TRICKS LEFT. JUST DULL TEETH AND A WEAK BITE.
I HAVE TO STOP COMING BACK FOR MORE.
ILENIA'S GIRLS CANNOT USE THEIR MORKAI POWERS. TOO MUCH LIGHT.
AND YOU ARE SCARED TO INVOKE YOUR GIFT IN CASE THE DEVIL SEES YOU.
PITY. ONE MISSTEP WILL END OUR DANCE.
RATHE KEEPS BARKING. BUT HE IS BETTER THAN BEFORE. BETTER THAN THIS OLD DOG.
DOGS ARE IDIOTS.

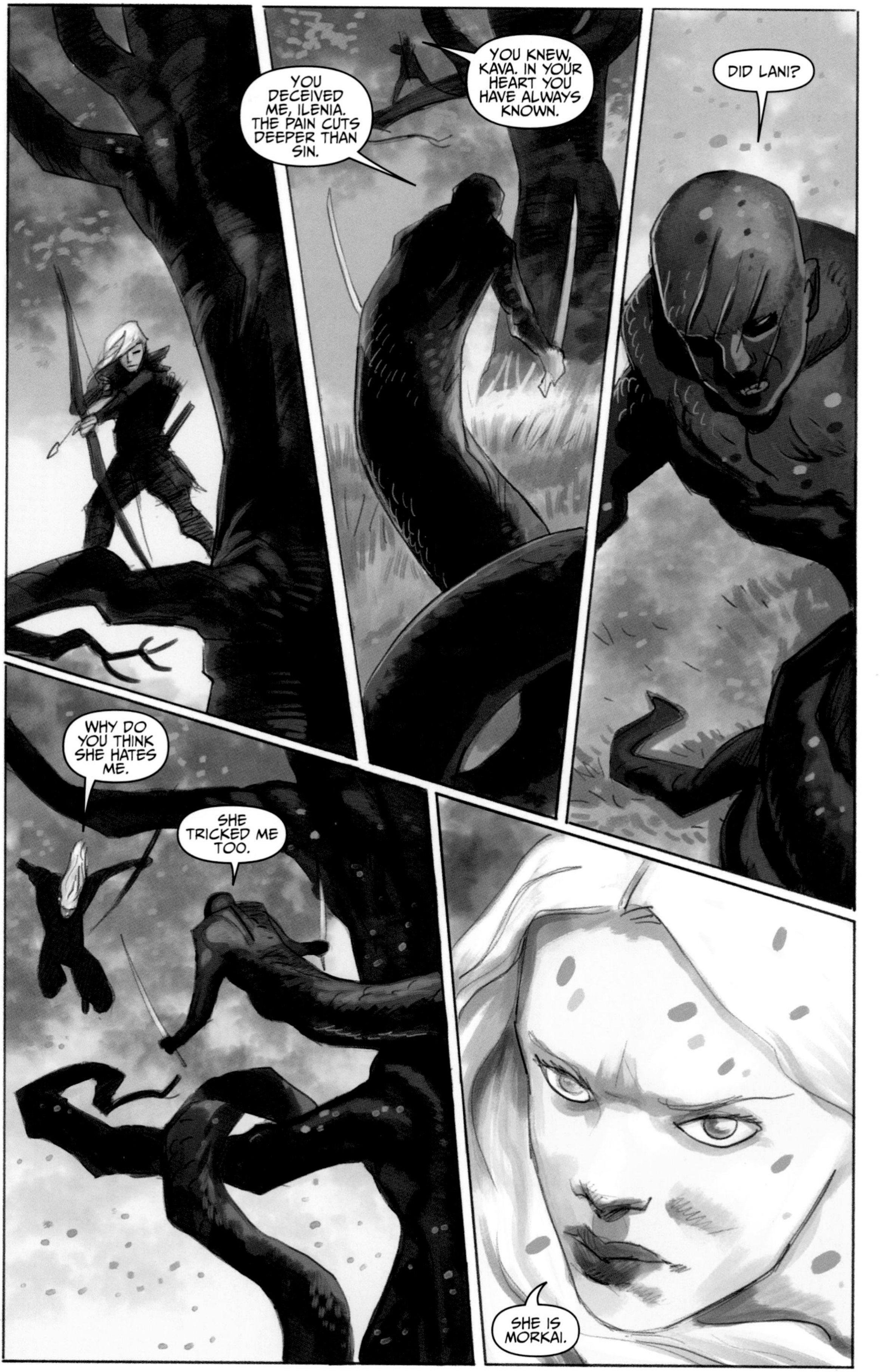
YOU DECEIVED ME, ILENIA. THE PAIN CUTS DEEPER THAN SIN.
YOU KNEW, KAVA. IN YOUR HEART YOU HAVE ALWAYS KNOWN.
DID LANI?
WHY DO YOU THINK SHE HATES ME.
SHE TRICKED ME TOO.
SHE IS MORKAI.

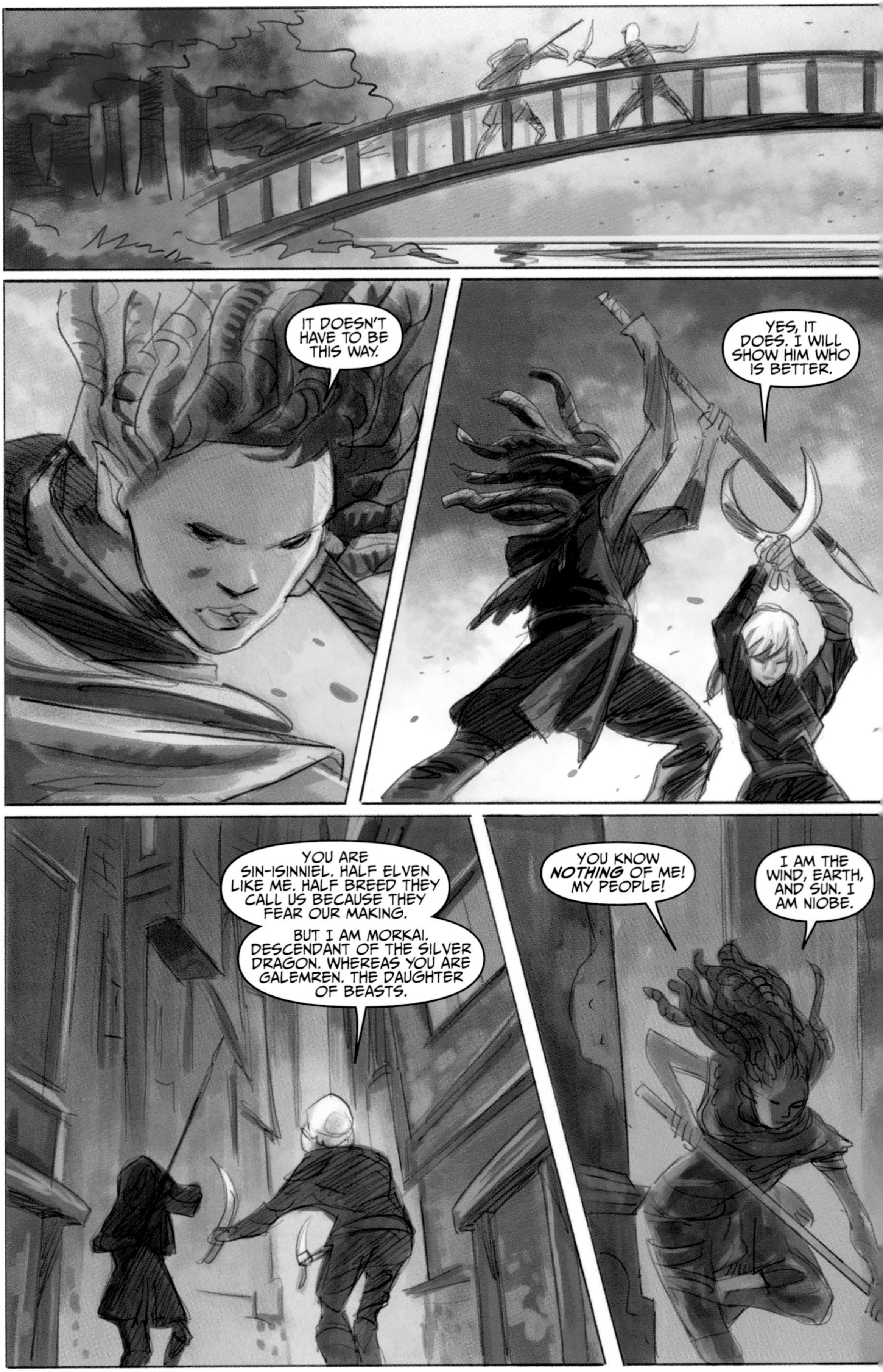
IT DOESN'T HAVE TO BE THIS WAY.
YES, IT DOES. I WILL SHOW HIM WHO IS BETTER.
YOU ARE SIN-ISINNIEL. HALF ELVEN LIKE ME. HALF BREED THEY CALL US BECAUSE THEY FEAR OUR MAKING.
BUT I AM MORKAI. DESCENDANT OF THE SILVER DRAGON. WHEREAS YOU ARE GALEMREN. THE DAUGHTER OF BEASTS.
YOU KNOW *NOTHING* OF ME! MY PEOPLE!
I AM THE WIND, EARTH, AND SUN. I AM NIOBE.

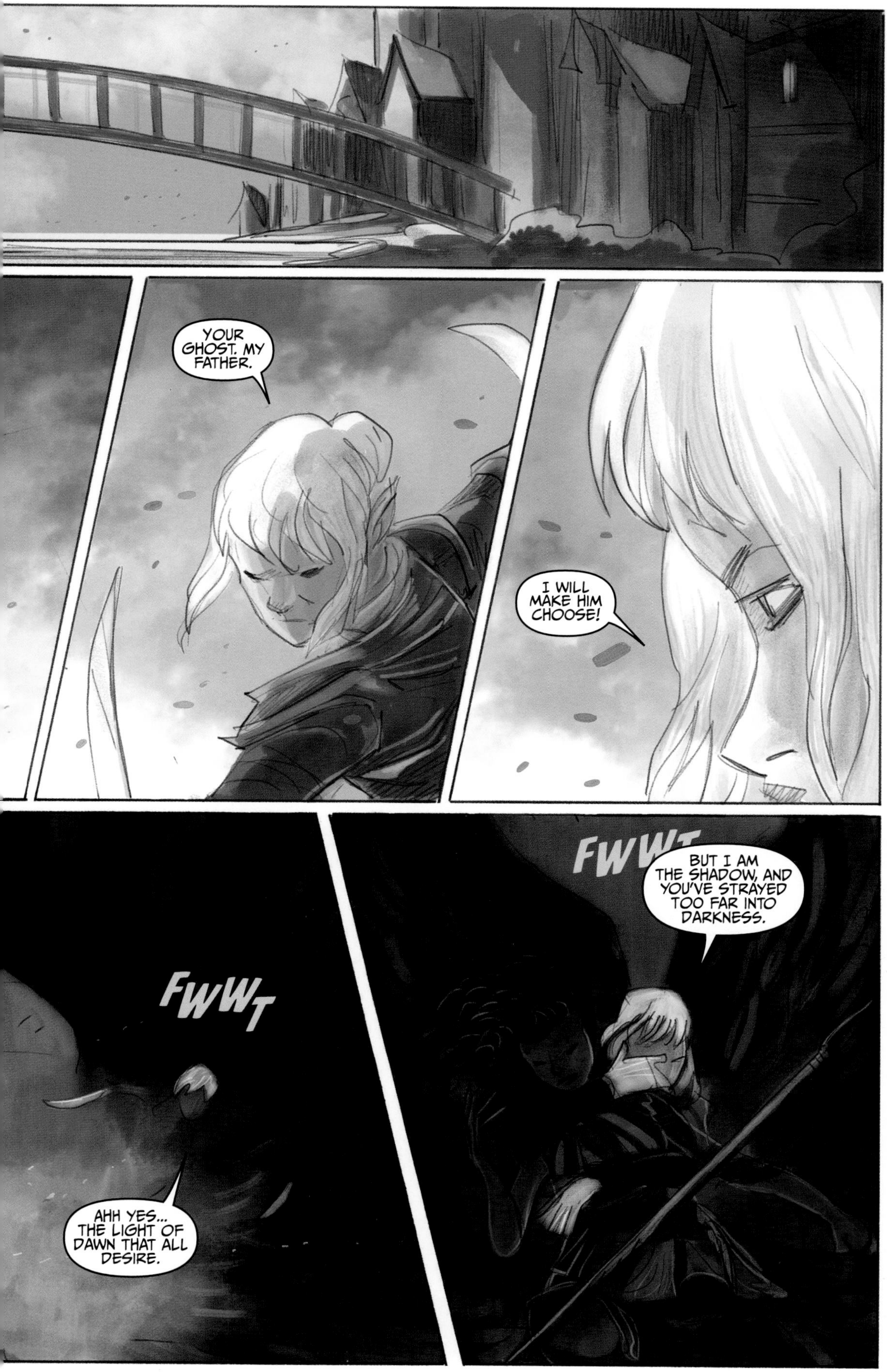
YOUR GHOST. MY FATHER.
I WILL MAKE HIM CHOOSE!
FWWT
AHH YES... THE LIGHT OF DAWN THAT ALL DESIRE.
FWWT
BUT I AM THE SHADOW, AND YOU'VE STRAYED TOO FAR INTO DARKNESS.

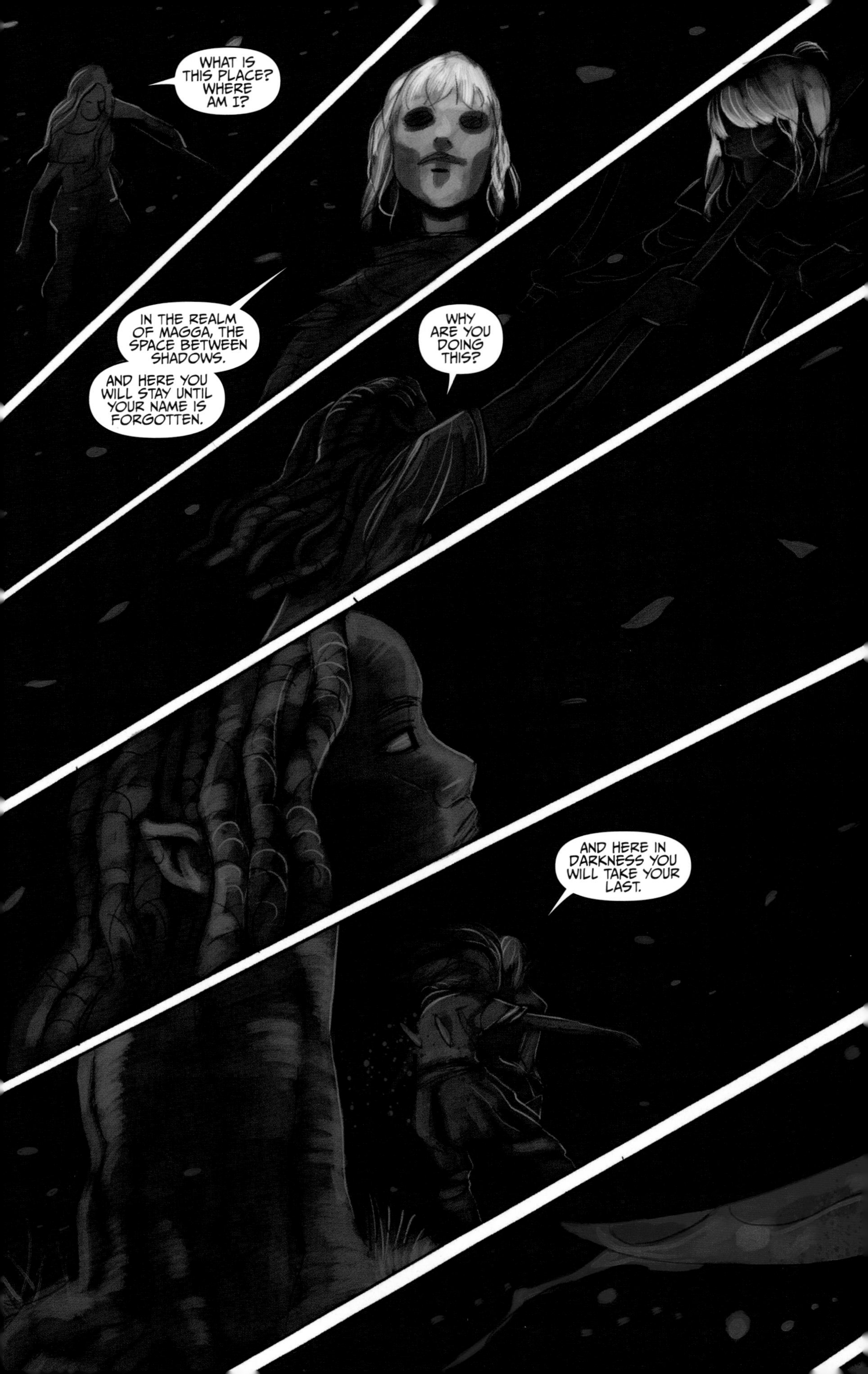
WHAT IS THIS PLACE? WHERE AM I?
IN THE REALM OF MAGGA, THE SPACE BETWEEN SHADOWS.
AND HERE YOU WILL STAY UNTIL YOUR NAME IS FORGOTTEN.
WHY ARE YOU DOING THIS?
AND HERE IN DARKNESS YOU WILL TAKE YOUR LAST.

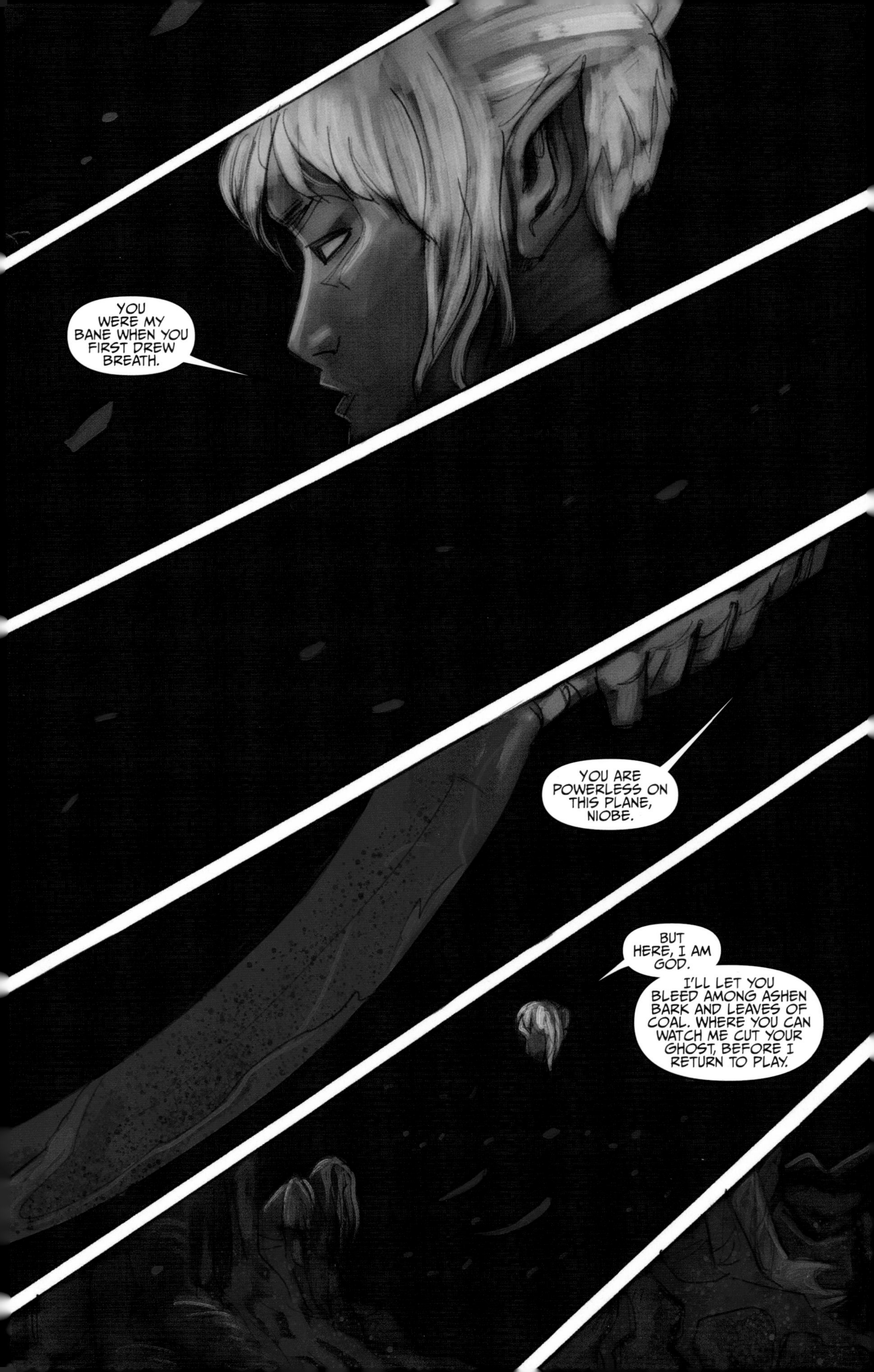
YOU WERE MY BANE WHEN YOU FIRST DREW BREATH.
YOU ARE POWERLESS ON THIS PLANE, NIOBE.
BUT HERE, I AM GOD.
I'LL LET YOU BLEED AMONG ASHEN BARK AND LEAVES OF COAL. WHERE YOU CAN WATCH ME CUT YOUR GHOST, BEFORE I RETURN TO PLAY.

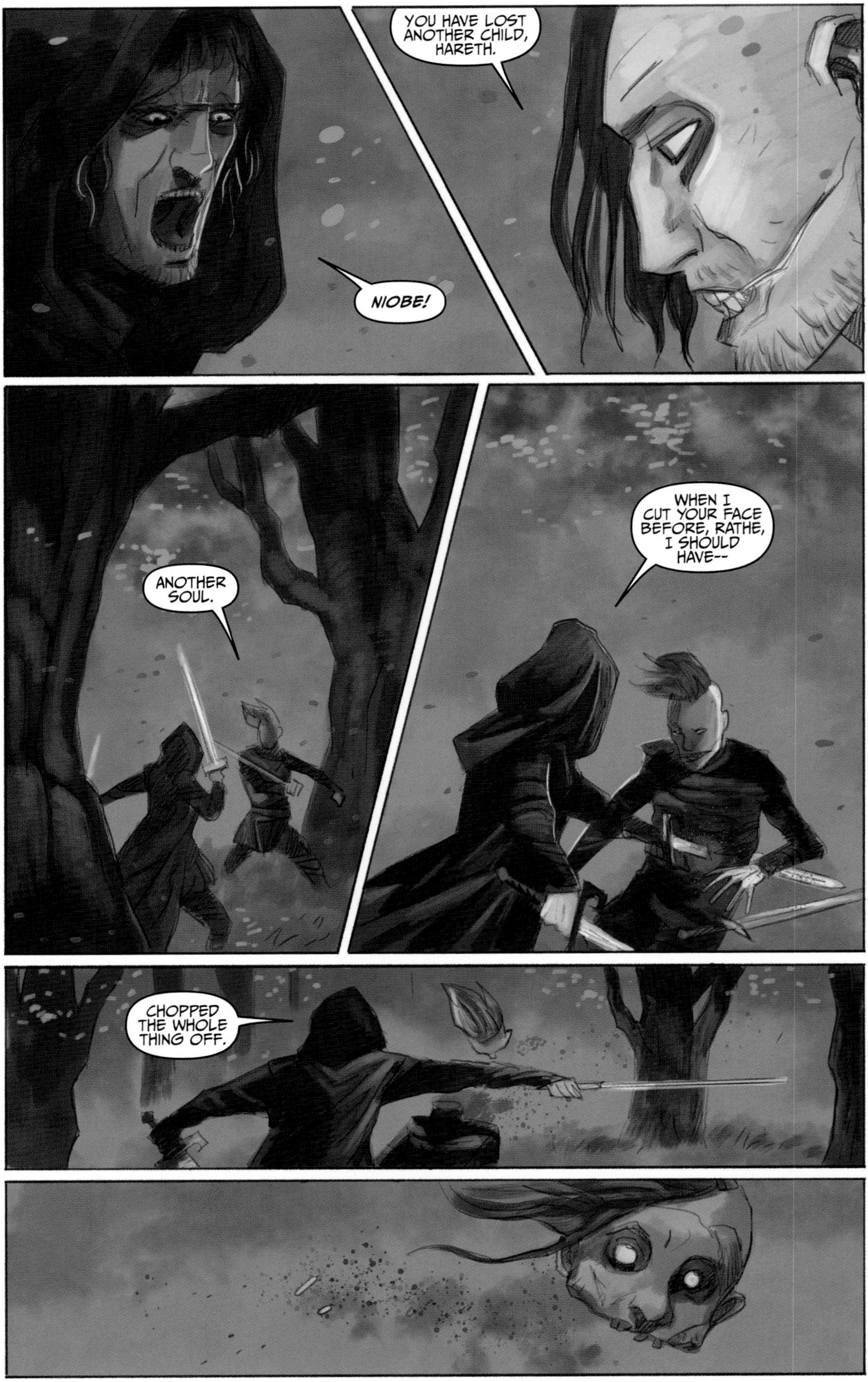
NIOBE!
YOU HAVE LOST ANOTHER CHILD, HARETH.
ANOTHER SOUL.
WHEN I CUT YOUR FACE BEFORE, RATHE, I SHOULD HAVE--
CHOPPED THE WHOLE THING OFF.

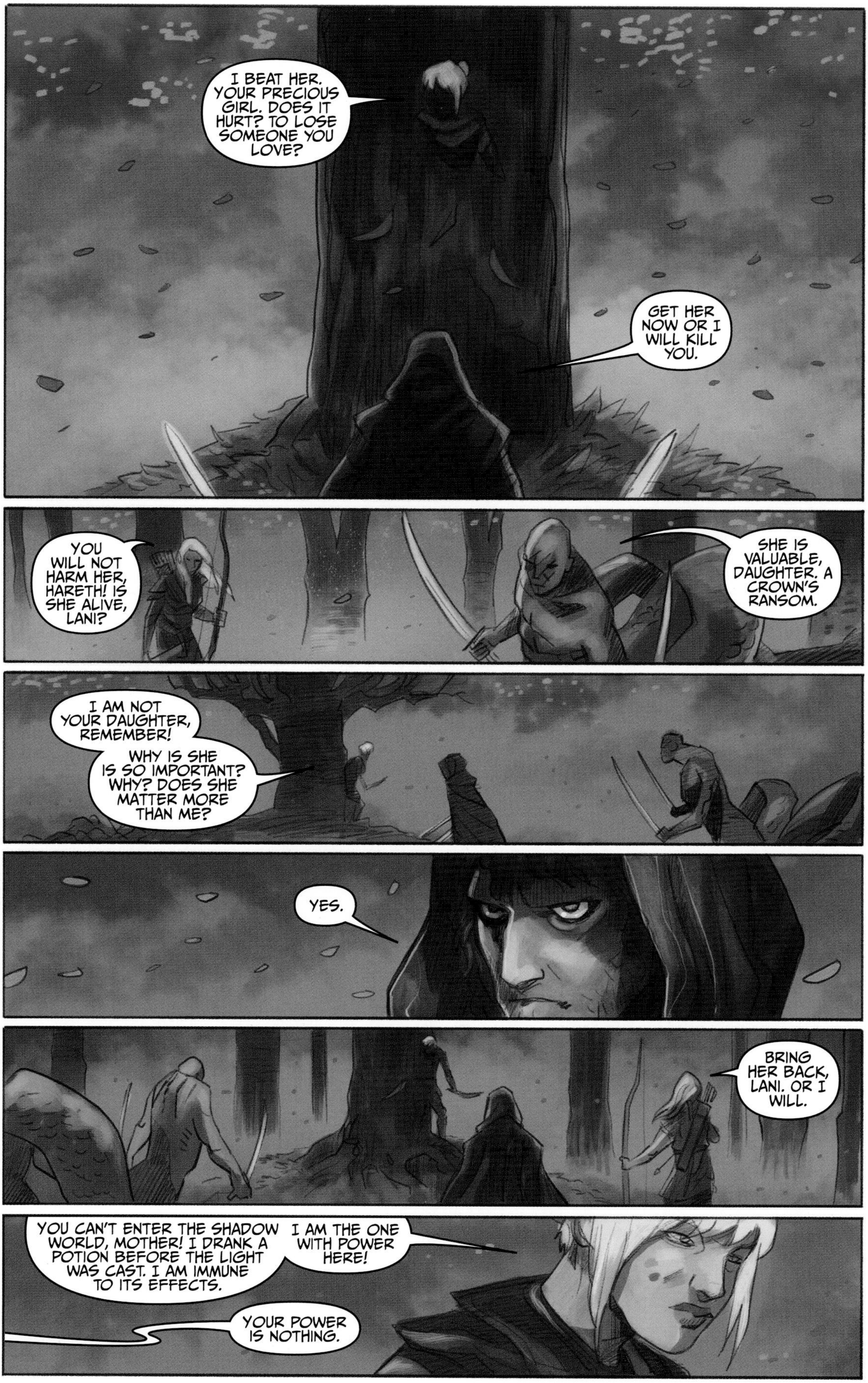
I BEAT HER. YOUR PRECIOUS GIRL. DOES IT HURT? TO LOSE SOMEONE YOU LOVE?
GET HER NOW OR I WILL KILL YOU.
YOU WILL NOT HARM HER, HARETH! IS SHE ALIVE, LANI?
SHE IS VALUABLE, DAUGHTER. A CROWN'S RANSOM.
I AM NOT YOUR DAUGHTER, REMEMBER!
WHY IS SHE IS SO IMPORTANT? WHY? DOES SHE MATTER MORE THAN ME?
YES.
BRING HER BACK, LANI. OR I WILL.
YOU CAN'T ENTER THE SHADOW WORLD, MOTHER! I DRANK A POTION BEFORE THE LIGHT WAS CAST. I AM IMMUNE TO ITS EFFECTS.
I AM THE ONE WITH POWER HERE!
YOUR POWER IS NOTHING.

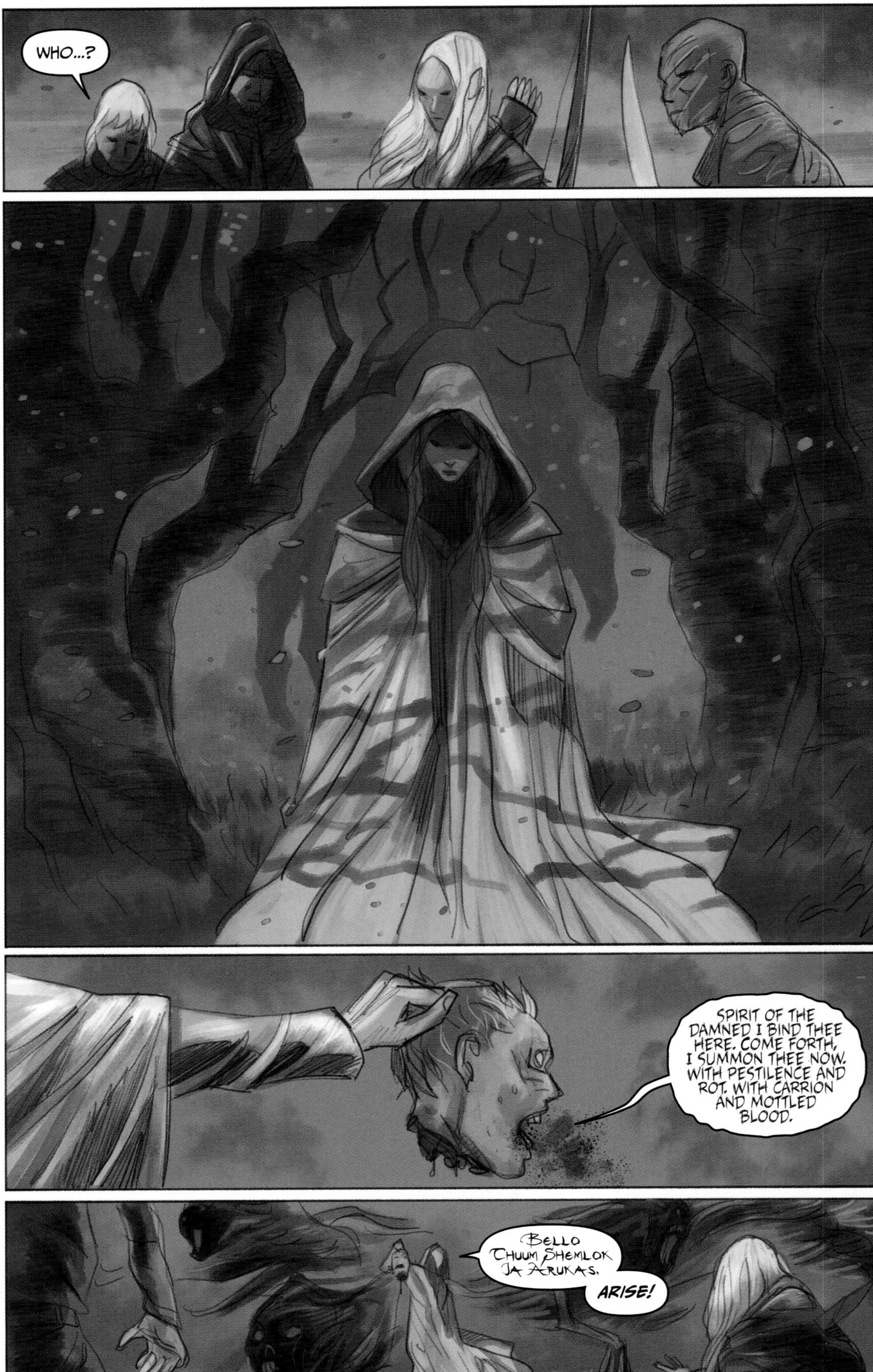
WHO...?
SPIRIT OF THE DAMNED I BIND THEE HERE. COME FORTH, I SUMMON THEE NOW. WITH PESTILENCE AND ROT. WITH CARRION AND MOTTLED BLOOD.
Bello Thuum Shemlok Ja Arukas.
ARISE!

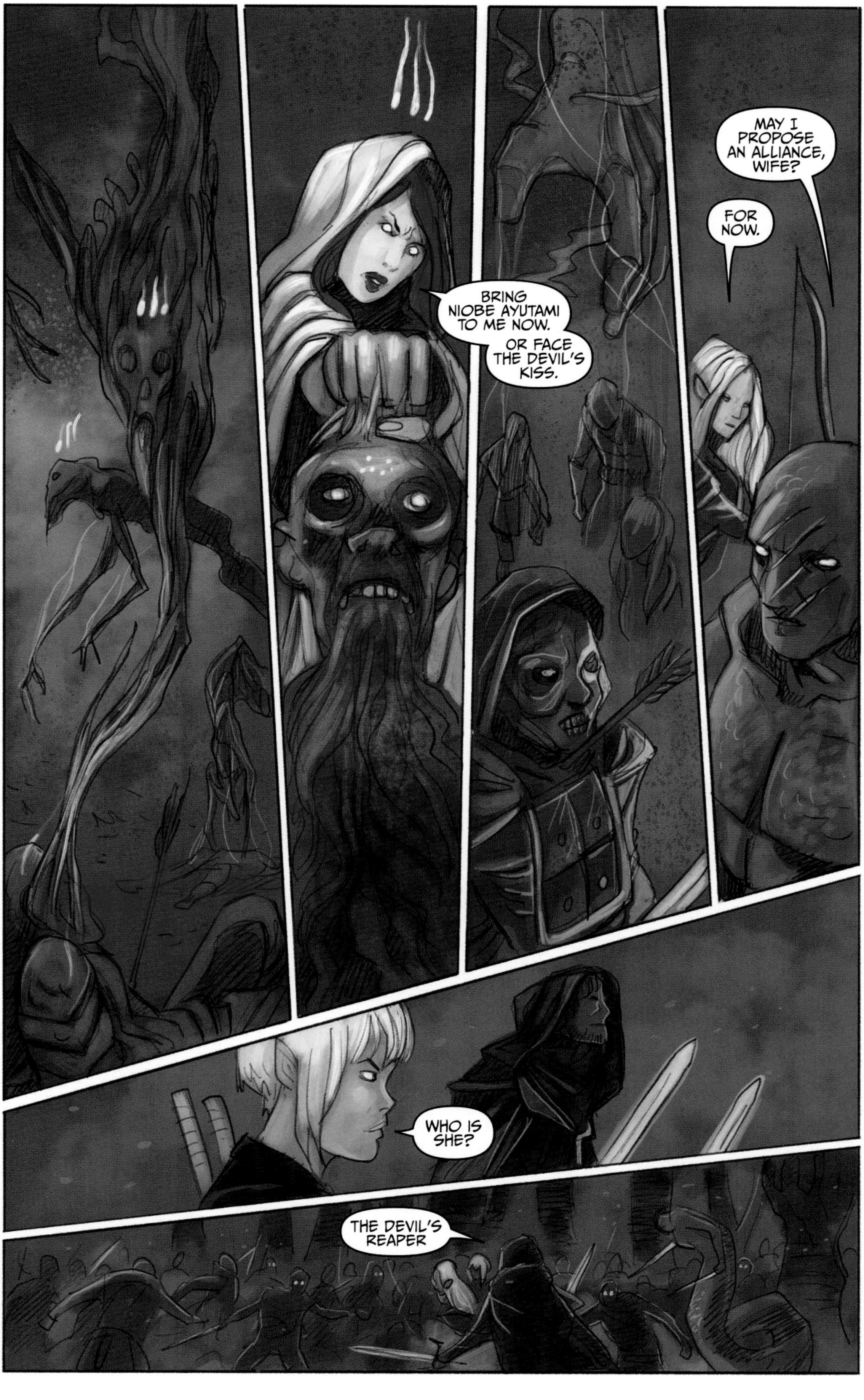
BRING NIOBE AYUTAMI TO ME NOW.
OR FACE THE DEVIL'S KISS.
MAY I PROPOSE AN ALLIANCE, WIFE?
FOR NOW.
WHO IS SHE?
THE DEVIL'S REAPER

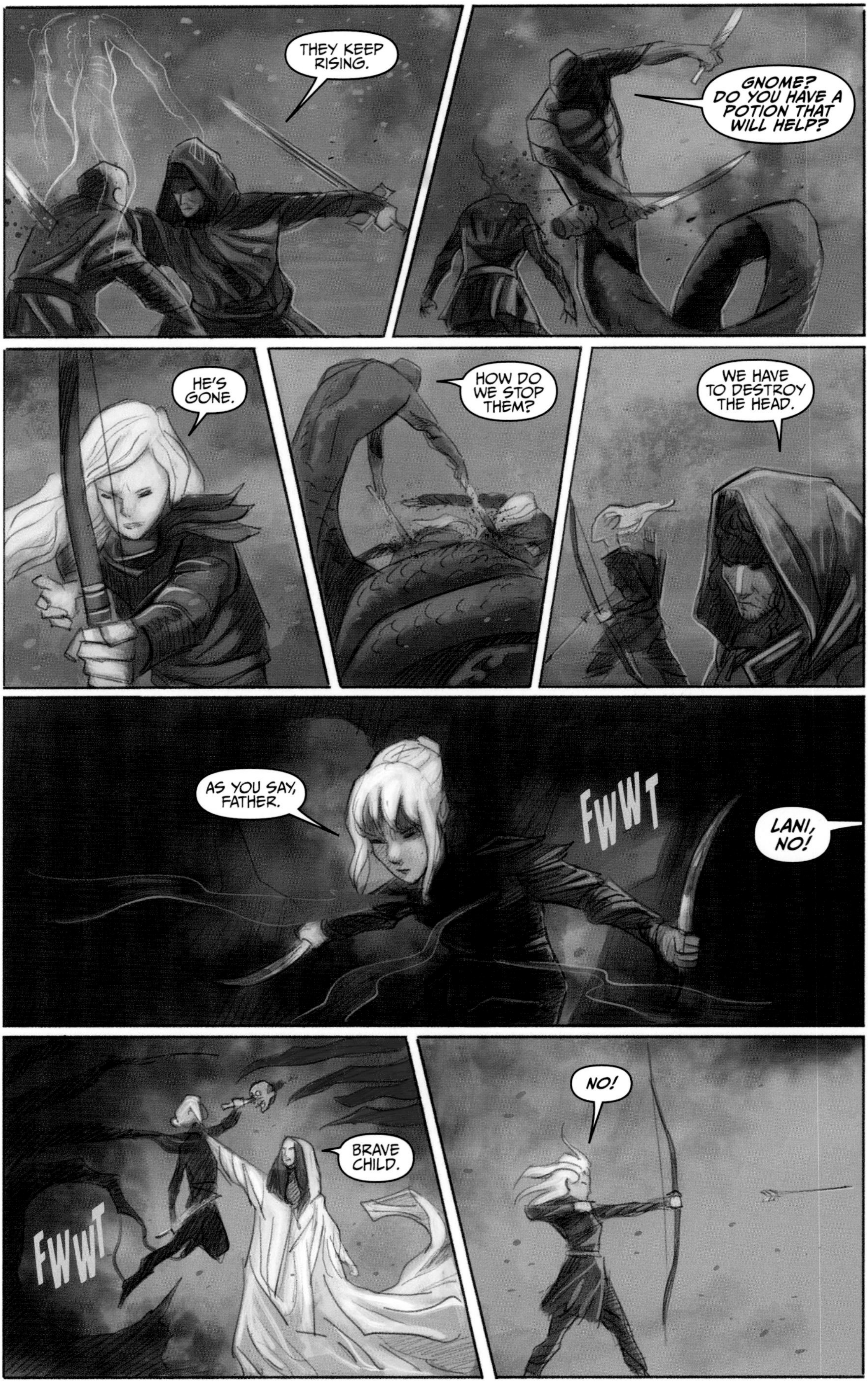
THEY KEEP RISING.
GNOME? DO YOU HAVE A POTION THAT WILL HELP?
HE'S GONE.
HOW DO WE STOP THEM?
WE HAVE TO DESTROY THE HEAD.
AS YOU SAY, FATHER.
FWWT
LANI, NO!
BRAVE CHILD.
FWWT
NO!

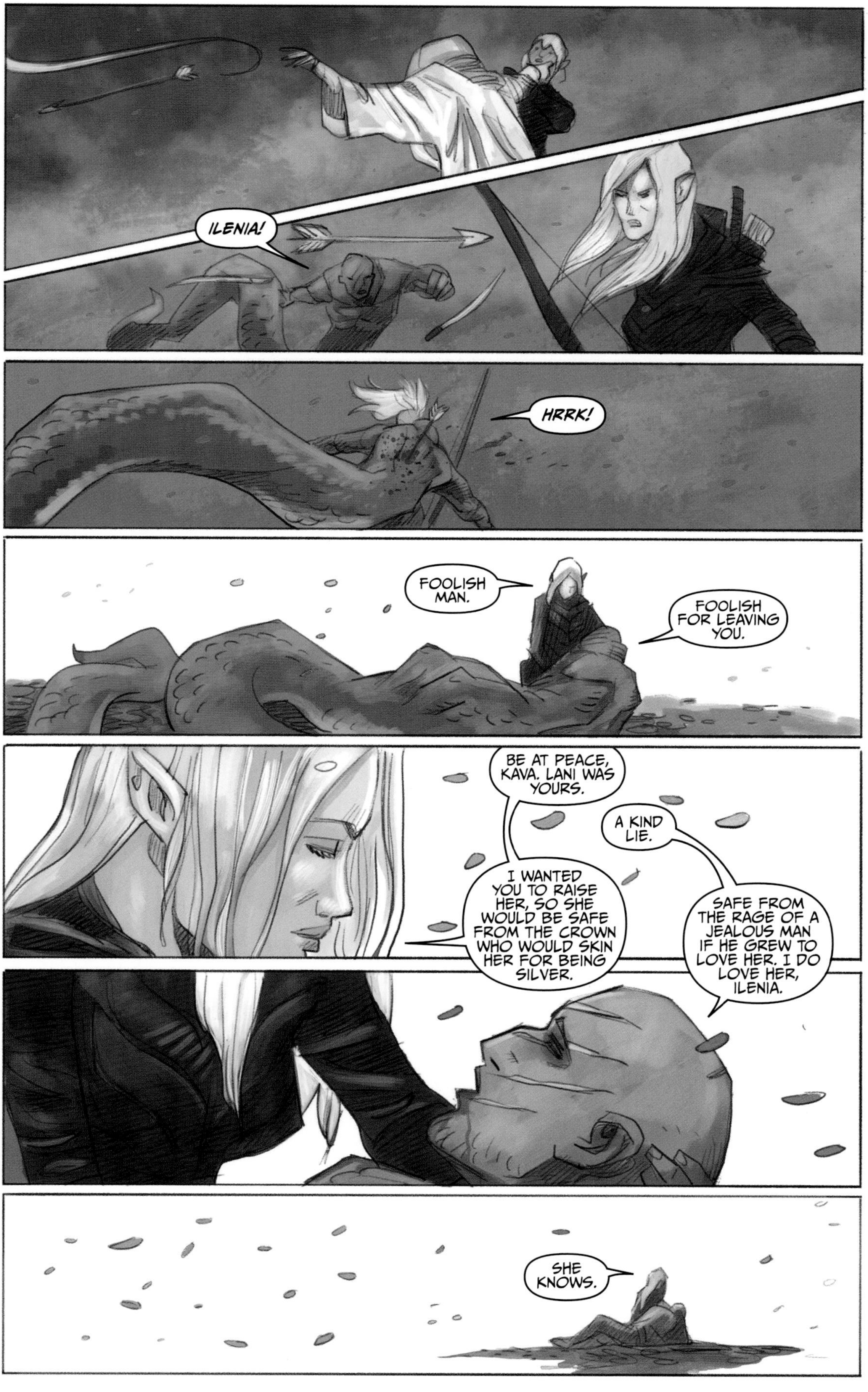
ILENIA!
HRRK!
FOOLISH MAN.
FOOLISH FOR LEAVING YOU.
BE AT PEACE, KAVA. LANI WAS YOURS.
I WANTED YOU TO RAISE HER, SO SHE WOULD BE SAFE FROM THE CROWN WHO WOULD SKIN HER FOR BEING SILVER.
A KIND LIE.
SAFE FROM THE RAGE OF A JEALOUS MAN IF HE GREW TO LOVE HER. I DO LOVE HER, ILENIA.
SHE KNOWS.

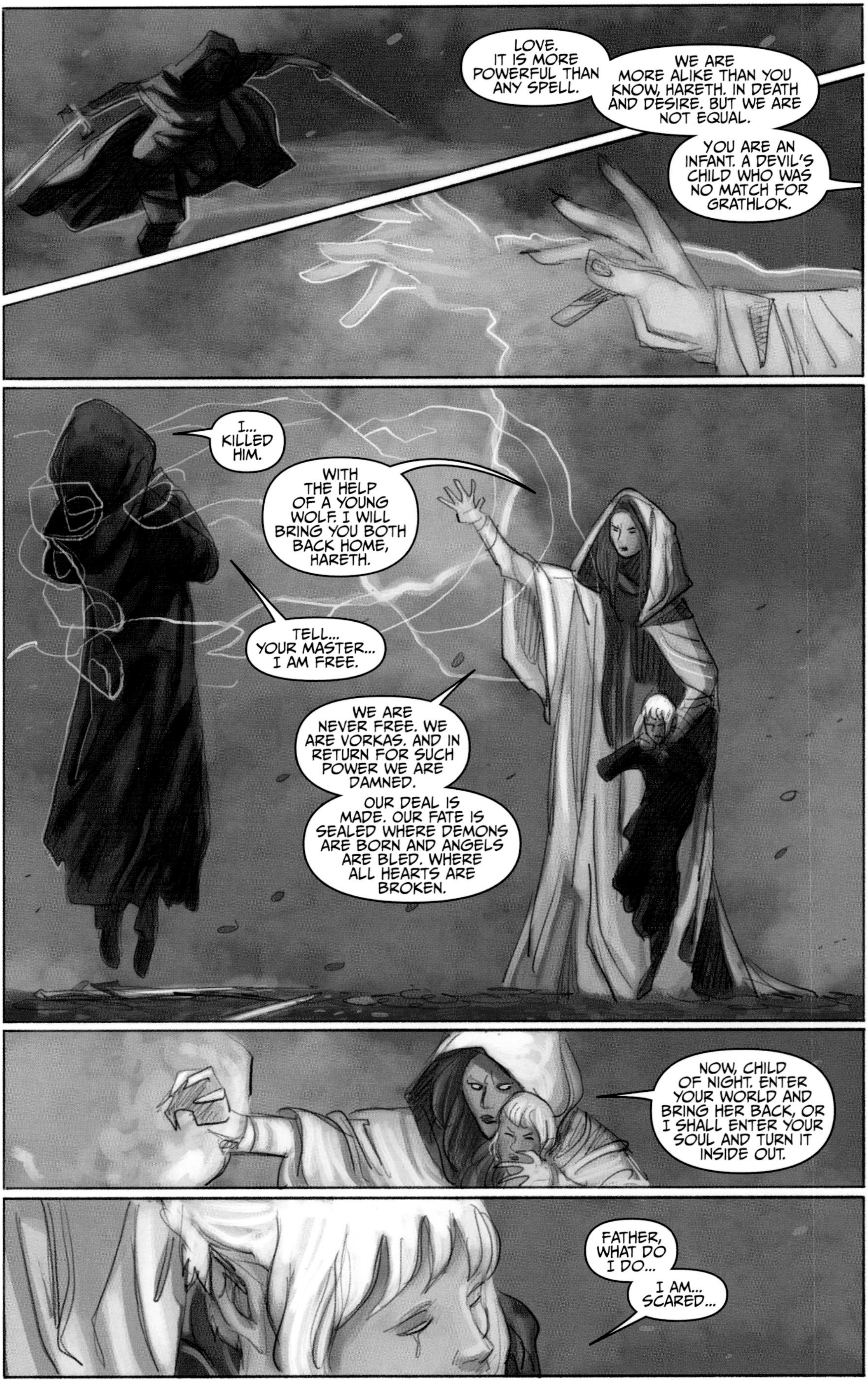
LOVE. IT IS MORE POWERFUL THAN ANY SPELL.
WE ARE MORE ALIKE THAN YOU KNOW, HARETH. IN DEATH AND DESIRE. BUT WE ARE NOT EQUAL.
YOU ARE AN INFANT. A DEVIL'S CHILD WHO WAS NO MATCH FOR GRATHLOK.
I... KILLED HIM.
WITH THE HELP OF A YOUNG WOLF. I WILL BRING YOU BOTH BACK HOME, HARETH.
TELL... YOUR MASTER... I AM FREE.
WE ARE NEVER FREE. WE ARE VORKAS. AND IN RETURN FOR SUCH POWER WE ARE DAMNED.
OUR DEAL IS MADE. OUR FATE IS SEALED WHERE DEMONS ARE BORN AND ANGELS ARE BLED. WHERE ALL HEARTS ARE BROKEN.
NOW, CHILD OF NIGHT. ENTER YOUR WORLD AND BRING HER BACK, OR I SHALL ENTER YOUR SOUL AND TURN IT INSIDE OUT.
FATHER, WHAT DO I DO...
I AM... SCARED...

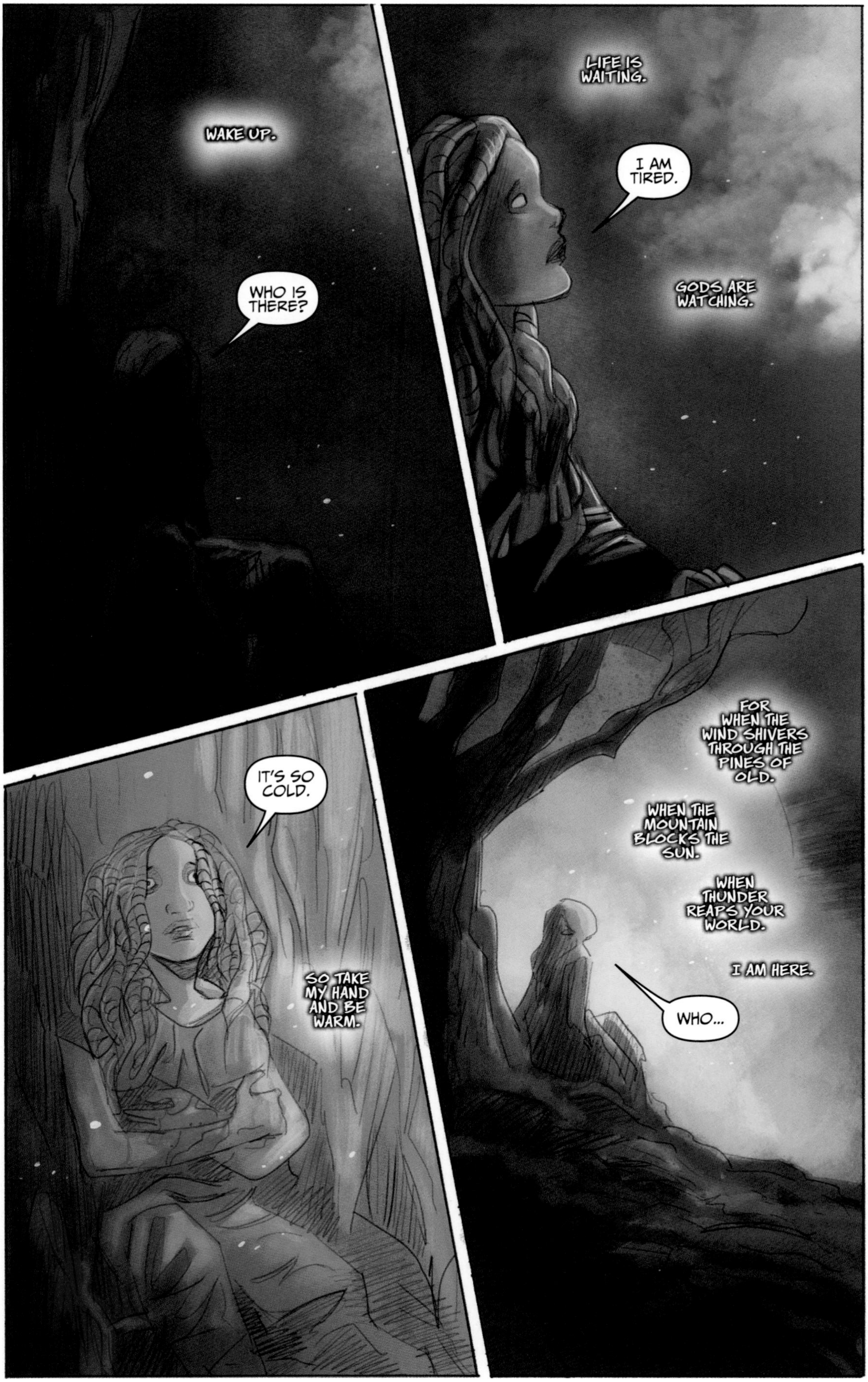
WAKE UP.
WHO IS THERE?
LIFE IS WAITING.
I AM TIRED.
GODS ARE WATCHING.
IT'S SO COLD.
SO TAKE MY HAND AND BE WARM.
FOR WHEN THE WIND SHIVERS THROUGH THE PINES OF OLD.
WHEN THE MOUNTAIN BLOCKS THE SUN.
WHEN THUNDER REAPS YOUR WORLD.
I AM HERE.
WHO...

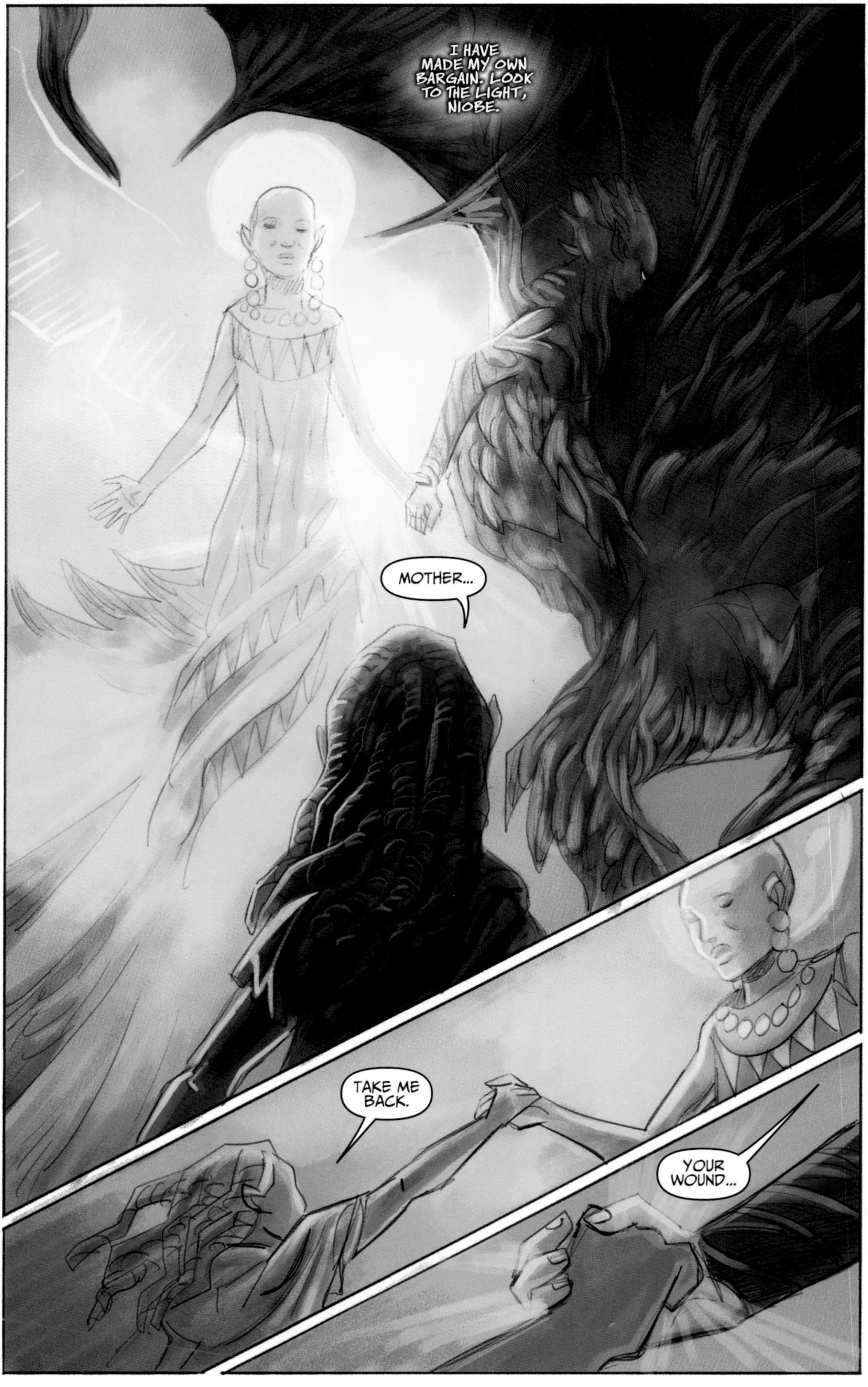
I HAVE MADE MY OWN BARGAIN. LOOK TO THE LIGHT, NIOBE.
MOTHER...
TAKE ME BACK.
YOUR WOUND...

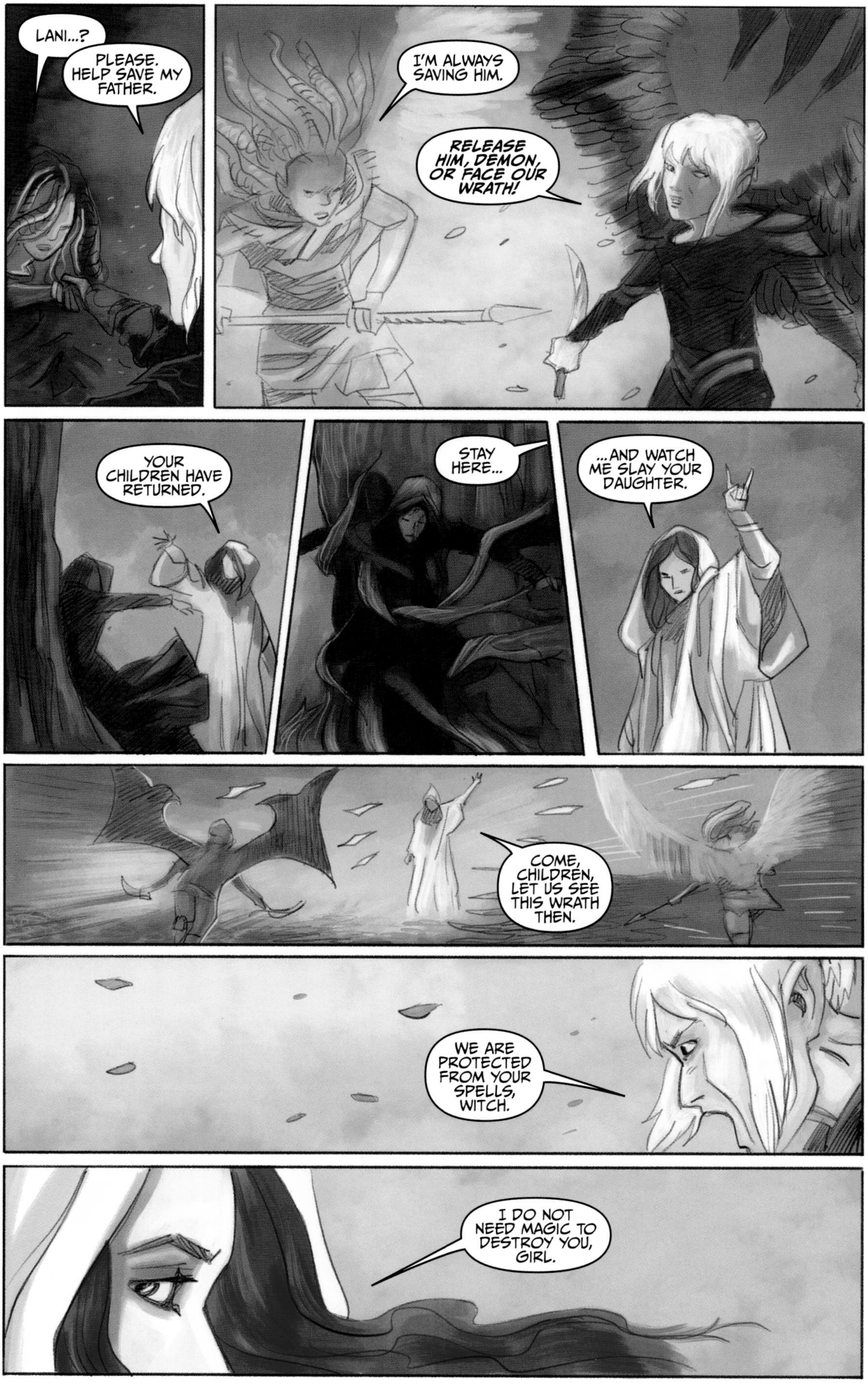
LANI...?
PLEASE. HELP SAVE MY FATHER.
I'M ALWAYS SAVING HIM.
RELEASE HIM, DEMON, OR FACE OUR WRATH!
YOUR CHILDREN HAVE RETURNED.
STAY HERE...
...AND WATCH ME SLAY YOUR DAUGHTER.
COME, CHILDREN, LET US SEE THIS WRATH THEN.
WE ARE PROTECTED FROM YOUR SPELLS, WITCH.
I DO NOT NEED MAGIC TO DESTROY YOU, GIRL.

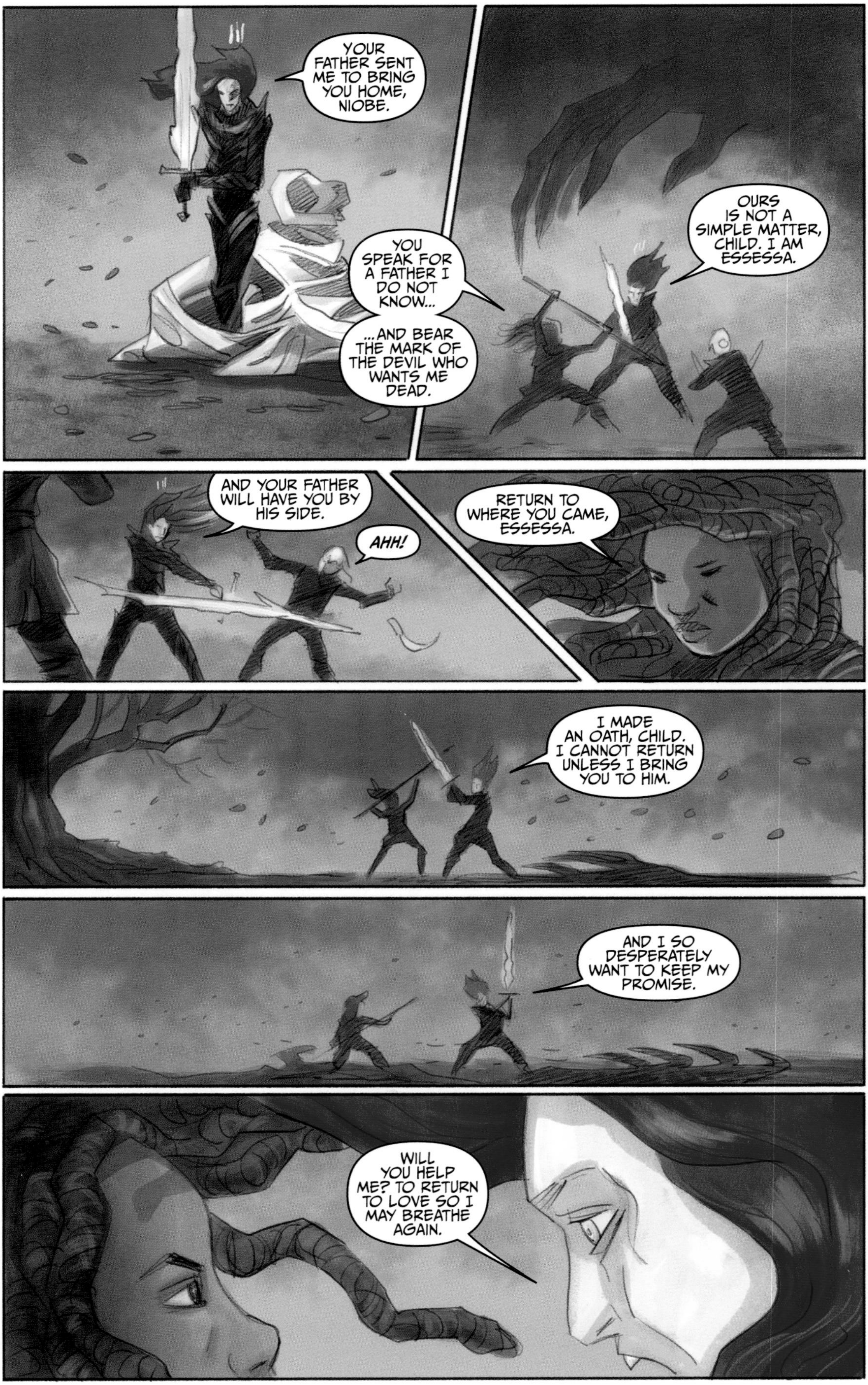
YOUR FATHER SENT ME TO BRING YOU HOME, NIOBE.
YOU SPEAK FOR A FATHER I DO NOT KNOW...
...AND BEAR THE MARK OF THE DEVIL WHO WANTS ME DEAD.
OURS IS NOT A SIMPLE MATTER, CHILD. I AM ESSESSA.
AND YOUR FATHER WILL HAVE YOU BY HIS SIDE.
AHH!
RETURN TO WHERE YOU CAME, ESSESSA.
I MADE AN OATH, CHILD. I CANNOT RETURN UNLESS I BRING YOU TO HIM.
AND I SO DESPERATELY WANT TO KEEP MY PROMISE.
WILL YOU HELP ME? TO RETURN TO LOVE SO I MAY BREATHE AGAIN.

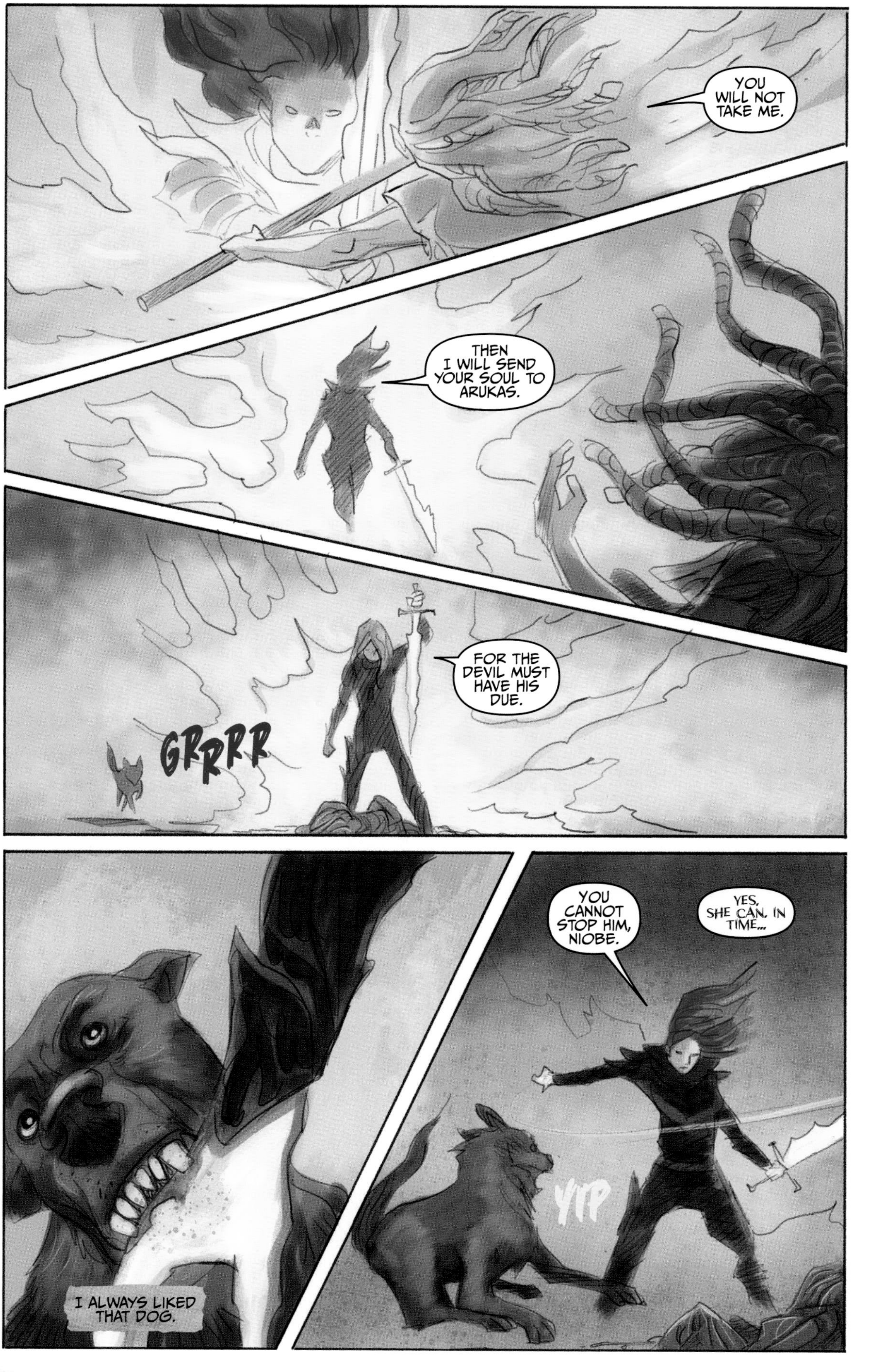
YOU WILL NOT TAKE ME.
THEN I WILL SEND YOUR SOUL TO ARUKAS.
FOR THE DEVIL MUST HAVE HIS DUE.
GRRRR
I ALWAYS LIKED THAT DOG.
YOU CANNOT STOP HIM, NIOBE.
YES, SHE CAN, IN TIME...
YIP

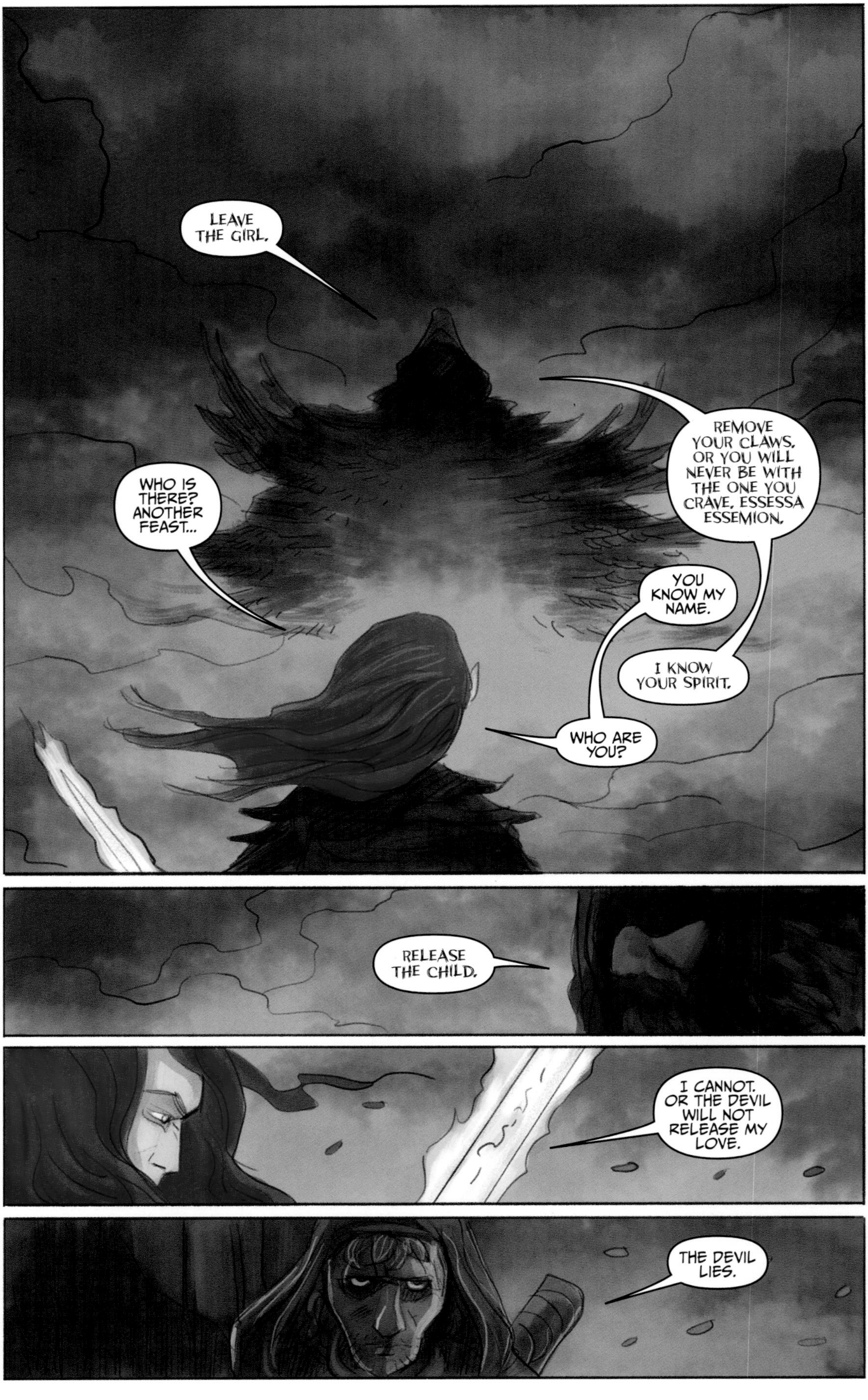
LEAVE THE GIRL.
REMOVE YOUR CLAWS, OR YOU WILL NEVER BE WITH THE ONE YOU CRAVE, ESSESSA ESSEMION.
WHO IS THERE? ANOTHER FEAST...
YOU KNOW MY NAME.
I KNOW YOUR SPIRIT.
WHO ARE YOU?
RELEASE THE CHILD.
I CANNOT. OR THE DEVIL WILL NOT RELEASE MY LOVE.
THE DEVIL LIES.

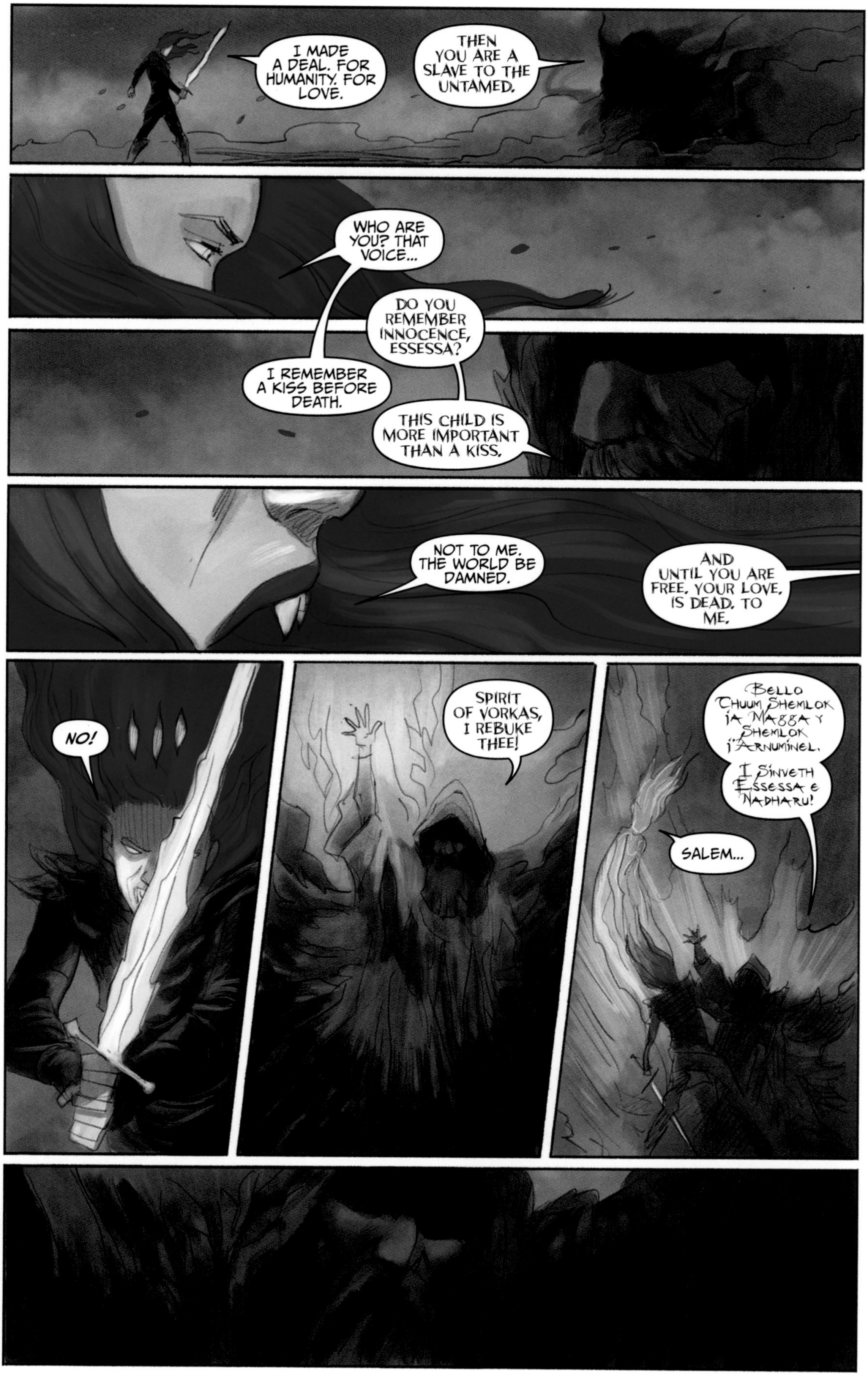

I MADE A DEAL. FOR HUMANITY. FOR LOVE.
THEN YOU ARE A SLAVE TO THE UNTAMED.
WHO ARE YOU? THAT VOICE...
DO YOU REMEMBER INNOCENCE, ESSESSA?
I REMEMBER A KISS BEFORE DEATH.
THIS CHILD IS MORE IMPORTANT THAN A KISS.
NOT TO ME. THE WORLD BE DAMNED.
AND UNTIL YOU ARE FREE, YOUR LOVE, IS DEAD, TO ME.
NO!
SPIRIT OF VORKAS, I REBUKE THEE!
BELLO CHUUM SHEMLOK IA MAGGA Y SHEMLOK I'ARNUMINEL.
I SINVETH ESSESSA E NADHARU!
SALEM...

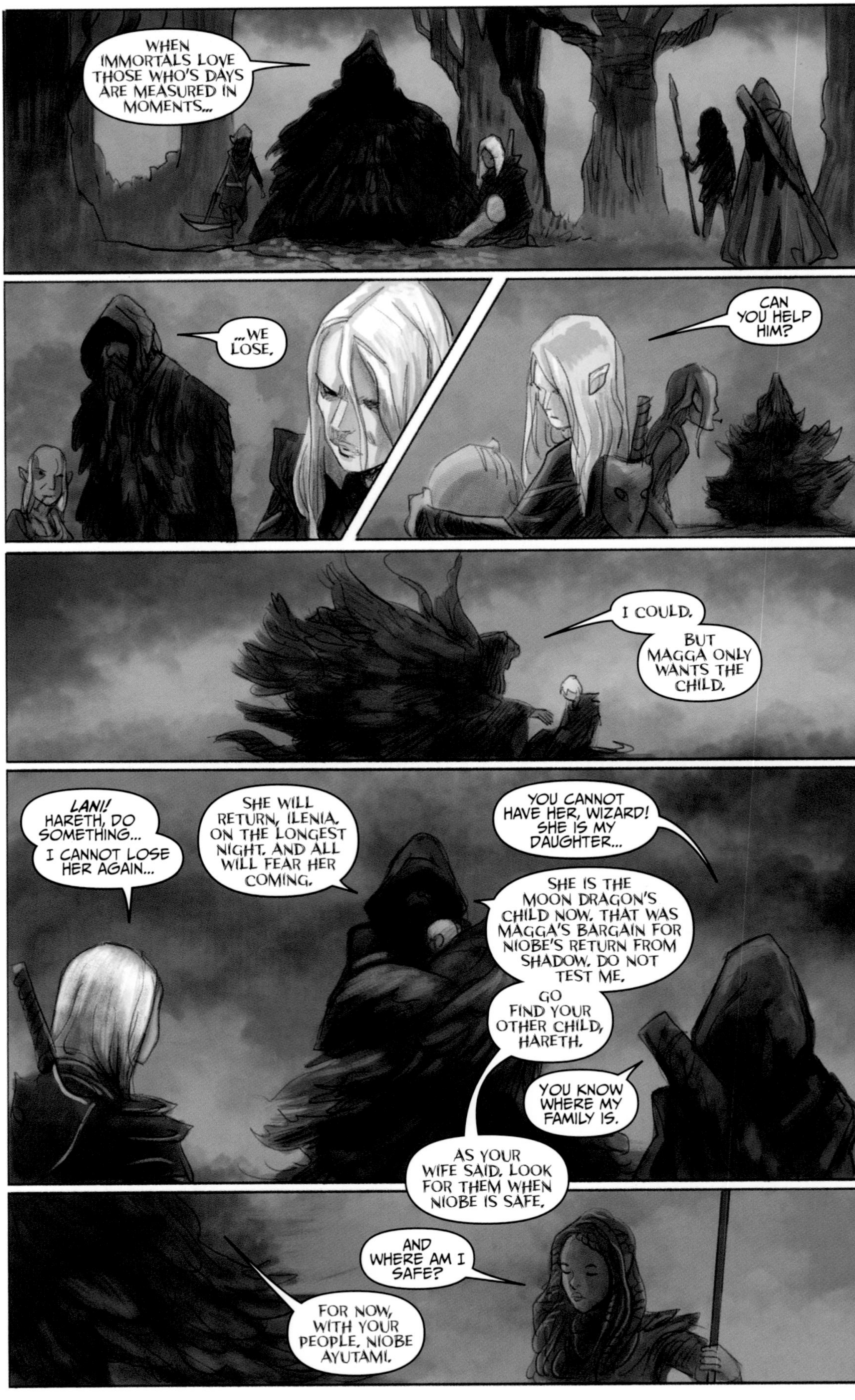
WHEN IMMORTALS LOVE THOSE WHO'S DAYS ARE MEASURED IN MOMENTS...
...WE LOSE.
CAN YOU HELP HIM?
I COULD.
BUT MAGGA ONLY WANTS THE CHILD.
LANI! HARETH, DO SOMETHING...
I CANNOT LOSE HER AGAIN...
SHE WILL RETURN, ILENIA, ON THE LONGEST NIGHT. AND ALL WILL FEAR HER COMING.
YOU CANNOT HAVE HER, WIZARD! SHE IS MY DAUGHTER...
SHE IS THE MOON DRAGON'S CHILD NOW. THAT WAS MAGGA'S BARGAIN FOR NIOBE'S RETURN FROM SHADOW. DO NOT TEST ME.
GO FIND YOUR OTHER CHILD, HARETH.
YOU KNOW WHERE MY FAMILY IS.
AS YOUR WIFE SAID. LOOK FOR THEM WHEN NIOBE IS SAFE.
AND WHERE AM I SAFE?
FOR NOW, WITH YOUR PEOPLE, NIOBE AYUTAMI.

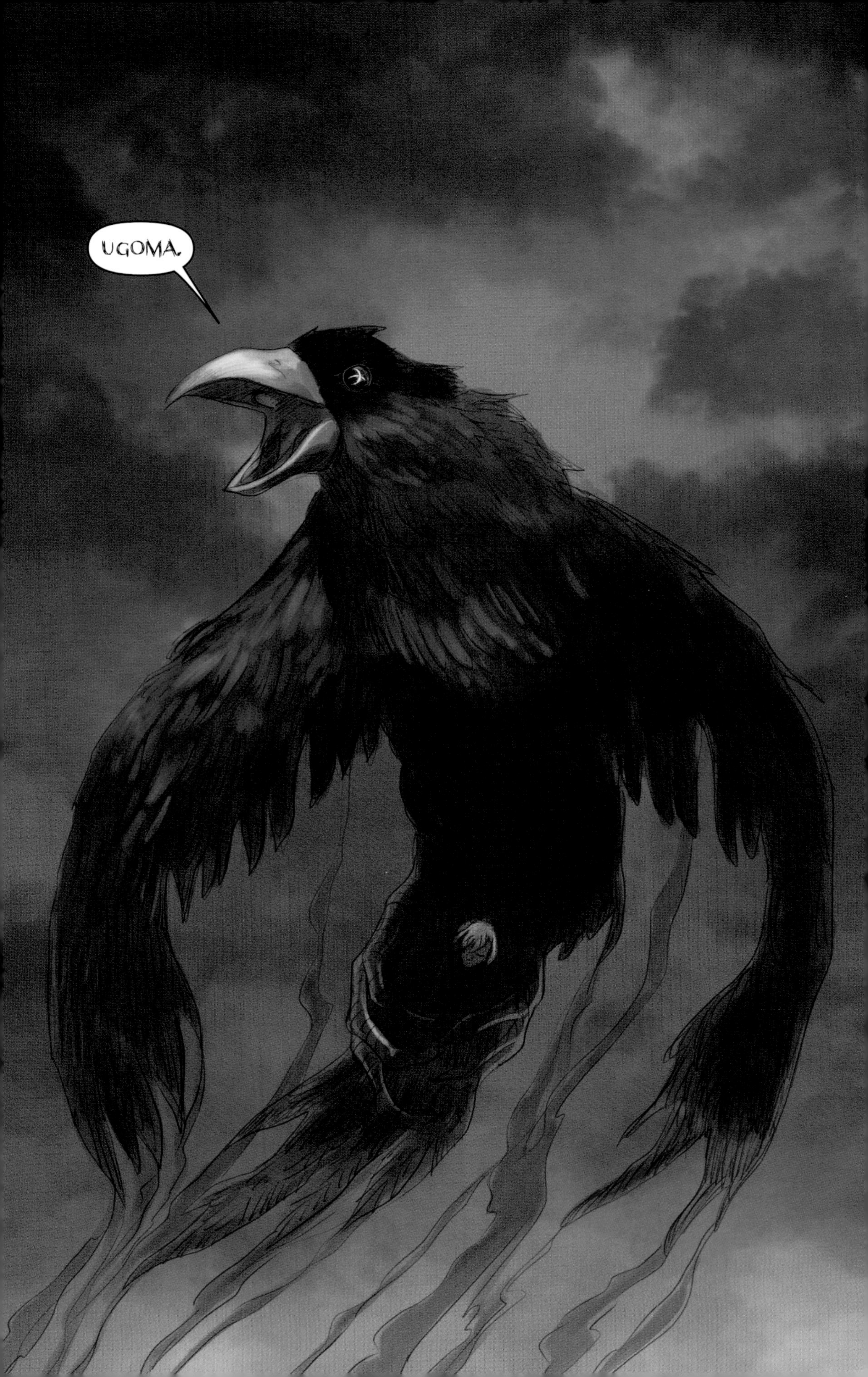
UGOMA.

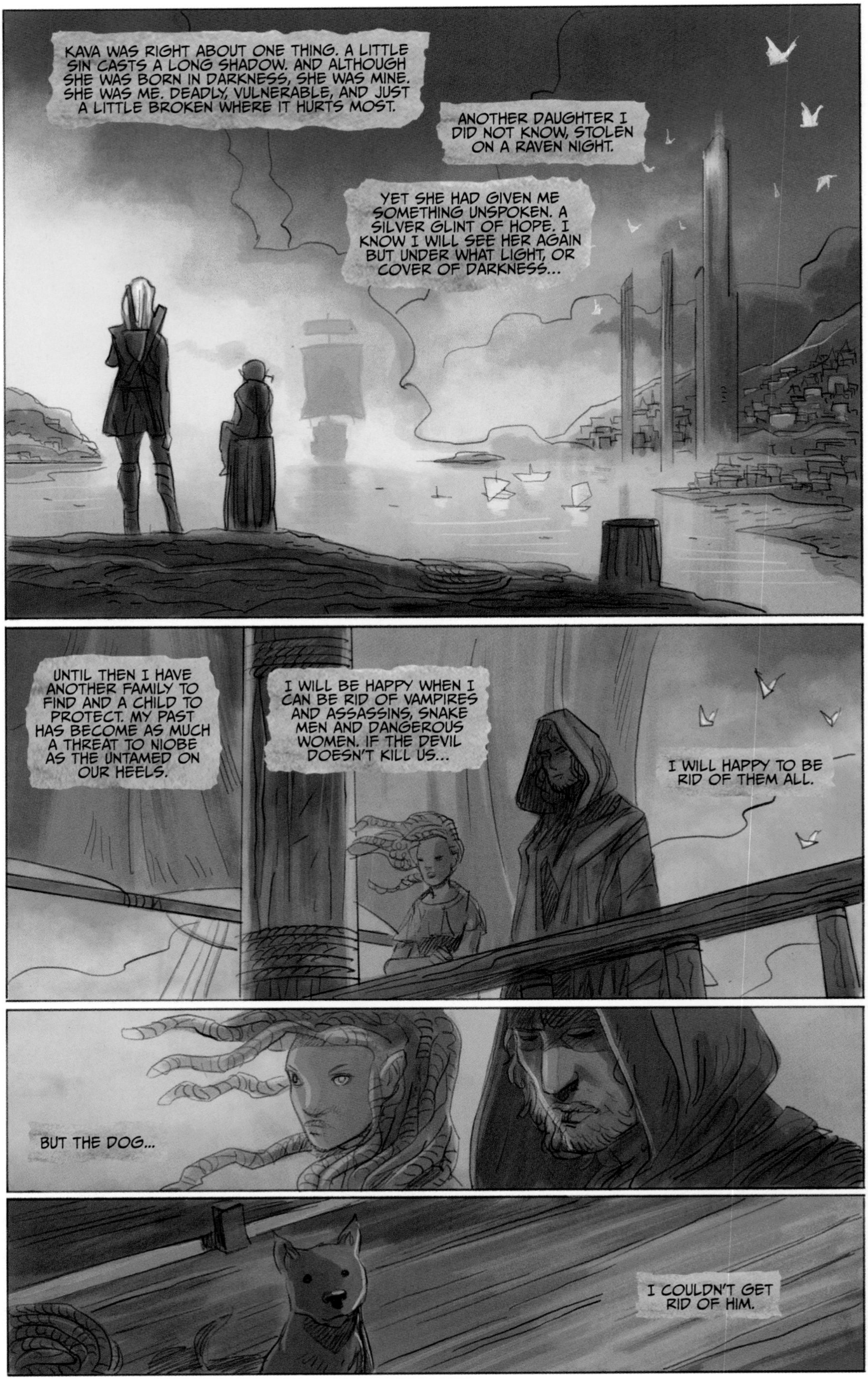
KAVA WAS RIGHT ABOUT ONE THING. A LITTLE SIN CASTS A LONG SHADOW. AND ALTHOUGH SHE WAS BORN IN DARKNESS, SHE WAS MINE. SHE WAS ME. DEADLY, VULNERABLE, AND JUST A LITTLE BROKEN WHERE IT HURTS MOST.
ANOTHER DAUGHTER I DID NOT KNOW, STOLEN ON A RAVEN NIGHT.
YET SHE HAD GIVEN ME SOMETHING UNSPOKEN. A SILVER GLINT OF HOPE. I KNOW I WILL SEE HER AGAIN BUT UNDER WHAT LIGHT, OR COVER OF DARKNESS...
UNTIL THEN I HAVE ANOTHER FAMILY TO FIND AND A CHILD TO PROTECT. MY PAST HAS BECOME AS MUCH A THREAT TO NIOBE AS THE UNTAMED ON OUR HEELS.
I WILL BE HAPPY WHEN I CAN BE RID OF VAMPIRES AND ASSASSINS, SNAKE MEN AND DANGEROUS WOMEN. IF THE DEVIL DOESN'T KILL US...
I WILL HAPPY TO BE RID OF THEM ALL.
BUT THE DOG...
I COULDN'T GET RID OF HIM.

Hello Stranger

I have no time for pettiness and even less tolerance for hate or those without compassion. If a path is not laid out for your brothers and sisters, your sons and daughters, pick up the hammer and help them pave the way. And do not let jealousy consume you, as it did for the man below.

The large man sat at the bar rapping ashen knuckles on old wood. It had been an age since he had been to Bandalak and visited his favorite hellhole tavern. Nothing had changed save the people. They seemed weaker, hiding behind store-bought tough guy outfits, and dock-side rehearsed accents. He took comfort in the sight of the gnome that poured the drinks though. He was the same. Dangerous and tough as the nail he chewed on.

"I'm looking for a girl. Elf. Different eyes," said the man in a gravelly voice, sliding a purse across the table. It snagged on a dirty splinter. "Traveling with a stranger."

"I know them," said the gnome, eying the man whose face was hidden behind strips of cloth. His stubby fingers gripped a mechanical crossbow under the bar. "They died. Some sort of town war. Even killed my dog. Nasty business."

"I don't think so," said the man.

"Are you calling me a liar in my own tavern?" said Obuds, biting on the nail with a toothy smile. A number of men stood up at this.

"I'm saying maybe you're confused. You see, I'd have felt it if my little brother died a second time. Now, are you going to pull the trigger or pour me a drink? Before I burn this whole damn town to the ground."

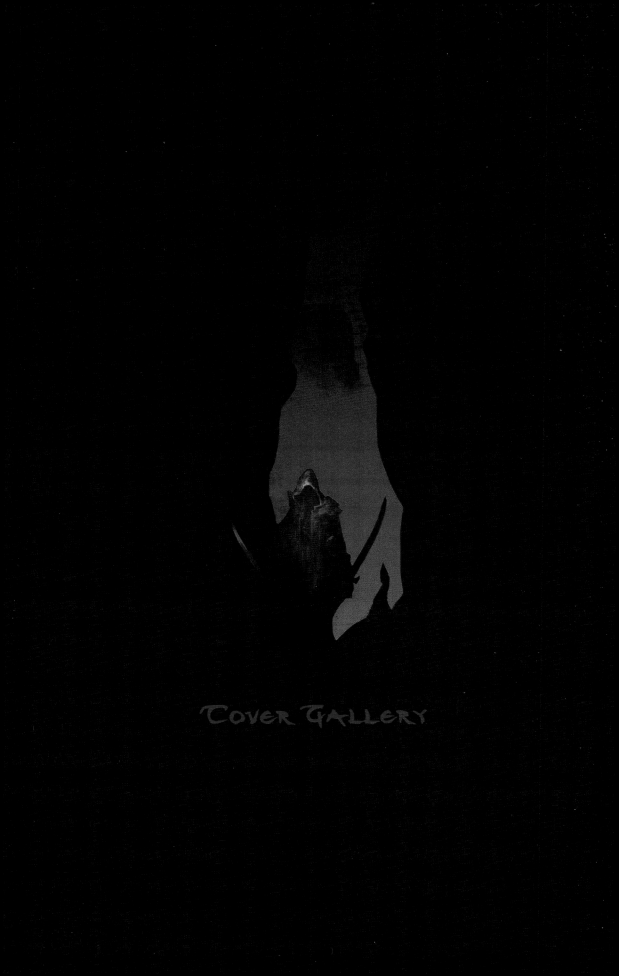

COVER GALLERY

JAE LEE

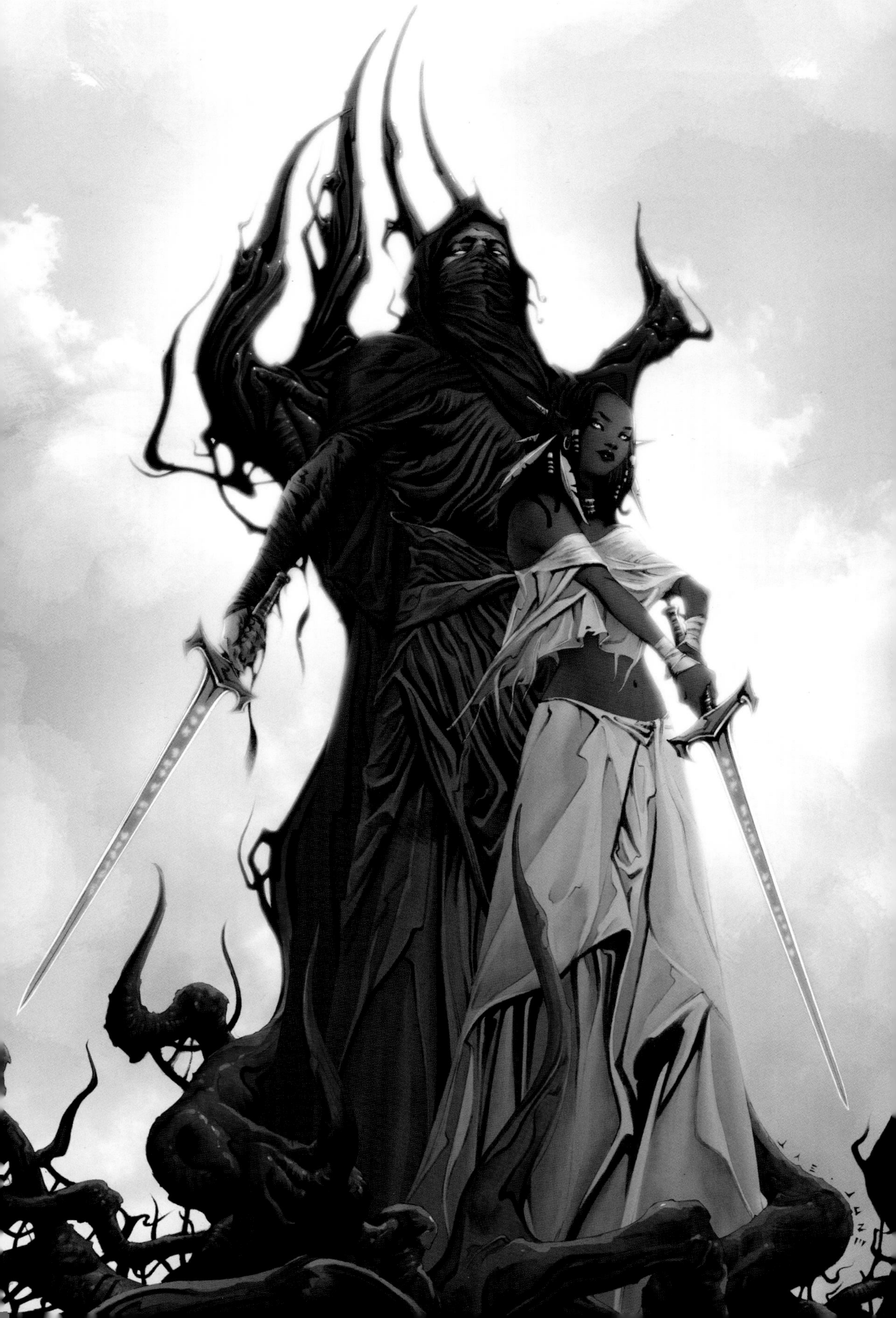

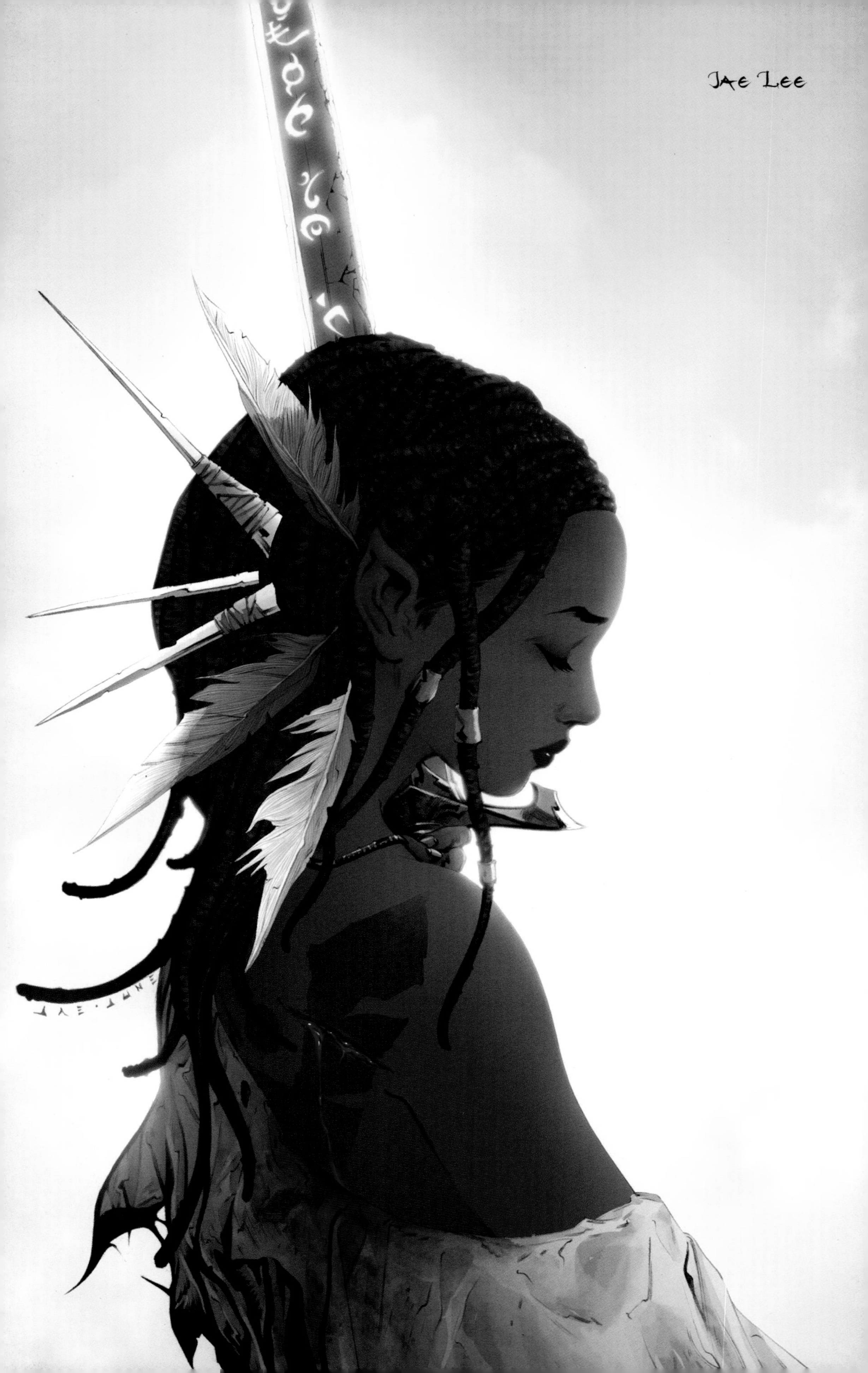
JAE LEE

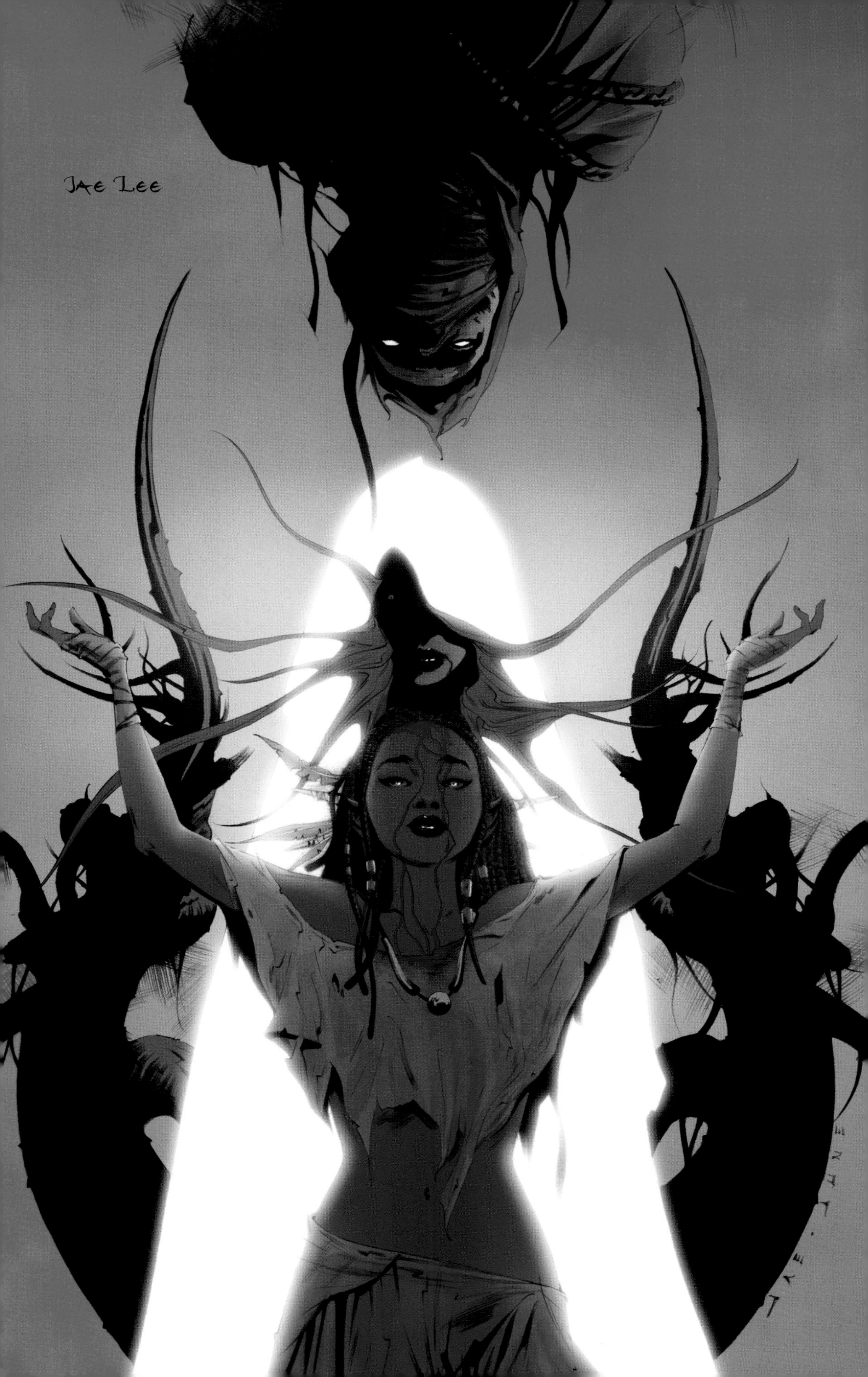
JAE LEE

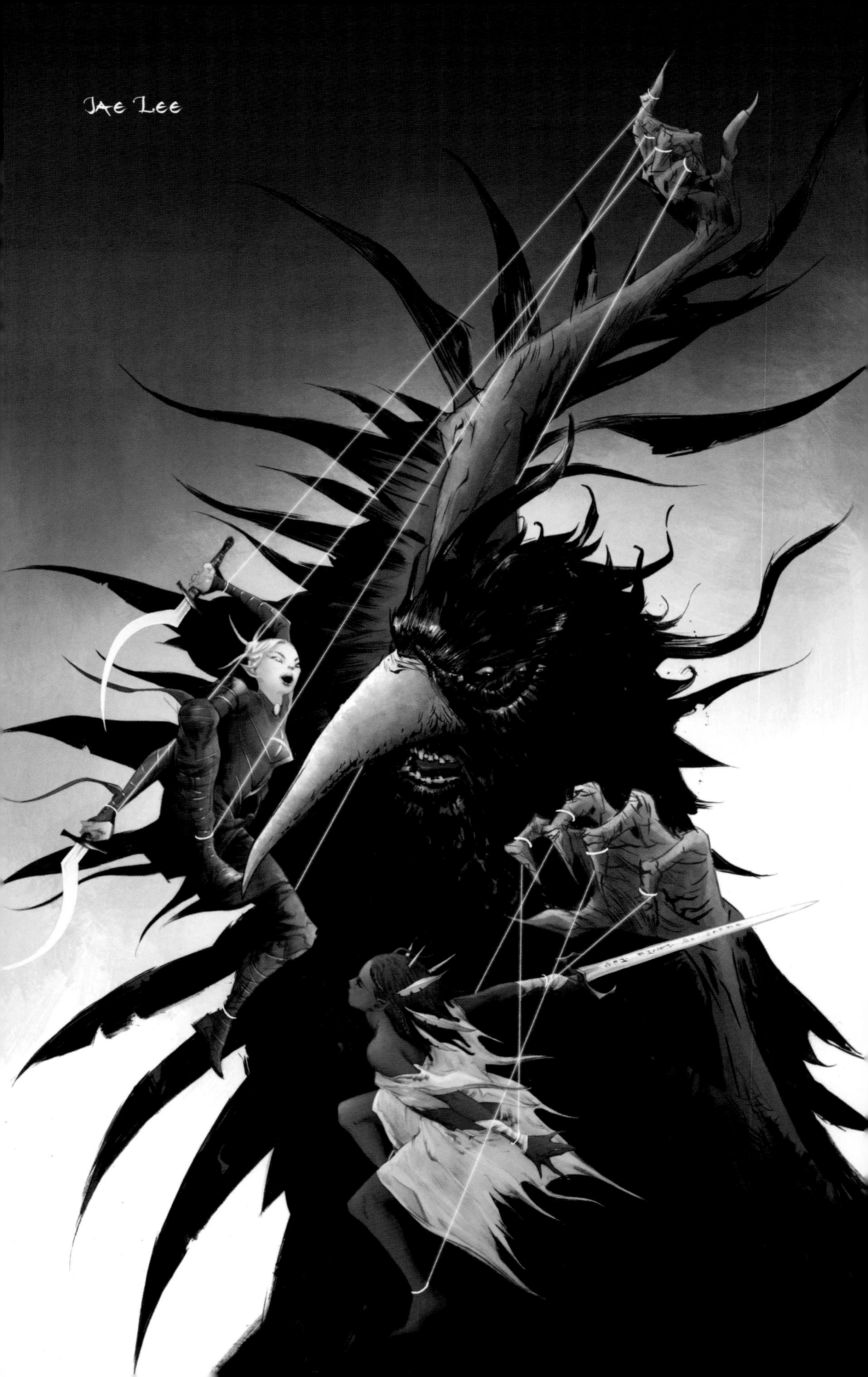
JAE LEE

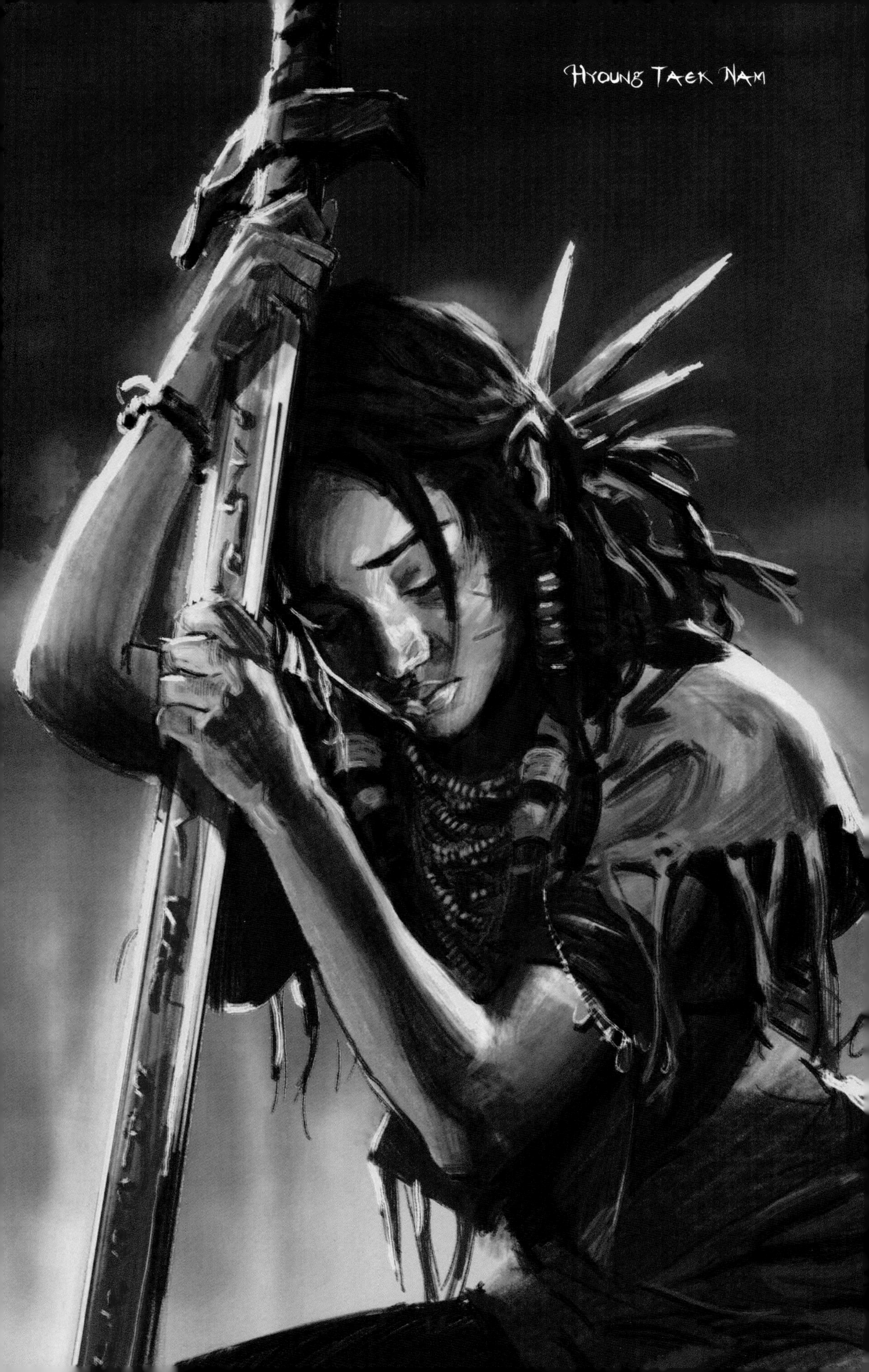
Hyoung Taek Nam

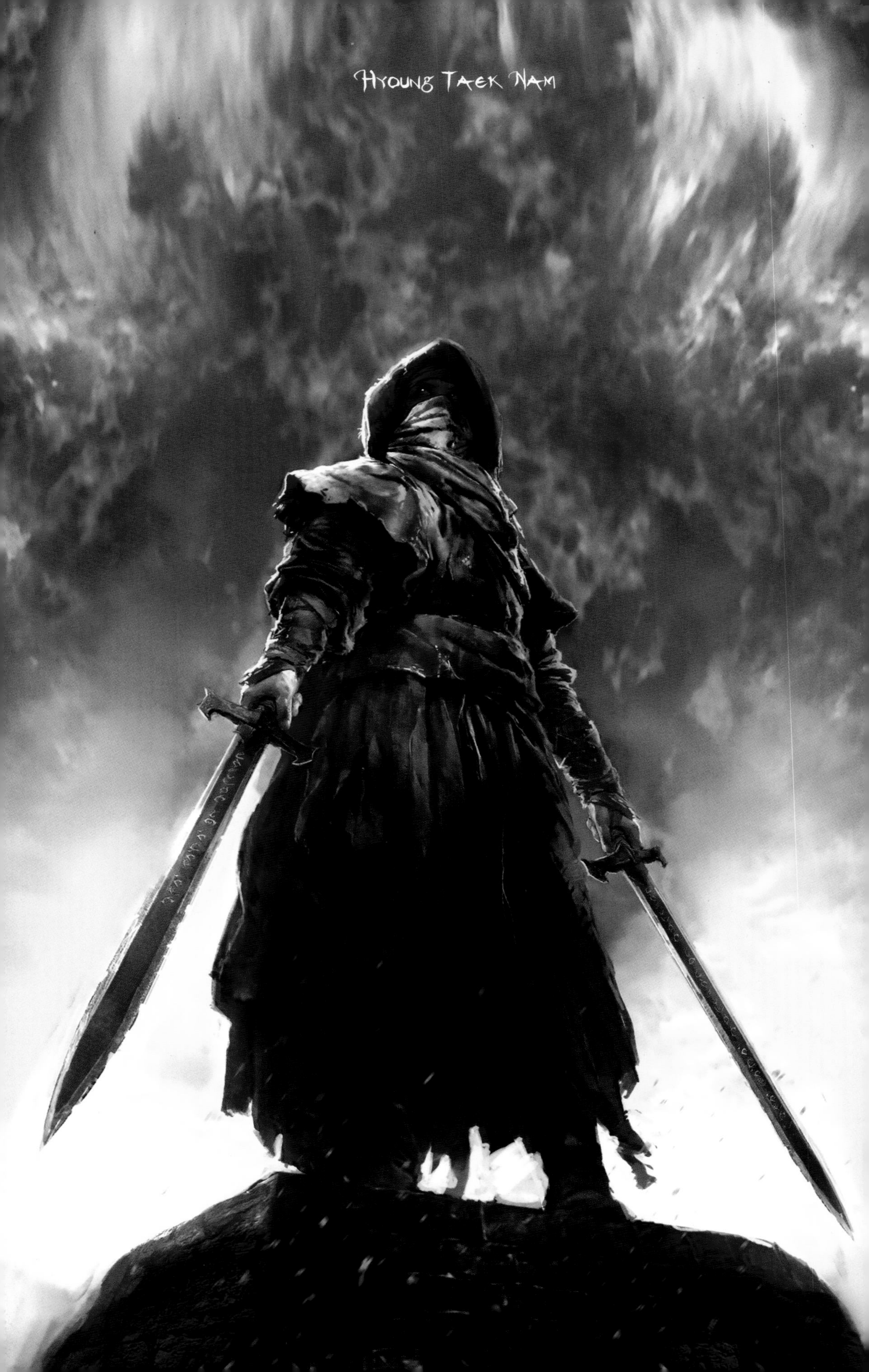
Hyoung Taek Nam

Soul of Ice

One-Handed Melee Weapon

Damage: 1d12 Slashing damage

Critical: 19-20/x3

Range: 10ft – magically enhanced range

Soul of Ice: +1d10 cold damage plus Special

Melee: +7 to attack and damage

Special: Soul of Ice is an exceptionally sharp enchanted sword that does an additional 1d10 cold damage. 3 times a day, upon a successful attack, target NPC or Monster must make a Will save or be frozen for 1d4 rounds. Soul of Ice does have a sister sword, Wrath of Fire, the wielder of which is immune to this freezing effect, just as the wielder of Soul of Ice cannot be burned by its flames.

Twin Blades gives Soul of Ice the ability to split into two blades and when split, it bestows the Two Weapon Fighting Feat on the wielder. This is effective only for the two blades and does not work with one blade and another weapon. The freezing effect of the Soul of Ice special is cumulative for the two blades and does not grant additional uses when split. Either of the twin blades, however, can trigger the effect.

Lastly, the two blades are twins and have an innate need to be together. For that reason, if they are separated by a distance of more than a mile, the wielder may call upon the other blade, and it will teleport to its twin sword. It should be noted that in the event someone is holding the other blade, however, they can make a Will save to resist the call. If they fail, they will be teleported with it.

LOOK FOR MORE NIOBE IN

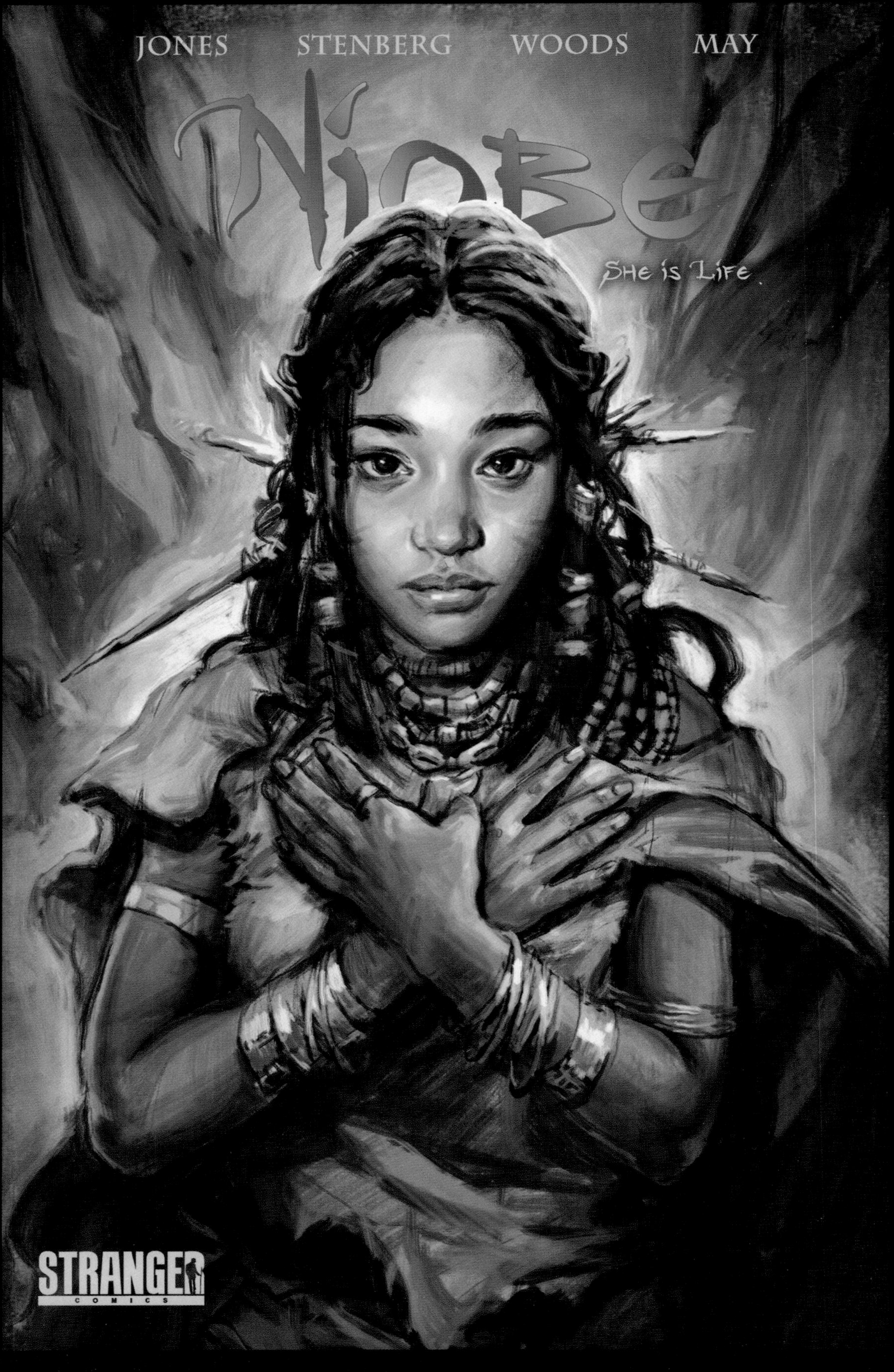

JONES STENBERG WOODS MAY
NIOBE
She is Life.
STRANGER
COMICS